READ BETWEEN THE LINES

The story of a Kindertransport survivor

LEON DWOLATZKY DUVAL

Read Between the Lines: The Story of a Kindertransport Survivor Copyright © 2025 Leon Dwolatzky Duval

All rights reserved. No part of this book may be reproduced in any form or by any electronic or mechanical means, including information storage and retrieval systems, without permission in writing from the publisher, except by a reviewer who may quote brief passages in a review.

Published by Nikkanor Gate in Israel
ISBN 978-965-597-114-9

To the memory of those murdered by Hamas terrorists on the 7th October 2023.

Age shall not weary her spirit
Martha at the ripe old age of ninety-five
(Portrait by Tal Hartuv)

Contents

Acknowledgements i
Prologue iii
Introduction 1

BOOK ONE: 1800-1899
Antisemitism evolves from religious to racial classification

Germany's Misfortune, Its Jewish Community 7
The Jews Are a Scattered Nation 26
The Hep, Hep Pogrom 28
The Wissenschaft des Judentums 30
The Jews Never Contributed to the Work of Civilization 35
Families Born into a Crucible of Hate 37
The Victory of the One, the Death of the Other 40
What's in a Name 46
The Jews Are Our Misfortune 47
The Antisemites Petition 50
Jewish Musicians Produce Shallow and Artificial Music 54
Unfortunately, the Fourth Child Survived! 60
Herr Ahlwardt, You Are Nothing More than a Petty Thief .. 62
The Antisemitism Virus Infects the Reichstag 66
Hitler's John the Baptist 69
Star-Crossed Families 77

BOOK TWO: 1900-1918
The Great War and the Jews in Germany

The Path to War 91
Daniel Braun Goes to War 98
And so, It Had All Been in Vain 118

BOOK THREE: 1918-1926
A noxious growth emerges from fertile ground

Armistices and Peace Treaties 121
Richter Der Geschichte 125
Gallery 1: The Evolution of a Stray Dog 128
Gallery 2: Prayers During Wartime, Celebrations During Peacetime 135
Friday Night Dinner at the Nissensohns – Scene One 148
Friday Night Dinner at the Nissensohns – Scene Two 157
Friday Night Dinner at the Brauns 163
Endings and Beginnings 168

BOOK FOUR: 1926-1939
Martha tells her story

Prologue 175
My Early Life in Altona 178
I Learn How to Swim 184
My Three Years of School in Altona Before Moving to Hamburg 187
The Beginning of the End 193
We Move to Hamburg 198

1938 to 1939, Two Years that Destroyed My Family 204
Read Between the Lines 209

BOOK FIVE: 1939-1958
Nineteen years living with a first cousin

Our Journey to Manchester 221
Our Introduction to Manchester 228
Life with Auntie Ella 233
My Contact with Tatti and Mutti 239
I Finally Go Ice-Skating 243
The Pig Farm 245
I Run Away 247
Epilogue 251

Illustrations 255

APPENDICES

First Interview with Martha Braun 269
Second Interview with Martha Braun 299
Notes 329

About the Author 335

Author's note

This book is not a biography, or an autobiography, it is a literary chimera that augments historical facts with personal memories, creating a compendium of stories that embed the history of one family into a chain of events which changed the world forever. Names have been changed when deemed to be appropriate.

Acknowledgments

I want to acknowledge the small group who were instrumental in facilitating the process that culminated with the writing of this book.

Marjorie Nadler became a friend and a confidante to Martha. Her friendship helped Martha unlock painful memories and find a degree of solace through the experience.

Marjorie's daughter, Lisa Nadler Revivi, recognised the importance of the story and facilitated our interviews with Martha.

Albee Kava, managed the interview process and proved himself to be an effective interviewer whose probing questions and patience stimulated Martha's memory, helping her to bring the past into the present.

And then, there is Tal Hartuv; her artistic genius was used for the front cover design of this book. Without her encouragement and positive criticism this book would never have been completed.

My grateful thanks to Denise Duval who devoted many hours to the difficult task of proofreading the edited manuscript.

Finally, thank you Kate Winter of From Manuscript to Book. Editor extraordinaire, she transformed the draft manuscript I gave her into a book suitable for publication.

Prologue

In October 1938 the Nazi government first arrested, and then expelled, around eighteen thousand Polish Jews living in Germany. If they did not have a valid re-entry authority stamped in their passports, the deportees were prevented from entering Poland. Expelled by Germany, and rejected by their country of birth, the deportees were effectively stranded and forced to live under extremely harsh conditions in makeshift camps on the border between the two countries.

The Grynspan family—a mother, father, and three children—were among those deported. In desperation, one of the children sent a message to her eighteen-year-old brother Herschel who was living in Paris, begging him to send money. Herschel appealed to family members living in Paris but was unable to collect the funds required. Finally, in an act of anger triggered by desperation he bought a gun, went to the German embassy and shot one of the diplomats, Ernst Vom Rath. Three days later Vom Rath succumbed to his wounds and Josef Goebbels, chief propagandist for the Nazi government, saw an opportunity for launching a retaliatory pogrom against all the Jews in Germany.

The pogrom began on the night of the 9th November 1938 and continued for two days. Urged on by Goebbels, Nazi party stormtroopers rampaged through the streets of Germany burning synagogues, looting Jewish shops, and beating defenceless Jews in their homes and in the streets. According to Yad

Vashem, the world Holocaust remembrance centre based in Jerusalem, over this two-day orgy of violence more than one thousand four hundred synagogues were torched, and ninety-one Jews murdered. The looting of Jewish shops left the streets under a layer of shattered glass and for this reason the pogrom became known as Kristallnacht, the night of broken glass.

In the aftermath of the pogrom some thirty thousand Jewish men were arrested and thrown into concentration camps, and to add insult to injury, the Jewish community was forced to pay compensation for the damage "they had caused" during the pogrom. The systematic persecution and marginalisation of the Jews in Germany which began as state policy after Adolf Hitler became German Chancellor in January of 1933 had now turned violent and for most of the approximately two hundred thousand Jews still living in Germany and Austria emigration became an imperative. Unfortunately, there were very few gates open and the embattled Jewish communities in Germany and Austria were effectively trapped.

In response to the perceived danger a number of Jewish and non-Jewish organisations lobbied the British government and in 1939 were successful in getting the British Parliament to approve a visa program that would bring unaccompanied Jewish children from Germany and Austria to Great Britain. This program ultimately became known as the Kindertransport and as a result around ten thousand children were allowed to enter Great Britain on the understanding that when the situation in their home countries allowed for it, they would be returned. The situation never allowed for it, and for a large number of children when the war ended their families had been murdered and there was no one left they could return to.

There are therefore around ten thousand stories that may be told about the journeys undertaken by the Kindertransport children, and about their new lives after they were sent away for their safety by heartbroken families. *This book is about only one of those stories; it is not intended to be, nor can it be, a representation of the total Kindertransport experience.*

If Martha's story should encourage a desire to understand more about the Kindertransport program and its impact, not only on the children, but also on the carers and parents of the children, a recent publication by Jennifer Craig-Norton is a valuable resource.[1] Just two insights from her book will offer some appreciation for the complexity of the subject. On the one hand Craig-Norton notes that the Kindertransport is frequently characterised as a model response to a refugee crisis.[2] However elsewhere in the book, from the testimony of a Kindertransport survivor, we find this: "I know I can never be one of them, I am and always shall be a foreigner."[3]

---

[1] Craig-Norton, J. *The Kindertransport: Contesting Memory.* Indiana University Press, 2019.
[2] Ibid., p11.
[3] Ibid., p211.

Introduction

When Martha Braun and her sister Margot boarded a train at the Hamburg railway station, a journey began that in its wake obliterated every childhood hope and dream they both carried with them on to the platform that late spring morning. How were they to know that events occurring decades earlier, many in the previous century, had become a torrential river of fate under which their heartbroken parents would later be submerged, victims of their own country's obsession to rid the world of every living Jew.

Where to start their story? I really struggled with that; and oh, by the way, begging your pardon, I have not yet introduced myself although my name is really unimportant—I am nobody, just a storyteller. But I suppose everyone needs to have some sort of calling card, don't they. A wonderful teller of Yiddish stories called himself Mendele Mocher Sforim, Mendel the Bookseller, so how about to you I am Ani Korim Sforim, which in English is simply "I read books". Incidentally, the Hebrew version is grammatically incorrect but it rhymes and has a nice ring to it so, what the heck!

And, you may very well ask, what stories do you tell, Ani Korim Sforim? I have this fascination, you see, some say it is an obsession, to look for time warps trapped inside historical kaleidoscopes. You can peer into these for hours watching how the lives of the people trapped inside the time warp react to the changing conditions thrown up by the revolving kaleidoscope.

It is a strange pastime I admit, not always satisfying; the colours within a particular historical kaleidoscope are often drab, grey, uninteresting, evoking little emotion, no excitement, a disappointing experience you quickly throw aside. At other times, however, what you find inside the historical kaleidoscope evokes a plethora of emotion and stimulates your every sense. It is in these experiences, some uplifting and inspiring, others horrifying yet edifying, where I find material for the stories I tell.

In the life of a time warp storyteller there are rare moments when someone will pull you aside, look you in the eyes and say, "You think you really know me, come with me and I will help you find the real me, and after you have discovered the real me, I give you permission to go and tell everyone about the me you discovered." And then, somewhat shyly and reticently, they hand over their own personal and very private historical kaleidoscope. That is a rare privilege, but it also brings with it a very heavy burden of responsibility for any storyteller.

I was privileged to be one of a small group to whom Martha, the older of the two Braun sisters, handed over her own personal historical kaleidoscope. When she said to us "you can ask me anything", we did, we peered into her life for untold hours, turned that kaleidoscope around and around, tried to understand what happened in the decades before she was born, how the past impacted on and moulded her life, the lives of her family, and those of her community. We discovered so many stories, a 'storyteller's feast you could say. We laid them out like pieces of a jigsaw puzzle, discovering matching themes that allowed us to connect story to story which in turn illuminated and clarified the big story, which was always Martha's story. Her story was emotionally ripping, and heartbreaking; we cried with her, laughed with her, and when it was over truly believed we had taken away some of her pain and transferred it on to ourselves.

Before I ask Martha to tell you her own story, it is necessary for us to travel back in time so that we can first identify and then piece together a sequence of events which ultimately brought Martha and Margot to the Hamburg railway station on the 21st May 1939. Our journey will not be unlike making a movie. First many scenes are filmed and then a skilful editor splices them together, creating what you eventually view as the completed production. I am going to show you a number of scenes from history and it is then up to you, dear reader, to decide how you splice them in order to develop your own understanding of Martha's story.

BOOK ONE

1800-1899

Antisemitism evolves from religious to racial classification

GERMANY'S MISFORTUNE, ITS JEWISH COMMUNITY

———◆———

The German Jewish community numbered around six hundred thousand at the end of the nineteenth century. A tiny minority which accounted for less than one percent of the general population, German Jews, as the saying goes, punched far above their fighting weight.

Many had the foresight to recognise the opportunities unfolding as the Industrial Revolution changed economic life in Europe. Utilising both the new technologies and production processes, they established large factories, employed large numbers of workers, and in the process, many became very wealthy.

The lives of Jews in Germany were not only impacted by the benefits derived from harnessing the opportunities presented by the Industrial Revolution. The evolution of intellectual and philosophical thinking we know as the Age of Enlightenment that began in seventeenth century Europe also gave birth to an age of Jewish enlightenment, the Haskalah. This movement, with its emphasis on moral and cultural renewal, was to radically alter Jewish life and community not only in Germany, but also in other European countries. As a result, German Jews became prominent in science, medicine, music, philosophy, political life, law, finance, literature, publishing, theatre, chemistry, mathematics, physics and engineering.

The Haskalah movement also became a catalyst that encouraged many prominent German Jews to abandon their religion and community by converting to Christianity. Their motivation was either because they found traditional Jewish religious observance too restrictive, or that the stigma of being Jewish became a barrier to acceptance in wider German society. It has been estimated that at least half of Berlin Jews were baptized during the first decades of the nineteenth century. Ironically, after Hitler and the Nazi party gained control Jewish identity was determined through blood inheritance, not religious affiliation. If one grandparent was Jewish you were Jewish, it did not matter which church you attended on Sunday!

I believe I am a competent storyteller but I do understand my limitations. I have to accept that it will just not be possible to list every contribution made by Germany's Jews during the nineteenth century and in the thirty-two years before Adolf Hitler became Chancellor in January 1933. I would however like to provide you with sufficient information to consider the validity of an allegation made in 1880 by Heinrich von Treitschke, prominent German historian, political writer, and Reichstag member; he wrote, and I quote, "the Jews are our [Germany's] misfortune."[4]

Let me begin with by telling you about a very early champion of the German Jewish Haskalah movement, Moses Mendelssohn. His father Mendel was a poor sofer,[5] and the family lived in Dessau, a large city situated at the confluence of

---

[4] H. Von Treitschke, *Ein Wort Uber Unser Jude.* January, 1880.
[5] A scribe who writes manuscripts in ornate Hebrew lettering.

the Elbe and Mulde rivers. The young Moses was brought up in a strictly Orthodox family environment and at the age of fourteen, he followed his rabbi and moved to Berlin. His initial education followed traditional lines, however a number of close friendships and an innate inquisitiveness driven by his huge intellectual capability drew him into the secular world. Mendelssohn's later writings encompassed the fields of metaphysics, aesthetics, political theory and theology, placing him at the forefront of the Haskalah movement in Germany. Immanuel Kant, a Lutheran who some consider to be one of the most important contributors to the world of philosophy since Plato and Aristotle, acknowledged Mendelssohn as a genius who created a new epoch in metaphysics and intellectual criticism. In Jewish circles Mendelssohn is probably best remembered for translating the traditional Hebrew text in which the Old Testament is written into German.

In 1819 leading Jewish intellectuals in Germany created the Society for Promotion of Jewish Culture and Science, its stated objectives being to initiate scientific method into the study of the Jewish religion history and culture. Two of the leading promoters of the society were Heinrich Heine and Eduard Gans. Heine, who was named Harry at birth, was the son of Samson, a successful textile merchant living in Dusseldorf. At the age of twenty-eight Harry Heine converted to Lutheranism and became Heinrich Heine. He was a poet, a writer, and a literary critic, recognised as a leading member of the young Germany movement, a group of writers dedicated to maintaining the principles of democracy, socialism, and rationalism. Heine's radical political views eventually led to many of his works being banned by the German authorities.

Although this added to his fame, he was forced to spend the last twenty-five years of his life as an expatriate in Paris. Eduard Gans was also born into a wealthy Jewish family, he initially studied law but became more interested in philosophy. After converting to Christianity in 1825 his career opportunities changed significantly and in 1828, he was appointed a professor in the Berlin University faculty of law.

Germany's first iron foundry and smelter was built by three Jewish industrialists, Moritz Friedlander, Simon Levy and David Lowenfeld. The coke necessary for steelmaking in Germany was produced by another Jew, Moritz Friedlander.

Albert Ballin founded the Hamburg American Line which for a time was the world's largest shipping company. He is also accredited with being the inventor of the cruise ship concept and is considered to be the father of modern cruise ship travel.

Emil Rathenau acquired the rights to manufacture electrical products based on Thomas Edison's patents. The company he founded was known as Allgemeine Elektrizitäts-Gesellschaft or AEG in abbreviation; it became one of the largest electrical product supply companies in the world. One of his sons was Walther Rathenau, an industrialist, politician, and progressive economist who served as German Foreign Minister for the Weimar Republic. Walter was assassinated in June 1922 by a right-wing terrorist group.

Jews were also prominent in the retail sector. Georg Wertheim established the Wertheim retail store chain (which was Aryanized by the Nazis) and Hermann Tietz was the founder of the Tietz department store.

A name synonymous with banking and finance is Rothschild. Mayer Amschel Rothschild was born in 1744 to an

Ashkenazi Jewish family in the Jewish ghetto of Frankfurt. He was one of eight children born to Amschel Moses Rothschild and his wife, Schönche Rothschild. Mayer Rothschild, who established the Rothschild banking dynasty, is often referred to as a founding father of international finance. In 2005 he was ranked seventh by *Forbes* magazine on a list it prepared of the twenty most influential businessmen of all time. The empire he created was inherited by his five sons and the Rothschilds became the premier bankers of Europe. They were hugely instrumental in contributing to the commercial development and industrial growth for Germany and the rest of Europe. And it was not only the Rothschild family—Gerson Bleichröder, a Jewish banker, managed German Chancellor Otto von Bismarck's private banking arrangements and negotiated large financial transactions on behalf of the Prussian state and the German Empire. He was also intimately involved with the inner dynamics of the process leading to the unification of Germany.

Jews were also prominent in the world of publishing. Leopold Ullstein was the founder and publisher of several successful German newspapers, many of which are still published today. He also established the leading German publishing house Ullstein-Verlag which at one time was publishing a hundred daily newspapers, weekly and monthly magazines. Following the rise of Adolf Hitler and the Nazi Party in 1933, the Ullstein publishing empire was forcibly Aryanized; valued at sixty million marks it was sold under duress for six million. Another publisher of note was Bernhard Wolff who established Wolffs Telegraphisches Bureau. It was among the first press agencies in Europe and one of three great European telegraph monopolies before World War II, the other two being the English Reuters and the French Havas.

In the field of medicine Jews contributed way above their status as a small minority within German society.

Moritz Heinrich Romberg, a German physician and neurologist, revolutionized European neurology, publishing the first systematic textbook on the subject. One of Romberg's significant contributions was to identify that the slow degeneration of the nerve cells and nerve fibres carrying sensory information to the brain was a disease now known by its medical name Tabes. Among his other significant clinical contributions are descriptions of achondroplasia, a genetic disorder leading to dwarfism, and the impact tertiary syphilis has on the pupils in the eye of someone stricken by the disease.

Robert Remak, embryologist, physiologist, and neurologist discovered that the origin of cells was by the division of pre-existing cells. As a Jew he was denied full professor status until late in his life and then had to make do with an appointment as assistant professor.

Ludwig Traube, the son of a Jewish wine merchant, became a physician and is acknowledged as being the founder of experimental pathophysiological research in Germany. He is also more widely recognised as the father of experimental pathology. His Jewish ancestry was also a major impediment to gaining any academic appointments but ultimately, he became adjunct professor, and then ordinary professor at the Friedrich-Wilhelms-Institute in Berlin. After the title "Geheimer Medizinalrath"[6] was bestowed on him in 1872, Traube was appointed a professor at the University of Berlin.

---

[6] An award for outstanding contributions to medicine.

Friedrich Gustav Jakob Henle, physician, pathologist, and anatomist, is credited with the discovery of the "Loop of Henle" in the kidney, its principal function being the recovery of water and sodium chloride from urine. Henle's essay "On Miasma and Contagia" was an early argument for the germ theory of disease.

Julius Cohnheim, a pathologist, was the first to use the now universal method of freezing fresh pathological objects for examination. He was the pioneer in the theory of inflammation, and his research in the field of pathological circulation and the causes of embolism marked a new departure in the methods of medical treatment.

Ferdinand Julius Cohn was one of the founders of modern bacteriology and microbiology. Karl Weigert is credited with the discovery of vascular tuberculosis and was the first to demonstrate how tuberculous material could enter the bloodstream.

Paul Ehrlich, a physician and scientist, made many notable discoveries in the field of medicine. He is best known for discovering a cure for syphilis and for developing a method to stain tissue, allowing for distinguishing between different types of blood cells and enabling the diagnosis of numerous blood diseases. In 1908 he was awarded a Nobel prize in Physiology or Medicine for his work on immunity.

Heinrich Finkelstein was the medical director of the Emperor and Empress Frederick Children's Hospital. His ideas for a program of comprehensive public infant care were ahead of time and reduced the infant mortality rate to 4.3%, a value not to be exceeded in Germany until many decades later. Together with Ludwig Ferdinand Meyer, he also developed the first artificial protein milk, which saved the lives of thousands of infants suffering from eating disorders. Finkelstein was respected and honoured internationally as a paediatrician, but being a Jew, he never received an ordinary professorship in his own country.

Paul Gerson Unna, a German physician who specialized in dermatology, described for the first time what was to be called Unna's disease, a chronic disease of the skin. Unna and a non-Jewish colleague, Arthur Thost, identified a rare hereditary skin disease affecting the soles and palms which is known as the Unna-Thost syndrome. Unna's research also contributed to developing treatments for leprosy, syphilis, and tuberculosis.

Julius Hirschberg, an ophthalmologist, was the first to use an electromagnet to remove metallic foreign bodies from the eye. He also wrote a nine-volume history of ophthalmology, *Geschichte der Augenheilkunde*,[7] which is considered to be one of his greatest achievements. Another German Jewish ophthalmologist, Ernst Fuchs, became well known throughout the ophthalmology world through his more than two hundred and fifty scientific publications. His collection of microscopic samples laid the foundation for anatomical and pathological understanding of blood vessels, muscles, and most other tissues of the eye. Fuchs' *Textbook of Ophthalmology* first published in 1889 was, for many decades, the most extensively used reference book in the field of ophthalmology worldwide.

Albert Ludwig Sigesmund Neisser discovered the strain of bacteria which caused gonorrhoea; a particular strain, *Neisseria gonorrhoeae*, was named in his honour.

Otto Fritz Meyerhof, a physician and biochemist, together with a non-Jew, Archibald Vivian Hill, was awarded

---

[7] *History of Ophthalmology.*

the Nobel Prize in Physiology and Medicine in 1922. The citation given was for their work on muscle metabolism, including glycolysis. Meyerhof became one of the directors of the Kaiser Wilhelm Institute for Medical Research, a position he held until 1938 when he was forced to escape the Nazi regime. He fled to Paris in 1938 and was fortunate to obtain papers allowing him to relocate to the United States in 1940.

In the world of chemists and chemistry Jews were again prominent.

Richard Martin Willstatter was an organic chemist whose study of the structure of plant pigments, including chlorophyll, won him the 1915 Noel Prize for Chemistry. In 1924 Willstatter brought his career to a premature end in protest against the rising tide of antisemitismin Germany. As a counter to the antisemitic rhetoric in 1933 the Central Union of German Citizens of the Jewish Faith published an encyclopaedia with one thousand and sixty pages that documented in detail the contributions of Jews to German life and culture during the previous two centuries. Willstatter was asked to write the introduction. In 1934 the Berlin State Police confiscated all the copies that had already been printed. Willstatter left Germany in 1939.

Adolph Frank, the son of a Jewish merchant who ran a general store, was a chemist, engineer, and businessman best known for having discovered uses of potash and then going on to help establish the potash industry in Germany. Together with the German-Polish chemist Nikodem Caro, Frank also is known for developing the Frank-Caro process of extracting calcium cyanamide. This became the foundation of the nitrogen and calcium cyanamide fertilizer industry. The brown colouring of bottles, which protects the contents from the effects of light, can also be attributed to him. Frank also researched the extraction of hydrogen for use in blimps together with a non-Jew, Carl von Linde.

Heinrich Caro was a German chemist who together with Adolf von Baeyer, the founder of the Bayer chemical company, synthesized the first indigo dyestuff in 1878. He also patented the dye alizarin on behalf of the Bayer company.

Richard Wolffenstein discovered acetone peroxide by reacting acetone with hydrogen peroxide and the so-called Wolffenstein-Böters reaction, which he discovered in 1913, became an alternative production method for explosives.

Fritz Haber received the Nobel Prize in Chemistry in 1918 for his invention of the Haber–Bosch process, a method used in industry to synthesize ammonia from nitrogen gas and hydrogen gas. This invention is important for the large-scale synthesis of fertilizers and explosives. It is estimated that one-third of annual global food production uses ammonia from the Haber–Bosch process. Haber is also considered the father of chemical warfare after his years of pioneering work developing and weaponizing chlorine and other poisonous gases during World War I. Tragically, his work was later also used to develop Zyklon B which the Nazis used to murder over one million Jews in the gas chambers at Birkenau. Haber has been called one of the most important scientists, if not the most important, in human history and possibly the greatest industrial chemist who ever lived.

From chemistry to the world of physics, once more the German Jewish community's contribution was significant.

Moritz Hermann Jacobi established Jacobi's Law, which is of use when driving a load such as an electric motor from a battery. He discovered galvanoplastics, or electrotyping, a method of making printing plates by electroplating, worked on the development of the electric telegraph and developed the Jacobi naval mine.

Heinrich Rudolf Hertz, whose parents had converted to Lutheranism before his birth, first conclusively proved the existence of electromagnetic waves. The unit of frequency was named the "hertz" in his honour. Hertz's proof of the existence of airborne electromagnetic waves led to an explosion of experimentation with this new form of electromagnetic radiation, which were called "Hertzian waves" until the term "radio waves" became current. Hertz's research on contact mechanics also facilitated the age of nanotechnology. In spite of the fact that Hertz's family had converted from Judaism to Lutheranism two decades before his birth, the Nazi government removed his name from streets and institutions and even tried to remove his name from the hertz unit of frequency.

James Franck won the 1925 Nobel Prize for Physics with another Jewish physicist, Gustav Hertz, for their discovery of the laws governing the impact of an electron upon an atom. Franck served as a volunteer in the German Army during World War I, was seriously injured in a gas attack, and was awarded the Iron Cross 1st Class. Born into a traditionally orthodox family, Franck once commented that science was his God and nature was his religion. When the Nazis came to power Franck was initially protected because of his military service but resigned all of his positions anyway as an act of protest against the antisemitic discrimination and actions of the Nazi government. He was in fact the first academic to resign in protest over the Nuremburg laws. Franck left Germany in November 1933 and went to the United States where he participated in the Manhattan Project which developed the atom bomb. He was also the chairman of the Committee on Political and Social Problems Regarding the Atomic Bomb, which is best known for compiling the Franck Report recommending that atomic bombs should not be dropped on Japanese cities without warning.

Gustav Ludwig Hertz was a Nobel Prize winner for his work on inelastic electron collisions in gases. At the end of 1934, he was forced to resign his position because he was classified as a "second degree part-Jew"; his paternal grandfather was born Jewish before the family converted to Lutheranism. Hertz then worked for Siemens as director of a research laboratory and avoided deportation during the war years. In 1945 he left Germany to live the rest of his life in the Soviet Union.

Albert Einstein was born into a family of secular Ashkenazi Jews. His father and uncle founded Elektro-technische Fabrik J. Einstein & Cie, which manufactured electrical equipment based on direct current. Albert Einstein is widely acknowledged as one of the greatest and most influential physicists of all time. He is best known for developing the theory of relativity, but he also made important contributions to the development of the theory of quantum mechanics. His mass–energy equivalence formula $E = mc^2$, which arises from relativity theory, has been dubbed "the world's most famous equation". Einstein received the 1921 Nobel Prize in Physics "for his services to theoretical physics, and especially for his discovery of the law of the photoelectric effect", a pivotal step in the development of quantum theory. His intellectual achievements and originality resulted in the name "Einstein" becoming synonymous with "genius". Einsteinium, one of the synthetic elements in the periodic table, was named in his honour. In 1933 Einstein moved to the United States as a protest against the antisemitism of the newly elected Nazi government. On the eve of World War II, Einstein endorsed a letter to President Franklin D. Roosevelt alerting him to the potential German nuclear weapons program and recommending that the US begin similar research.

German Jews also contributed significantly to German literature.

Ludwig Anton Salomon Fulda was a playwright and poet with a strong social commitment. He became a member of the Prussian Academy of Arts and the first president of the PEN[8] association of Germany. He attempted to gain refuge in the United States after the Nazis came to power but was refused. A disillusioned and broken man, Fulda committed suicide in 1939 after he was turned down for asylum.

Jakob Wasserman's work includes poetry, essays, novels, and short stories. The two most recognised publications are the novel *Der Fall Maurizius*[9] and his autobiography, *Mein Weg als Deutscher und Jude*,[10] in which he discussed the tense relationship between his German and Jewish identities. In 1933 his books were banned in Germany and he died on 1st January 1934 at his home in Altaussee of a heart attack at age sixty-one.

---

[8] Poets Essayists Novelists.
[9] *The Maurizius Case.*
[10] *My Life as German and Jew.*

Georg Hermann, who was born Georg Borchardt, was an internationally renowned author of novels, essays, and commentary. His writings portrayed his pacifism and this together with his Jewish inheritance drove him and his family to flee Germany and seek refuge in Holland after the Reichstag burned down in 1933. Hermann was sent to the Dutch concentration camp of Westerbork and then transported to Auschwitz where he either died during the deportation or shortly after his arrival.

In the sphere of German music Jews were exceptionally prominent.

Giacomo Meyerbeer was possibly the most frequently performed opera composer during the nineteenth century. His grand opera style was achieved by the merging of German orchestra style with Italian vocal tradition. Meyerbeer was born into a wealthy Jewish family and began his musical career as a pianist. He decided, however, to focus on the opera and moved to Italy where he studied and also began composing. Meyerbeer held appointments as Prussian Court Kapellmeister[11] and also as Prussian General Music Director. Ironically, he was an early supporter of Richard Wagner and facilitated the first production of Wagner's opera *Rienzi*. After Meyerbeer died Wagner repaid the support by launching a concerted critical assault on his work which ultimately led to a decline in the popularity of his works. In his scurrilous publication "Jews and Music" Wagner accused Meyerbeer of being only interested in money and not in music. The Nazis suppressed Meyerbeer's operas after they gained power in 1933 and his works were largely not performed during the rest of the twentieth century. Today

---

[11] Director of Music.

however his operas have begun to reappear in the repertory of numerous European opera houses.

Jakob Ludwig Felix Mendelssohn Bartholdy, widely known as Felix Mendelssohn, was a composer, pianist, organist, and conductor of the early Romantic period. His compositions include symphonies, concertos, piano music, organ music, and chamber music. Among his best-known works are the famous "Wedding March" which is included in the incidental music he composed for *A Midsummer Night's Dream*. The melody for the Christmas carol "Hark! The Herald Angels Sing" is also his. Mendelssohn's "Songs Without Words" are his most famous solo piano compositions. Felix was the grandson of Moses Mendelssohn and was initially brought up in a family devoid of religion. When his family elected to convert to Christianity, he was baptized at the age of seven.

Ferdinand David was raised Jewish but later converted to Protestant Christianity. Initially trained as a violinist, David became concertmaster at the Gewandhaus in Leipzig and the first professor of violin at the newly founded Leipziger Konservatorium für Musik. David worked closely with Mendelssohn, providing him with technical advice while he was composing the "Violin Concerto in E Minor". When the concerto was first performed David was the soloist. Another outstanding German Jewish violinist was Heinrich Wilhelm, who many considered to be the successor to one of the most celebrated violinists of all time, Niccolò Paganini.

Hermann Levi was the son of a rabbi who began his music studies at the Leipzig Conservatory. He held position as music director at Saarbrücken and Mannheim and for a two-year period was chief conductor of the German Opera in Rotterdam.

Levi's name is closely linked with the increased public appreciation of Wagner's music. While preparing for the inaugural Bayreuth Festival, Levi stated in a letter that Wagner was the best and noblest of men and he was grateful for the privilege of being able to work so closely with him. Levi also conducted the first performance of *Parsifal* at Bayreuth despite the fact that Wagner initially objected and wanted Levi to be baptized before conducting the opera.

Bruno Walter was born into a middle-class Jewish family and began his musical education at the Stern Conservatory at the age of eight, making his first public appearance as a pianist when he was nine. When Hitler became Chancellor in January 1933, Walter was scheduled to conduct a series of concerts with the Gewandhaus Orchestra but the ministry of the interior threatened to cancel the concerts if Walter was to be the conductor. The same threat, this time emanating from none other than Joseph Goebbels, resulted in Walter withdrawing from conducting a series of concerts in Berlin at which point he left Germany, not returning until after the war.

Kurt Weill grew up in a religious Jewish family in the "Sandvorstadt", the Jewish quarter in Dessau where his father was a cantor. At the age of twelve, Weill began his musical career on the piano and soon began writing music. His earliest preserved composition was written in 1913 and is titled "Mi Addir: Jewish Wedding Song". Weill fled Nazi Germany in March 1933, and became a prominent and popular composer who together with Bertolt Brecht created a revolutionary kind of opera that was effectively social satire.

One of the most influential persons in the development of German theatre and film is Max Reinhardt; his innovative stage productions made him one of the most prominent directors of German language theatre in the early twentieth century. Reinhardt introduced powerful staging techniques that integrated stage design, language, music and choreography. He also established the Salzburg Festival. Reinhardt left Germany after the Anschluss between Austria and Germany in 1938.

Despite the attempts to discriminate against and marginalize the Jews in Germany, its members were prominent in the political life of the emerging unified German nation.

Edward Lasker, born Yitzchak Lasker, was both politician and jurist. A spokesman for liberalism, he became the leader of the left wing of the National Liberal party, which represented middle-class professionals and intellectuals. He was a vocal proponent for the unification of Germany and had a major role in the codification of the German legal code. In 1881, Lasker left the National Liberal party and helped form the new German Free Thought Party.

Ludwig Bamberger was an economist, politician, revolutionary and writer. In 1848 he was actively involved in the movement that promoted pan-Germanism, and demanded that the autocratic political structure dominating the loosely aligned independent states of the German confederation be changed. In 1849, with other leaders of the movement, Bamberger was condemned to death but managed to escape to Switzerland. An amnesty enabled him to return to Germany in 1866 and he was elected as a member of the Reichstag representing the National Liberal Party. In 1868 Bamberger published a short life of Bismarck in French, and in 1870 he and Jewish banker Gerson Bleichröder were sent to Versailles by Bismarck to participate in negotiating the peace terms that brought an end to the

Franco-Prussian War. Bleichröder was Bismarck's personal banker and also responsible for negotiating major funding arrangements on behalf of the Prussian state and the German Empire. In the German Reichstag Bamberger was one of the leading authorities on matters of finance and economics; he was actively involved in the campaign to introduce a gold currency and assisted in the formation of the Reichsbank. Ultimately his free market philosophies brought him into conflict with Bismarck and he left the National Liberal Party to join a breakaway movement that became the German Free-Minded Party. Bamberger was also co-founder of Deutsche Bank which today is a leading multinational banking institution.

Three Jews also served in Bismarck's cabinet after the unification of the German states. They were Eduard von Simson, Heinrich Friedberg and Rudolf Friedenthal. Stahl, whose original name was Julius Jolson, converted to Lutheranism at the age of seventeen. Awarded the degree Juris Doctor, he became an ordinary professor and ultimately held the chair at Berlin University for ecclesiastical law and policy. He became one of Bismarck's closest advisers and is famous, or possibly infamous, for coining the phrase "not majority authority".

Ferdinand Lasalle was born Ferdinand Johann Gottlieb Lassal but changed his name to avoid any association with Judaism. His father, Heyman Lassal, was a Jewish silk merchant. Lasalle established the world's first organised trade union movement, The General German Workers Association, which ultimately morphed into the Social Democrats party in Germany. His life had a tragic end when he fought a duel over a woman and lost; he died in the exchange of fire!

And in conclusion, no overview of German Jews connected to the world of politics can be complete without mentioning the man whose name was indelibly linked with the word Jew in the mind of Adolf Hitler: Karl Heinrich Marx. Marx's family was originally Jewish, but had converted formally to Christianity before his birth. His maternal grandfather was a rabbi in the Netherlands and on the father's side there were generations of rabbis. Karl Marx's father Herschel was the first in his family to receive a secular education, became a lawyer and also owned a number of vineyards. Karl Marx was a philosopher, economist, historian, sociologist, political theorist, journalist, critic of political economy, and socialist revolutionary. His most famous publications are the 1848 pamphlet he named "The Communist Manifesto", and the four-volume *Das Kapital*. His influence on the future debate regarding social, political, and economic theory has been enormous and enduring, and his name is now both noun and adjective.

And so dear readers, this is not by any means an exhaustive summary of the contributions made by Jews in Germany to the country they were loyal to and considered to be their home. Now, if you were the presiding judge in a trial where Von Treitschke was being sued for defamation, how would you rule?

THE JEWS ARE A SCATTERED NATION

———•◆•———

When I introduced myself to you, dear readers, I spoke about my fascination, some would say obsession, with a phenomenon called time warps. I also told you that to study time warps a time kaleidoscope is required. You peer into the kaleidoscope's interior all the while turning the barrel around and around, and then, like an entomologist with a net attempting to snare that elusive rare species of butterfly you deftly swoop, trapping the image you see before it disappears once more. How about we do a test run; I will pick up the kaleidoscope, peer into it, turn the barrel, and let's see what image we can trap.

We are in Berlin, outside the University; it is 1815. Given my fascination with the past I decide to amble over to the department of history; its incumbent professor, Christian Friedrich Ruhs, is one of Germany's most eminent and influential historians. I find the day's schedule on a notice board and see with some excitement that Professor Ruhs is to deliver a lecture titled, "About the Claims of the Jews to German Citizenship". I am intrigued; here is an opportunity to understand how the issue of Jewish emancipation is being discussed in a proper academic context. The lecture hall is packed but the subdued level of conversation communicates an air of some solemnity. When the professor enters the room silence descends immediately. He is quite young, in his forties I think, very fashionably dressed, the wig on his head creating an image a little at odds with his reputation as a serious historian.

"The Jews", he begins, "are a scattered nation, they are only accountable to their rabbis and therefore should never qualify for German citizenship. Their population growth should be restricted and they must be encouraged to convert to Christianity".[12]

There are a few murmurs around the room and I notice some students shifting uncomfortably in their seats; I cannot tell if they are Jewish. Ruhs then continues, "The Jews are an alien race in our midst and should be made to wear the mediaeval yellow star".[13]

This is enough for me; I get up quickly and leave. I had hoped to be informed, and possibly even comforted by the arguments presented by an eminent German academic. I depart very disturbed by the illogicality and underlying viciousness of his arguments.

---

[12] In 1815 Ruhs published these thoughts in a pamphlet titled "Ueber die Ansprüche der Juden an das Deutsche Bürgerrecht" (About the Claims of the Jews to German Citizenship).
[13] Ibid.

The Hep, Hep Pogrom

———◆———

We are now travelling back in time to the German city of Wurzburg, arriving on the 2nd August 1819. I am not all that comfortable about being here, this was the town where in 1621 a priest put men, women, and children on trial for the crime of witchery. For five years, in an orgy of burnings torture and beheadings, hundreds of innocent souls were judicially, or should I rather say religiously, murdered. The streets I am walking through on this very warm summer day are strangely quiet but they exude a palpable tension. In the distance I hear the sound of a regular chanting, "hep, hep"—shepherds urging on their flock in the middle of the town? There is something different; these chants are angry, almost hysterical, and in the background I can hear screaming and crying. What is this, sheep don't scream, don't cry?

I am walking down a narrow alleyway; the closer the exit, the louder the noise. I emerge from the alleyway and confront mayhem.

To my right an elderly man is crouched over, his arms raised trying to block blows raining down on his head by a broom wielded by a young woman. Not only is he under attack from the woman, but he is also trying to fend off a snarling, barking dog lunging for his legs, teeth bared. Behind them two men are struggling; one heavyset and well-dressed is beating his hapless victim with a club while simultaneously trying to choke him with his free hand. I can hear the terrified victim pleading, crying, "Josef, we are neighbours, why are you doing this?" Broken furniture and household possessions are strewn all over the small square and, with shock, I see an old lady lean out of her window and pour a bucket of boiling water over a young woman standing below.

There is a larger thoroughfare opening out from the small square; in its centre a uniformed figure on horseback is urging his mount forward, sword raised in preparation for a downward swing. In front of him others on horseback are chasing a gaggle of panicked humans who are desperately trying to outrun the charging horses. In panic these poor souls keep throwing quick glances behind them hoping that the race against their pursuers is being won. The backward glances cause many to trip and fall, and they in turn become obstacles for others to trip and fall over. The swords that catch up with the people on the ground are merciless, and blood runs freely over the cobbled street. "Where are the police?" I shout out, but they are nowhere to be seen and of course nobody can hear me, I am an onlooker from the future. Eventually I see a few policemen arrive and watch the mayhem unfolding in front of them. What I am seeing here is too horrible to watch. I leave hurriedly; visiting the past is at times a painful experience. Who were the victims and what was their crime? The victims were the Jews in Wurzburg, there had been a Jewish presence here from the 1100s. Their crime: requesting emancipation, wanting to live as equals with their fellow citizens in the state of Bavaria.

The Wissenschaft des Judentums

———◆———

Now that I had the kaleidoscope focused on the year 1819, I thought it might be interesting to have a peek at some of the activities being undertaken by the Berlin Jewish community in that year. Date, 27th November. I am standing in front of the imposing entrance to the University of Berlin. The university was founded by the Prussian philosopher, linguist, government functionary and diplomat, Friedrich Wilhelm Christian Karl Ferdinand von Humboldt. Today the university bears his name and is known as the Humboldt University of Berlin. The building has only been used as an academic institution for nine years; its original purpose was as a palace built for Prince Henry of Prussia.

In a small, rather gloomy and austere room allocated for group study sit three men: Leopold Zunz twenty-five years of age, Eduard Gans twenty-one years of age, and Moses Mosser twenty-three. Zunz is talking animatedly and the others are listening intently without interruption. Leopold Zunz is a student at the university and already quite well known within selected intellectual and academic circles. Two years previously he published a booklet which was a plea for the recognition of Judaism and its literature in university research and teaching. As we enter the room, incognito of course, Zunz is talking animatedly about the general level of ignorance displayed by the books non-Jewish scholars write about Judaism and the Jews. And then he abruptly changes tack, observing quietly with a tinge of bitterness in his voice, "Jews have made valuable contributions to science, medicine, music and philosophy here in Prussia and elsewhere, and yet we are reviled in the halls of academia. To be accepted we choose baptism, it is the only gateway for acceptance into the intellectual world in which we live."

Gans, who comes from a prosperous Jewish family, immediately enters the conversation. He has made the journey to Berlin from Heidelberg, where he was reading philosophy and jurisprudence under the supervision of two renowned scholars, Georg Wilhelm Friedrich Hegel, and Anton Friedrich Justus Thibaut. "Zunz, what you are saying is correct, and what is more I am confronting this very situation at the moment. I am seeking a position in either the law or in academia and all doors are shut to me when they find out I am Jewish. We all agree that this is the reality but the question becomes, are we able to change the reality?"

"That, my dear Gans, is exactly why we are here today," responds Zunz excitedly, "we must establish a Verein für Kultur und Wissenschaft der Juden,[14] we can call it Wissenschaft der Juden. I have given this much thought, even formulated the two primary objectives for the association, which will be to combat assimilation and conversion in our Jewish community, and to initiate a scientific method into the study of the Jewish religion history and culture. This will promote understanding in the world of academia of the intellectual rigor underpinning our

---

[14] An association for culture and science of the Jews.

Jewish religion. It will open the doors for advancement into that world for our people."

Zunz then leans forward in his chair and earnestly launches into a lengthy explanation of his vision for the Wissenschaft. "We will enlist many Jewish scholars into our association. They will open up our ancient texts and commence to study these in the same way that scholars study the classical Greek and Latin texts. We will begin an analysis of our holy texts using the disciplines of history and linguistics and, in this way, we will develop a whole new approach to the understanding of Jewish tradition and history. Our search will be to understand how our religion has changed and developed over the millennia by asking questions that are based on a scientific and historic methodology. Now, my friends, I do understand this approach will bring us into direct conflict with the traditional rabbinical authorities and with those who would seek to ensure our religion is forever shackled by precepts created by the social and cultural demands of past eras. This, however, cannot be helped because our mission must be to bring our religion into the present and in so doing prepare it for a different future."

The third member of the group, Moses Mosser, a well-to-do German merchant, has for a time also been an assistant to the banker Moses Friedlander. Mosser is known to possess considerable mathematical talent, has studied philology, and is a close friend of Harry Heine who is currently enrolled as a student at the University of Bonn. Zunz understands that his fledgling association requires a financial benefactor and has invited Mosser for precisely that reason. Mosser's friendship with Heine also provides Zunz with a contact into a group of emerging young Jewish intellectuals who will be invaluable resources for the Wissenschaft.

Zunz stops mid-sentence and is looking at Mosser expectantly.

"My dear Zunz," Mosser begins, "I believe this is a most worthy enterprise. As you know I am a very cautious fellow and will need to understand a great deal more about who will lead and organize this association. You must also explain what money will be required to ensure its success, no doubt that is one of the prime motivations for my presence here today. But these are details, we will discuss them in the weeks to come. Your rationale for establishing the Wissenschaft is compelling, I have heard sufficient here today that will allow me to give you my qualified support. This support will begin in a tangible form. I will arrange for a small sum to be transferred to a lawyer I work with here in Berlin; he will make those funds available to you for undertaking the initial procedures required for establishing the Wissenschaft. As you know, I have a close association with Harry Heine, a young man whose reputation in academic and literary circles is growing. He would be an ideal candidate to contribute towards the work of this association, and I will appraise him of the discussion here today."

Gans, who has been busily scribbling notes into a small notebook, quickly breaks in before Mosser can continue, "Zunz, if this association of yours can support the emancipation of the Jews living in the German states, I pledge whatever resources I have to assist you in your endeavour."

Zunz, by nature severe and strictly formal, stands, smiles briefly, and replies, "Gut, meine Herren, we shall arrange to meet again, next time with a formal agenda and an expanded attendance. I bid you guten Tag."

Roll the kaleidoscope forward and arrive in the year 1821. Harry Heine becomes a member of the Wissenschaft des Juden.

Roll the kaleidoscope forward and arrive at 1825. Eduard Gans converts to Christianity.

Roll the kaleidoscope forward and arrive in the year 1826. Gans is appointed a professor in the Berlin University faculty of law.

Roll the kaleidoscope forward and arrive in the year 1828. Harry Heine converts to Lutheranism and changes his name to Heinrich Heine.

Roll the kaleidoscope forward and arrive in the year 1832. Zunz completes what has been described by some as the most important Jewish book published in the nineteenth century, *Gottesdienstliche Vorträge der Juden*.[15] The book's intellectual foundations become a fork in the road of Jewish religious scholarship, demonstrating that Judaism could be a growing force rather than an ossified body of religious laws. The publication is also to become a significant influence on the reform Judaism movement although Zunz himself is not a supporter of this.

---

[15] "*The Worship Sermons of the Jews, Historically Developed* is a historical analysis of Jewish homiletical literature and its evolutionary development up to the modern-day sermon." (*Encyclopedia Britannica*)

THE JEWS NEVER CONTRIBUTED TO THE WORK OF CIVILIZATION

———— ♦ ————

In my wanderings through the past, I had come across a book published in 1843 that was titled *The Jewish Question*. The author, Bruno Bauer, was not only recognised as both historian and theologian, but also known to have very controversial views that put him at odds with the mainstream intelligentsia of German society. It appeared that for him the Jews presented for German society a major dilemma, and this was long before the Nazis attempted to solve the same question one hundred years later. I was intrigued, there had to be a story in this.

The kaleidoscope takes me to the city of Bonn, to the university where Bauer was teaching. As luck would have it, I see that Bauer is to be debating a member of the theology department this very day; the topic for the debate is advertised as "The Origins of Christianity". I find the room and walk into an atmosphere of animated discussion, a stark contrast to what I had found in Berlin. It appears that when religion is discussed, passions are ignited! The protagonists walk in, severe-looking gentlemen, no smiles or camaraderie as they shake hands and bow formally to each other. After a brief introduction by the chairman Bauer begins speaking. His opening remarks cause much consternation for the audience. "Christianity," he states, "owes more to Greek philosophy than to the ancient teachings of Judaism."[16] Although I am unable to follow the complexity of the many arguments which follow; it appears that Bauer sees Jesus of Nazareth as a fictional personality created in the second century through a fusion of Jewish, Greek, and Roman theology. As for the Jews, Bauer justifies their oppression by a Christian state. Oppression, he says, will force their conversion to Christianity and ultimately solve the Jewish question. "The Jews," he argues, "are only loyal to their own history, therefore, they will always be permanently separated from the rest of mankind. Because of their Judaism, Jews are incapable of becoming perfect and, what's more, they have never contributed anything to the work of civilization."

A young man in the audience immediately interjects, shouting over the demands of the chairman who stridently warns him to sit down and not interrupt. "You claim Jews have never contributed to the work of civilization, what about Maimonides, Mendelssohn and Spinoza?" Bauer, who had paused mid-sentence in response to the interjection, looks calmly at his challenger and retorts, "The works of Maimonides and Mendelssohn are irrelevant. As for Spinoza he was no longer a Jew when he wrote his signature work, he had converted to Christianity!"

---

[16] The quotations accredited to Bauer are to be found in his book *Die Judenfrage (The Jewish Question)*, originally published in 1843.

FAMILIES BORN INTO A CRUCIBLE OF HATE

———— ♦ ————

This is an appropriate point in our journey to try and discover some information about Martha and Margot's family. The earliest information we have dates back to the year 1847 when her paternal grandfather, Joachim Braun, was born. Looking into the kaleidoscope no images about his birth appear so I am left with the only option, conjecture.

I find the choice of Joachim's first name to be interesting; it has both Jewish and Christian connotations. According to Christian tradition Joachim was the father of Mary the mother of Jesus, and according to Jewish tradition it is the transliteration of the Hebrew word יְהוֹיָקִים (Yehoyakim) which means "lifted by God". But then the father of Mary was Jewish, so why would he not have a Hebrew name? Is there some hint here that the Braun family were attempting to straddle both their Jewish culture and the German environment in which they were living?

The likelihood is that Joachim was born in Altona, an independent town until 1937 when it was absorbed into the area of greater Hamburg. Altona is situated on the banks of the River Elbe and was home to an active Jewish community from 1641.

The Jewish presence in Altona actually predates 1641 because the town became the final resting place for members of a Portuguese Jewish community who were living in Hamburg and were banned from burying their dead within city boundaries. Altona therefore is acknowledged for having the oldest Sephardi Jewish cemetery in Northern Europe.

Ultimately Jewish settlement in Altona was made up predominantly from Ashkenazi Jews who were engaged in commerce, shipping and whaling. In the 1700s the community also established a number of Hebrew printing presses and the town became an important centre for the publication of Hebrew texts. When Joachim was born the Jewish community would have numbered around two thousand souls, a mere four per cent of the total population.

When I attempt to find early images of the Nissensohns, once more the kaleidoscope is revealing no images so I resort to conjecture.

Siegmund Nissensohn, Martha and Margot's maternal grandfather, was born on the 3rd June 1863 in Hamburg. Jewish settlement in that city dates back to the end of the sixteenth century when Converso Jews[17] from both Portugal and Spain sought refuge there. Initially they concealed their Jewish identities but as they became more comfortable in the new environment many began observing Jewish customs once more. The presence of Jews in their city angered segments of the Hamburg population and a movement emerged demanding the expulsion of this "undesirable element". The city fathers,

---

[17] Converso Jews is the name given to Spanish Jews forced to convert to Catholicism in the fourteenth and fifteenth centuries. They are also referred to as Marranos which is a pejorative term—Marrano is the Spanish word for swine.

however, were more pragmatic and opposed the expulsion because of the economic benefits flowing into the city from the commercial activities of the Converso community.

From the early 1600s the community diversified when Ashkenazi Jews began settling in Hamburg. By 1800 they numbered around six thousand three hundred souls and represented the overwhelming majority of the Jewish community. The Hep! Hep! riots of 1819 were especially severe in Hamburg and there were other serious anti-Jewish riots in 1830 and 1835. Despite this, Jewish life thrived and like Altona, Hamburg became an important centre for the printing of Hebrew texts. Its small printing shops produced prayer books, the Hebrew Bible, texts about mystic lore, and books of popular literature.

In 1850 the Jewish community of Hamburg was granted full citizenship rights and, on the 3rd July 1869, the newly created Reichstag of the North German Federation abolished all restrictions on civil and political rights based on the criteria of religious affiliation. This pronouncement opened the door for Jews to actively participate in the work of the German state at both local and federal level, becoming an important milestone on the path to full emancipation.

Little Siegmund Nissensohn at six years of age would not have understood the spontaneous outpourings of excitement and relief coming from his parents, their relatives and friends. At last, in the Germany they embraced as home, Jews were on the way to becoming recognised as full citizens.

The Victory of the One, the Death of the Other

———◆———

The 1870s are important both for Germany and in the search to find the beginnings for Martha's story. For Germany the decade marks the date when, on the 18th January 1871, twenty-five independent states united and became the Empire of Germany. For Martha's story we do know that sometime during this decade her paternal grandparents, Joachim and Minna, were married.

History is packed with pomp and ceremony so I decided to have a peep at the celebrations marking the beginnings of a unified Germany—the German story is part of Martha's story, you see. Come with me to the Hall of Mirrors in the magnificent Palace of Versailles and let's find a good vantage point to view the proceedings. I can see the Kaiser, Wilhelm I, standing on a raised platform; he is resplendent, his military uniform bedecked with medals. On his right stands his son, Crown Prince Friedrich, and on his left the Grand Duke of Baden who with raised hand is exhorting the crowd below to cheer loudly. Most of the crowd are dressed in military finery and are raising drawn swords in the air in time to the cheers. In the centre of the cheering crowd, dressed in a white military uniform also bedecked with medals, stands the imposing figure of unified

Germany's first Chancellor, Otto Von Bismarck, also known as The Iron Chancellor.

The scene disturbs me greatly; the raised swords, the uniforms and medals, would leave an imprint of military adventurism within the DNA of the emerging German Empire. I imagine how out of place a representative of the traditional German Jewish community would feel standing on that platform next to the Kaiser. Smartly dressed, with sombre black suit and tie, maybe even a top hat for the occasion, wanting to be part of it all but struggling to determine how.

Now that we are visiting the 1870s I thought it would be interesting to discover how unification impacted the Jews in Germany. Sadly, the promise of a new and glorious future for the citizens of the unified Germany did not apply to all who saw themselves as German. The first setback for the Jewish community occurred when the 1873 global financial crisis caused many small investors to lose all their savings. Who did they blame? The Jews, of course. I had also heard some stories on my various travels about a journalist and writer called Wilhem Marr. Marr is not only accredited with inventing the term antisemite, he is also referred to as the "patriarch of antisemitism". I turn the kaleidoscope vigorously, arriving in the year 1879 and a scene comes into view where a prominent German Jewish novelist, Berthold Auerbach, is interviewing Marr about his recently published pamphlet "Der Weg zum Siege des Germanenthums über das Judenthum", which in English translates as "The Way to Victory of Germanism over Judaism".

When the patterns inside a time kaleidoscope are shaken up so vigorously there is no way of knowing whether the scene it eventually throws up actually happened. Between us, I don't think it really matters, we are only telling stories aren't we![18]

The two are sitting in Marr's study. His lodgings are quite ordinary, and it does not appear that the man is enjoying a very salubrious financial situation. Auerbach is approaching seventy years of age; his flowing white beard and receding hairline give him the appearance of the Moses depicted by various Renaissance artists. Marr, with his back to an untidy writing desk, is seated facing Auerbach. Marr's face is pinched, I can only describe it as somewhat avian. The stand out feature are the intense dark eyes, watchful and suspicious.

"If you don't mind, Herr Marr," Auerbach is saying, "I would like to understand a little about your life, it may help me understand how you arrived at the views expressed in the pamphlet published some months ago. You are a writer, I am a writer; so, we have common ground to debate these matters. Your second wife was Jewish I understand, in fact her maiden name was Israel. I find that a little incongruous given the views you expressed about Jews in your pamphlet."

"My second wife was a pure Jewess and since pure blood is always preferable to mixed blood, my life with her was happy."

"I apologise, Herr Marr; I am not sure what you mean. How do you somehow connect the concept of mixed blood with a state of happiness?"

"My first wife was half Jewess, and so was my third; both marriages were a disaster and ended in divorce. So, you see, I

---

[18] The quotations ascribed to Marr in this story are all derived from Marr's pamphlet *The Victory of Judaism over Germandom*, published in March 1879, and other statements attributed to him.

came to know the Semitic race in a thorough manner, in its most intimate details, and I consequently warn against the mixing of Aryan and Semitic blood. With my second wife it was all different. We would have been very happy, but she died, you know, after giving birth to a premature child who also died."

On saying this Marr chokes up a little but quickly pulls himself together. "We were very close. I was not even bothered when she brought the whole mishpoche[19] with her into the marriage."

"So, your thesis is that Jews are acceptable if they are pure blood, it is the mixed blood Jews who are the danger?"

"No that is not what I am saying at all! What applies at the personal level cannot apply at the national level. My personal experiences are not relevant; in my pamphlet I am warning about existential threats to the whole German nation."

"We will come to your pamphlet in a minute, I just want to know a little bit more about your personal philosophies. You are an avowed atheist I understand, in fact you once wrote that Christianity was an attempt to seize world rule; it was despotic and antisocialist, the rule it sought to impose was immoral, and its growth was only based on the social insecurity and ignorance of the population. Am I correct, then, in concluding that since you are not a Christian your hatred of Jews, your antisemitism, as you call it, is a divergence from the traditional religious foundations for Jew hatred?"

"In a way I can accept that, but it is a little bit more complex. We also have to consider the danger presented by the Jew Ferdinand Lassalle and his followers. This pursuit of state socialism invented by him and his fellow Jews will destroy

---

[19] The Yiddish word for "family".

everything we hold dear in our Germany. I therefore reject the whole premise of Jewish emancipation and even Jewish assimilation. Our German liberalism allowed the Jews to control all of German finance and industry and as a result we, the Germans, are locked in a longstanding conflict against the Jews living in our midst. The foundation on which this conflict is based is all about race—the Jews, as you know, are a separate race, they can never be German—and what is more, I believe they are winning that conflict right now. The struggle between Jews and Germans can only be resolved by the victory of one and the ultimate death of the other. A Jewish victory will result in the end of the German people. I am proud to say that I founded the League of Antisemites which is the first German organization committed specifically to combating the threat to our Germany posed by the Jews. We advocate their forced removal from the country."

"Herr Marr, I have one observation to make in response. The Jews in Germany number around one percent of the total population. I fail to understand how that tiny percentage could muster the numbers and the resources to wipe out the other ninety-nine percent of the population. If you and others like you actually consider this outrageous proposition to be possible then clearly you have little confidence in the capability of your fellow Germans—which I, by the way, do not share."

Auerbach can see that Marr is not only becoming very agitated, he is also looking very uncomfortable. He resolves to press his advantage.

"I understand you moved to Berlin a few years ago and have been heard to complain that it is now a city half Jewish and half socialist, both of which you deplore. I also heard that since your arrival here you have experienced difficulty in finding work, possibly because the views you publicly express do not endear you to the fairly eclectic demographic now prevalent in the city. Herr Marr, and I will conclude on this point, I believe you arrived here in 1877 after a very difficult divorce; you were not able to find work; your pamphlet, the subject of our discussion, was rejected by respectable publishing houses and the only person who showed interest was a renowned Jew hater, Rudolf Kostenobel. He, by the way, was dismissed from his position in the Jewish-owned Mosse publishing company for a number of reasons I will refrain from discussing. One of Kostenobel's more outrageous public utterances is a wish for the promised land to be established allowing all the 'rabble', his adjective for the Jews in Germany, to go there and cheat one another instead of us Germans. And so, Herr Marr, I wonder whether this outpouring of antisemitism, as you yourself call it, laced as it is with coarseness and deceit, is nothing more than an expression of your own personal shortcomings which you blame on others rather than yourself."

Berthold Auerbach gets up from his chair, turns around, and without a word of farewell walks out of the room.

What's in a Name

———◆———

The kaleidoscope is refusing to change the date, it is the year 1876. We are in a nondescript office in a very ordinary building in the Waldwiertel, a rather picturesque area of lower Austria. A very severe looking thick-set man in his early forties is signing an official document using the desk of the clerk sitting behind it. The signer is sporting a horseshoe moustache with long straggly ends that waggle rather amusingly as he moves his head. His name is Alois Schicklegruber, illegitimate son of Maria Anna Schicklegruber and Johann Georg Hiedler.

"So, mein Herr," the clerk is saying, "you came into my office as Alois Schicklegruber and are now leaving as Alois Hitler. I wish you good fortune and a guten Tag."

Schicklegruber, now Hitler, gives a curt nod and without a word turns and walks out of the office.

THE JEWS ARE OUR MISFORTUNE

———•———

For some reason the kaleidoscope will not allow us to leave 1879 and peering down the tube, I am surprised to find we are once more in front of the University of Berlin. The image begins to transform and settles on an elderly heavy-set man with an enormous head, his face covered with a grey Santa Claus beard and moustache. He is sitting behind a large desk, scowling, intently studying a heavy tome, and occasionally banging his fist on the desk shouting "dieser verdammte Jude Graetz". Who is this, I ask, and why is he cursing that damn Jew Graetz—I assume he is referring to the Jewish historian Heinrich Graetz? I look around the room, notice a number of testimonials on the wall, and see the name Heinrich von Treitschke. Now I am really interested, this man is an influential German historian, political writer, and member of the Reichstag. He has a reputation as an authoritarian with little time for convention and believes that the might of Prussia should take the lead in forging German unity.

While I was searching for his name Von Treitschke had lifted himself off the chair and is now pacing around the room, while alternately shouting and mumbling. The door suddenly opens and a student walks in, his face expressing concern. Taking Von Treitschke by the arm he sits him down and shouts loudly in his ear, "Herr Professor, what is wrong?" I realize then that the professor is not only hard of hearing, he is probably almost deaf. Von Treitschke points at the book in front of him and shouts at the student to get out. The poor man, who had entered the room out of concern for the professor's welfare when he heard loud shouts pierce through a closed door, shrinks visibly and without a word slinks out. Von Treitschke sits for a moment then heaves himself up and ponderously walks out of the room. I walk up to the desk and close the book he was reading so that I can see its cover; it is the eleventh volume of Graetz's history of the Jews, the one containing a number of rather disparaging observations about Christians and Christianity.

The image suddenly disappears and immediately transforms. I find myself in a bookshop that is running a promotion for a pamphlet titled *Ein Wort über unser Judenthum*, translated as *A Word about Our Jews*; the author is Professor Heinrich von Treitschke. I pick up a copy and begin paging through. Much of what I am reading is all about German nationalism which I skip over and then, towards the end of the pamphlet, one passage catches my eye.

"Year after year, out of the inexhaustible Polish cradle, streams over our eastern border a host of hustling, pants-peddling youths, whose children and children's children will someday command Germany's stock exchanges and newspapers."

Suddenly the image transforms and I am in October 1938, thousands of Polish Jews are in refugee camps on the Polish German border. They have been expelled from Germany.

The image fades and transforms, another page of the pamphlet comes into view. I am reading the phrase "die Juden sind unser Ungluck", the Jews are our misfortune. Once more the image fades and transforms, we are in the year 1932 and I am looking at the front page of a newspaper called *Der Sturmer*.[20] In bold black print emblazoned across the front page I read "Die Juden sind unser Ungluck".

---

[20] *Der Sturmer* was a weekly tabloid in German published from 1923 to February of 1945. It was virulently antisemitic and although not a publication of the Nazi party became part of the Nazi propaganda war against the Jews.

The Antisemites Petition

―――◆―――

The image the kaleidoscope fixes on is that of a street corner in a city I do not recognise. It must be in one of the German states because in front of me there is a newspaper stand and all the papers on offer are in German. I am able to make out the year which I see on one of the papers, it is 1880. A man standing next to a small table to the left of the newspaper stand is approaching every passerby, trying to engage with them. Many shrug their shoulders and walk away, others stop to listen and abruptly walk away without comment. As he approaches a new target, I move closer trying to hear what he is saying. I hear the name Ludwig Förster; I know all about him, a teacher by profession and a leading light in the world of antisemites. One of his claims to fame is that he married the sister of the hugely influential German philosopher Friedrich Nietzsche. Forster himself has become a prolific writer about "Die Judenfrage", the Jewish question, and his works frequently refer to Jews as "a parasite on the German body". The second name I hear mentioned is Liebermann von Sonnenberg; I also know of him, an officer in the German Imperial Army and now another luminary in the world of antisemites.

Now I am really intrigued, is the newspaper salesman promoting or decrying this rogue's gallery of antisemites?

Pretending to be looking for a paper to buy, I move closer so as to hear what is being said.

Realizing the word Juden had sparked some interest in his listener, table man launches into a prepared tirade that begins with an appeal to sign a petition demanding the law emancipating the Jews in Germany be immediately rescinded. "We Germans," table man urges, "need to be emancipated from this form of alien domination which we cannot endure for any length of time. Die Juden must not be allowed to come here from other countries, they must be expelled from their positions as judges, teachers and members of our civil service. What is more, we must guarantee that we maintain the Christian character of our grammar schools by ensuring that only Christian teachers be appointed to teach in them."[21]

His loud voice is beginning to attract other curious passersby and as a small crowd develops other petition organizers emerge from behind the newspaper stand and began engaging the newcomers.

The kaleidoscope image suddenly transforms, we are in the Prussian House of Deputies on the 22nd November 1880, and a debate is in progress. The matter under discussion is "Der Judenfrage". A spokesman for the government is offering a half-spirited defence for Jewish emancipation.

Once more the image transforms, we are in the office of the Iron Chancellor, Otto Eduard Leopold von Bismarck. The date is sometime in April 1881. In front of him is the petition I had seen promoted on the streets which now bears the signature of around two hundred and sixty-five thousand adult German males, a very disappointing result for the organisers. The

---

[21] Derived from the writings of Ludwig Forster.

Chancellor peruses the content carefully, summons an aide, hands him the petition with a curt "nein", and turns to the next document on the neat pile in front of him. My cynical mind thinks that the reason for his rejection is the fact that a prominent Jewish banker, Gerson Bleichröder, manages the chancellor's private banking arrangements and is also negotiating large financial transactions on behalf of the Prussian state and German empire.

It was clear that the exhortations of William Marr were starting to find a modicum of support within certain segments of German society. How did the Jews respond? Prominent Jews in Germany reacted in different ways. The despondence it invoked in Berthold Auerbach, a prominent novelist and an ardent German nationalist, is clearly apparent in this public comment from him, "The horrible fact remains that such coarseness deceit and hatred are still possible,"

Leopold Zunz, however, went on the attack. He remarked scornfully, "Thus I live unconcerned by anti-Jewish swine eaters; their din is a childish imitation of the crusades no longer in style. World literature today, and in the newspaper press, is more powerful than all the blockheads aping the Middle Ages." Sadly, he grossly miscalculated the groundswell of support the antisemitic movements were attracting.

The publication of the Antisemites petition resulted in some violent aftershocks. One of the schoolteacher sponsors, Ernst Henrici, took advantage of the social momentum and established a rabidly antisemitic political party which he named The Reich Social Party. He went on a speaking tour to drum up support for the new party and wherever he appeared violence against the local Jewish community broke out. In July of 1881, the baying mobs screaming "Juden Raus"[22] attacked Jews in the streets of Neustettin, smashed the windows of Jewish shops, and burnt down the synagogue.

Throughout the 1880s more and more of the deputies securing seats in the German Reichstag either actively or subtly promoted an antisemitic agenda. By the end of the decade the Social Democrats, with thirty-five seats out of three hundred and ninety-seven, were the only major political party that actively opposed the rising tide of antisemitism.

---

[22] "Jews get out."

JEWISH MUSICIANS PRODUCE SHALLOW AND ARTIFICIAL MUSIC

———◆———

The kaleidoscope spins and stops. The year, 1882, the date, 29th August. I am in a theatre looking at heavy curtains fronting the stage. With some excitement I realise I am in the famous opera house in Bayreuth, the Bayreuth Festspielhaus. The curtains are ochre, orange and gold, the colours synchronise beautifully with the rather subdued glow coming from the gaslit lights arranged around the auditorium just below the private boxes. I look around me, the theatre is very full but I see a few seats at the back and make my way there. The person in the seat next to me is discussing the production and I glean from the conversation that it is a performance of *Parsifal* by Richard Wagner. The third act is about to begin.

Now I am really excited, I am about to witness one of the more bizarre episodes in the life of this very controversial composer.

I see the conductor enter the orchestra pit, ascend the podium, and in the midst of thunderous applause turn and bow to the audience. The applause fades into a moment of silence which becomes the swirling sound of muttered astonishment followed by the outpouring of thunderous applause. The audience had expected Hermann Levi—son of a rabbi, admirer and friend of Richard Wagner, who had conducted the first two acts—to ascend the podium. In his place the maestro now bowing stiffly and somewhat unsteadily to an exuberant audience is Richard Wagner himself.

A drama had played out backstage. Levi was preparing to enter the orchestra pit when he was summarily pushed aside by Wagner who grabbed the baton, and walked out in his place.

Music maestros tend to be somewhat imperious, a little arrogant, hugely talented and like many artists sensitive to criticism. Therefore, one cannot but imagine Levi's devastation, his feeling of betrayal and humiliation as he was summarily pushed aside without explanation. He had opened this Bayreuth season, tonight was the sixteenth and last performance of *Parsifal*; it should have been a time for celebration, a time to enjoy the adulation showered on a maestro after a successful performance, a time to gracefully accept huge bouquets of beautiful flowers while acknowledging the thunderous applause from a rapturous audience. All that was now to be showered on the composer himself.

Without warning the kaleidoscope spins and I find myself in a large, cluttered room. The man sitting at the desk is reading aloud from a neatly written sheet of paper on the blotter in front of him. The man is Hermann Levi.

"Mein liebe Meister," he is saying, "we have known each other for many years, I have had the honour of working with you and conducting the music produced by your brilliant mind. I glossed over the unkind remarks and obscenities which many times were directed against me and others close to you. I made excuses for this, shrugging them off as nothing more than expressions of impatience that comes with artistic brilliance. I was estranged from many friends and family when I glossed over your reported criticisms of Jewish musicians that you published in 1850 under the pseudonym K. Freigedank.[23] Only seven years ago I wrote to my father and told him, 'Wagner is the best and noblest of men...I thank God daily for the privilege to be close to such a man. It is the most beautiful experience of my life.' But then, your arrogant dismissal of myself, someone who was your friend, an admirer, and defender, and what is more in the middle of a performance was a shock, and it forced me to reevaluate the underpinnings of our relationship.

"Meister, I want you to know that I did not want to write this letter, I wanted to tell you what I feel directly. However, when I tried to get an audience with you, Cosima refused to invite me into your home. She informed me, somewhat rudely I might add, that you were too ill to receive visitors and summarily slammed the door in my face. And so, I am now forced to commit my feelings to the written page, a rather unsatisfactory medium for this particular situation I might add.

"At the outset I want to discuss the incident at Bayreuth and I recall the emotions of both pride and gratitude which swept over me when I was asked to conduct the first public performance of Parsifal that was to open the sixth Bayreuth Festival. Then, I received your note informing me you would only permit this if I immediately converted to Christianity! Meister, you of all people know that in my own way I have maintained a strong connection with my faith, I would never countenance such a bizarre request. Why would you have demanded this of me, was it your devious plan to ensure I did not open the festival? I confess when the festival organizers

---

[23] K. Freethought.

intervened and confirmed that the decision about choice of maestro was theirs alone, for a brief moment I demurred, but then, for the very first time in our relationship, I decided not to succumb to your bullying tactics.

"I turn now to your outrageous action on the twenty-ninth of August when, without explanation, you rudely barged in backstage, picked up the baton and walked out to the orchestra pit. You humiliated me, the critics are saying that Wagner considered Levi's performance to be unsatisfactory, decided he should be replaced, and did so personally in the third act of the last performance of the opera.

"These outrageous attacks on my personality, my art, and my integrity, Meister, became a catalyst for me to research the facts behind the many accusations against you, accusations that I, in my blind devotion, summarily ignored. What I discovered forced me to re-evaluate every opinion I cherished about you as composer and human being.

"I turn now to the essay to which I previously referred, the one you first published in 1850 using a pseudonym, and then again under your own name some nineteen years later. I am of course referring to 'Das Judenthum in der Musik'.[24] When this was published, I did not actually study it at the time. We had a relationship, you and I, German non-Jew with German Jew, so my experience was at odds with what others were claiming. Last week I actually read the essay. I will not repeat every unkind comment you make but mention some that shocked me. You claim that the German people are repelled by Jews due to their alien appearance and behaviour. Regarding the attempts to achieve emancipation for the Jews you say Germans are

---

[24] Jewishness in Music.

instinctively repelled by any actual, operative contact with them.

"And so, Meister, I ask you this: were you repelled by me when we were together?

"You further assert in that essay that Jewish musicians are only capable of producing music that is shallow and artificial because they have no connection to the genuine spirit of the German people. At the time it was assumed that these comments were designed to counter the enormous influence both Giacomo Meyerbeer and Felix Mendelssohn were having on music at the time. When colleagues confided in me and expressed their concerns about these extremely harsh criticisms I defended you, shrugging them off as mere artistic disagreements driven by your frequently expressed desire for the creation of a new German music genre. I now juxtapose these criticisms with your toxic comments about Jewish people and am forced to re-evaluate my early views. Meister, I recall one day when we were together you were reflecting on your difficult days in Italy and you told me, somewhat bitterly, that while Meyerbeer was experiencing fame and success with his operas you were impoverished, unable to create interest in your own compositions, and reduced to music copy editing in order to keep body and soul together. I now realise that your denigration of Jewish musicians was driven by jealousy which you tried to cloak within the garb of intellectual debate. It was a low and mean-spirited attack, especially since I have recently discovered that in these difficult times you actually had contact with Meyerbeer, that he loaned you money, and what is more used his considerable influence to arrange for the premiere in Dresden of *Rienzi*, your first successful opera. I recently discovered that at the time Meyerbeer publicly expressed his hurt and bewilderment over your abusive comments about him, his works, and his faith.

"Meister, I know not whether your refusal to meet with me was motivated by illness, or you are repelled by me. If you are indeed ill, I wish you a speedy recovery. If you are repelled, I wish you to know that I too am repelled; by you!

"Hermann."

Unfortunately, the Fourth Child Survived!

———◆———

There is a wintry, very grey atmosphere emanating from the image slowly appearing in the depths of the kaleidoscope. I check the date, it is the 20th April 1889. Why the greyness, I ask, it is spring, after all? I try to understand where we are and determine it is Braunau Am Inn, a small town on the border of Austria and Germany. I pass a small synagogue and peek in the front door. There is a service going on, I realise it is the evening prayer at the end of shabbat. On a small table in the tiny anteroom leading into the main prayer hall lie scattered the remnants of the Sabbath day third meal. I see a small pile of matzoth on the table and realise with amazement that this day, the 20th April, is within the eight days of Passover, the festival in which Jews celebrate their exodus from slavery and the defeat of the evil pharaoh who had enslaved them and attempted to eradicate them from the future pages of history. Just four nights earlier the Jewish community of Braunau Am Inn would have been sitting around a beautifully decorated table celebrating the second of two ceremonial meals at the start of the Passover festival when the story of the Exodus is told.

The first image fades and is replaced by the front of a rather odd square building. The ground floor windows in the front façade are rectangular in shape and those in the two upper floors are topped by arches. The image changes, I am standing outside a closed door and hear the cry of a newborn child. Suddenly a heavy-set man with a bushy horseshoe moustache comes up the stairs, opens the door and enters the room. I watch him walk to a bed where an exhausted woman is sitting back holding a child swathed in blankets. With a start I recognise him, it is Alois Hitler, the man who changed his name from Schicklegruber to Hitler. I watch as he walks up to the bed, bends over to look at the child in his wife's arms, and says gruffly, "Let us hope this one survives, Klara, we will name him Adolf", and walks out of the room.

When you are trapped inside a time warp you have no powers of intervention, what will be will be. The three previous children of Klara and Alois Hitler never survived to become adults, why was this the one to survive?

HERR AHLWARDT, YOU ARE NOTHING MORE THAN A PETTY THIEF

———◆———

I had heard quite a lot about a prominent antisemitic member of the Reichstag named Hermann Ahlwardt and begin a search to find a time warp in which he features. The kaleidoscope produces an image, a man stepping from a doorway being greeted by quite a large crowd. The year 1893, the month and day not visible. The man himself is rather comical, heavy set, a large head, round face, florid complexion, and a brush moustache under his nose. The pièce de résistance is a large tuft of hair on top of his forehead that resembles a wave curling over, about to break on the shore. It is Ahlwardt leaving his Berlin lodgings en route to the Reichstag.

The crowd in front of him appears to be mainly supporters who clap enthusiastically as he appears but I also notice a sprinkling of individuals with notebooks in hand, accompanied by photographers. Apparently, the Berlin newspapers are also interested in speaking to Ahlwardt on this rather chilly Berlin morning.

One of the newspaper men calls out loudly, "Herr Ahlwardt, Jurgen Meyer, *National Zeitung*, may I ask you some questions?"

Meyer is standing on the fringe of the crowd and it takes Ahlwardt some time to fix his gaze on the questioner.

"Aha, Herr Meyer, you work for that liberal newspaper controlled by the Jew Bernhard Wolff. I don't know what I have to say to you, whatever I say, you will just print lies, never truths. As I observed in my book published some years ago, Jews like Wolff are like an octopus whose tentacles reach everywhere in our beloved Germany, they squeeze the life from our nation."

There is a low murmur from the crowd and a few clap their hands in agreement.

"Yes, Herr Ahlwardt, this was one of my questions. Your words at that time appear to conflict with something else you wrote that appeared in a publication of the Association for the Defense of Antisemitism, you say and I quote directly, 'Antisemitism is illogical; I have always condemned it, and shall continue to condemn religious intolerance until my last breath.' I find this contradiction rather confusing, Herr Ahlwardt, and I am sure the good people around me here would agree with me. In the Reichstag you refer to the Jews in Germany as predators, cholera bacilli, you say they should be exterminated. You claim that Ludwig Loewe & Company, a Jewish enterprise, supplied guns that, and once more I quote your words, 'were worthless to the German army', and that together with the Alliance Israélite Universelle their aim was to facilitate the defeat of Germany in her next struggle with France, a claim I might add found to be totally untrue by a court of law. So, my question. Herr Ahlwardt. is what is your real position regarding the Jews in Germany?"

Ahlwardt appears to be rather at a loss for words and is about to ignore the question when a few voices in the crowd start shouting, "Yes, good question, what do you really think about Jews?"

Ahlwardt then launchs into a rather rambling statement quite difficult to understand. In summary it appears he only hates those Jewish bacilli who sapped the life out of Germany, these were the ones he was talking about. The average Jew could be acceptable, of course only when you got to know him.

"Herr Ahlwardt," Meyer persists, "our paper is about to publish a story about you, as you know you are quite a prominent member of the Reichstag and your views are important. It would be very helpful to have some background information that will assist me to write the story." At this Ahlwardt visibly puffs up and with an indulgent smile turns his attention once more to Meyer.

"I understand, Herr Ahlwardt, that until some years ago, 1889 in fact, you were the rector of a primary school." At this Ahlwardt's posture changes, he looks like a person searching rather desperately for an avenue of escape. "You were discharged from there because of some misappropriation of funds, monies apparently collected for the children's Christmas party in that year."

"That is a lie, a dirty lie," shouts Ahlwardt, then turning to the crowd who are exchanging questioning glances he says, almost pleads, "you see, the Jew Wolff sends his underlings to discredit me because I stand up to these predators. I was set up by whole cabal of Jewish money lenders, they were the criminals not me."

"But Herr Ahlwardt," Meyer continues, "I can prove that accusation to be totally untrue," and, turning to the crowd, "as for you good people, please feel free to contact me at the paper and I will provide you with evidence proving, let us say, Herr Alwardt's indiscretion."

"Herr Alwardt, I now turn to another incident from your past and ask for your comment. You wrote a book some time ago claiming that the German government was in the pay of the Jewish banker Gerson Bleichröder, the same Gerson Bleichröder who is the personal banker and adviser to our Chancellor. I have on record that you were jailed after an investigation into this claim disclosed that the documents you produced as evidence were forgeries actually written by yourself. And so, Herr Ahlwardt, my question to you is how can the people of Germany believe anything you say? Your history reveals you to be a petty thief stealing money from children, and in addition you were convicted of the crime of making fraudulent claims against one of Germany's most prominent citizens."

Ahlwardt's florid features are now burning red, he appears to be in a paroxysm of emotions that include indignation, anger and embarrassment. Saying nothing, he pushes through the now rather chastened crowd, makes his way to a waiting horse-drawn coach, climbs in, and disappears into the traffic; just another ubiquitous means of transport on a busy Berlin street.

The Antisemitism Virus Infects the Reichstag

———•◆•———

I turn the kaleidoscope and wait to see what image it throws up. I see the year 1894, I am standing in the Konigsplatz in Berlin facing an imposing edifice that I later discover had been completed only recently. It is the Reichstag building where unified Germany's elected parliamentary delegates meet to conduct the business required for ensuring the security and wellbeing of all citizens. The model used by the architect was Philadelphia's Memorial Hall wherein the 1876 Centennial Exhibition had been housed. On each corner of the Reichstag building stands a large tower, these represent one of the four German kingdoms that had come together: Prussia, Bavaria, Saxony and Württemberg. Flanking the columned main entrance are each kingdom's coat of arms as well as other heraldic symbols representing the various German city states. Ascending the stairs leading into the building one cannot help being not only awed by the magnificence of the structure, but also a little humbled by the hope it represents for the future. The interior is replete with decorative sculptures, reliefs, and inscriptions.

We find ourselves in the public gallery; a delegate is on his feet gesticulating wildly as he is speaking.

"Der Bund der Landwirte[25] was founded on the 18th February 1893 by ten thousand concerned citizens. And why was it established? Because, meine Herren, the Chancellor, Herr Caprivi, in his wisdom decided to reduce tariffs on grains with the result that cheap second-rate imports now flow into Germany. Does he realise what he has done to the lives of the men, women, and children who daily toil on the land dedicating their lives to growing the produce that feeds the citizens of this country? As a result, mein Herren, the people of this country showed him exactly what they thought of his stupidity. Just three months after our league was brought into existence, we fought an election and returned one hundred and forty delegates to this Reichstag, nearly one-third of the members here today. [Prolonged applause.] And why were we returned in such numbers? It was not only because we have a Chancellor who cares not about the ordinary people of this country, it is also because ordinary people, the backbone of this country, fear the creeping threat from the socialists on the one hand, and the blood-sucking financial capitalists on the other. And who is behind this creeping threat—the Jews, yes, the Jews. They use their influence and power to acquire a decisive say in our press and in our commercial life. Meine Herren, I will close my remarks with a warning. We the farmers who toil day and night to feed the people of this state are involved in a fight to the death with the Jewish socialists and capitalists. This war must continue until one or the other lies lifeless, or at least powerless, on the ground. In order to win this fight, the league urges the delegates in this place to boycott Jewish stores, prohibit rela-

---

[25] The Agrarian League.

tions between Jews and Germans, and finally to expel all Jews from Germany."

At that point he sits down accompanied by loud cheering from some delegates and muted clapping from others while the president of the Reichstag announces from the podium that the day's business is now done. As the delegates walk out, I hear one saying to a companion, "Did you hear the support he received? I told the party members only last week that this antisemitism as they now call it is a vote getter, we need to embrace this as our policy."

Hitler's John the Baptist

———•◆•———

Our journey into the nineteenth century using time warps is about to end. Looking back at the images we uncovered during our time there, we see clearly the billowing black clouds of hate that are roiling up on the horizon. Many Germans living in those times became disturbed, others frightened; some attempted to turn back the clouds of hate, while others sought refuge elsewhere. For the most part, however, those affected did nothing. Such is the nature of *Homo sapiens*, a species that was to reveal its darkest side in the century to follow.

In the nineteenth century Jew hatred had evolved into "antisemitism", certainly a more socially accepted description than just, "I don't like Jews". On our journey through nineteenth century Germany we met with many prominent antisemites, men who promoted the hatred of Jews using irrational emotional premises based on pseudo-intellectual foundations. However, this suited the more sophisticated strata of German society who may have shrunk from simply proclaiming publicly, "I hate those filthy Jews".

Leaving the nineteenth century without an encounter with the man we should award the title "antisemite of the century" would be equivalent to ploughing through a whodunit without finding out who actually did it! And so, we turn the kaleidoscope and arrive in the year 1899.

I see a balding man with a high forehead and dark piercing eyes. His aquiline features convey the image of a bird of prey. His name is Houston Stewart Chamberlain and he has just published *Die Grundlagen des Neunzehnten Jahrhunderts*[26] a rambling tome containing around one thousand pages which eighty-two years later would be described as representing "the ravings of a renegade".[27] The book was an immediate best-seller discussed widely by the upper levels of Berlin society and as a result Chamberlain became a celebrity of sorts.

A Jewish reviewer of the book, the Berlin banker Heinrich Meyer-Cohn, was scathing in his criticism asserting that the writing was not only bad, unclear, and unpleasing in style, it was also full of false modesty, ignorance, and a false affectation of learning. I thought therefore it could be rather interesting to arrange for Chamberlain to be interviewed by Meyer-Cohn. You can do these things when delving into time warps! Did it happen? Dear reader, never forget, I Ani Korim Seforim am just a teller of stories!

"Herr Chamberlain, you are originally an Englishman, would you prefer us to talk in English rather than German?"

"As you wish, I am of course fluent not only in English and German, but can discuss my book with you in French, a language I dare say escapes you; it is a far cry from the kitchen German you speak, Yiddish you call it."

---

[26] *The Foundations of the Nineteenth Century.*
[27] Joll James, "Ravings of a Renegade". *New York Review* 24th September 1981.

"We will speak in German; I hope I will be able to understand your version of our language. Herr Chamberlain let me begin by saying that I have considerable influence in Berlin, not only in Jewish circles, but as a banker of note with many prominent non-Jews as my clients. I intend on writing a review of your recently published book but before doing so thought it appropriate for me to develop some understanding of you as a person, get to hear first-hand what motivated you to produce such an extraordinary work. In this regard, I am rather intrigued by something you wrote as a young schoolboy attending Cheltenham College in England. You said, and I hope I am not misquoting you, 'The starlight exerted an indescribable influence on me. The stars seemed closer to me, more gentle, more worthy of trust, and more sympathetic – for that is the only word which describes my feelings – more than any of the people around me in school. For the stars, I experienced true friendship.' To be blunt, Herr Chamberlain, that is a rather bizarre worldview and could be indicative of a deep-seated mistrust you harbour for all humanity. It appears to me that you camouflage this psychological disorder by singling out the Jews as the sole reason for your insecurity, Jews by the way who, unlike you, were born in this country and are truly German."

"That is a gross misrepresentation and typical of your race. What do you, a banker, know about the feelings of people? You, who devote your life to destroying the lives of others by implementing usurious practices that make you wealthy and suck the life out of ordinary Germans! I fail to understand how the musings of a young boy in an intolerable environment could in any way represent the psychological state of a mature man;

we will not pursue this matter again or this discussion is ended now."

"Very well Herr Chamberlain, I am just trying to understand who you are as a person and apologise if you find my questions offensive. Let me turn then to music. It appears that you are an ardent Wagnerite; what is it in the music that you find so compelling?"

"I was twenty-three years old when I first heard an opera composed by the master. This experience can only be described as an epiphany, a moment that was intensely religious. I finally discovered in his music the spiritual force that is totally absent in British and French culture. I was privileged to meet Wagner twenty-three years ago and am honoured to say we became firm friends. He is a genius without parallel. I am also an admirer of his widow and am proud to say that Cosima has publicly referred to me as her surrogate son."

"Wagner is recognised to be one of the most prominent antisemites in Germany, so the question I have for you is this. Given the adoration you feel for this man is it not possible that you imbibed from him his hatred of Jews and that your publication, which I will discuss shortly, is merely a synthesis of the musician's ideas rather than your own?"

"That is a preposterous assertion and highly offensive. How dare you suggest that my lifetime of research has yielded no original thought and is merely a reproduction of someone else's worldview."

"Herr Chamberlain, there is no need to take offence, we are two adults debating a scientific publication. You agree I am sure that it is a scientific publication. As such your work should be open to critical review, that is the nature of science is it not?

Maybe I am mistaken, possibly you do not consider yourself a scientist and are therefore not subject to the strictures imposed by a process of peer review? Anyway, to move on, I still find it rather interesting that the intensity of the comments you make about Jews seem to increase after your relationship with Wagner is established. As an example, you begin to produce writings that are distinctly Völkisch in the early 1880s and I am told that in letters to your English family antisemitic statements become the norm from that time. You even proclaimed in 1888 that you were overjoyed when Kaiser Friedrich died, calling him a Jewish liberal. You then lauded the ascension of his son Wilhelm whom you say is a confirmed antisemite. As the decade evolved your anti-Jewish rhetoric became more and more odious. I hope you don't take offence if I use that adjective, I use it because you frequently utilise it yourself in your writings. I am told that at one time you visited a spa and later stated in a letter that the spa had unfortunately fallen into the hands of Jews and as a result every visitor is now being 'bled' as you describe it, and further you said, there is no longer any order or cleanliness in the place. I might add that I find to be odious your comments about fellow tenants from the apartment building you were living in when you claimed that because the building had been sold to a Jew it became impossible for ordinary people to now live there. You personally stated that you were now in a state of constant warfare with the vermin who had moved in. Now Herr Chamberlain, as the author of a scientific publication I put to you that these are rather unscientific conclusions about Germans who, like yourself, are *Homo sapiens*. I assume you still classify yourself as *Homo sapiens* and this Aryan race as you call it are also members of that genus? Possibly however the answers to all these questions are in your book, so Herr Chamberlain with your permission, let me now turn to this extraordinary publication.

"I refer to your rather curious conclusion where you assert that the founder of the Christian faith could not possibly have been a Jew, in your view he must have been pure Aryan. Herr Chamberlain, are you not aware of the research that has shown Aryan peoples to have migrated into the Western regions of Europe around four thousand years ago. There is also no evidence that they established any footprint in the fertile crescent where Jesus was born, raised, and died?"

"That is exactly the distortion of history you Jews promote in order to establish your credentials as the source from which Christianity sprang. Jesus could not possibly have been a Jew; you Jews are an inferior race and someone of such stature could never have originated from your blood. He could only have been Aryan, it is a logical deduction! What is more, you Jews contaminated the pure doctrine originally spoken by Jesus and this initiated a permanent war now being waged between your race and the Aryan race. In fact, the Catholic Church is a Jewish invention, you planned this as a means for destroying the Aryan people. Through the Catholic Church you now preach a Judaized version of Christianity which had nothing to do with the pure religion created by the Aryan Christ. The Germans on whom the mantle of pure Aryanism fell are the highest cultural achievers and saviours of humanity, they are fated to engage in a battle to destroy the Jews who are a bastard race of greedy, inferior foreigners."

"Herr Chamberlain, apologies, just one question if I may. You are not German, so are you not also an inferior foreigner, or is there a category in your racial classification that awards the title honorary Aryan?"

"Your question is facetious, in my work I do not talk of myself, I am merely an observer who discovered that the whole of European history is represented by a clash between two races, the superior Aryans and the inferior Jews. That fight to the death includes the struggle against capitalism, a destructive economic system which the Jews invented to enrich themselves at the expense of Aryans. The Jews also invented socialism which is nothing more than a strategy to divert the attention of ordinary people away from the economic devastation brought about by Jewish financiers."

"Herr Chamberlain, I am not sure if you are aware of the fact that capitalism and socialism are effectively two opposing systems. It seems quite ludicrous to me that these Jews, who you say are responsible for creating both, would seek to introduce two systems that counteract each other. It seems to me that since you are not an economist the subtle differences between the two are not immediately apparent to you."

"I am totally conversant with the philosophy underpinning both and what is more let me conclude this discussion with the following which you will find in my book. You Jews are a race, not a religion, and therefore the Jewish question cannot be resolved by allowing you people to convert to Christianity. Even if you convert you remain a Jew, it is in your blood. In this, I disagreed with Wagner; he believed Jews could annihilate their Jewishness through conversion. I stated conclusively, a Jew can never be a German. The resolution of this race struggle can only finally end when the Aryans completely destroy Judaism and rescue the world from racial chaos. This discussion has ended, please leave."

"Gladly, Herr Chamberlain, however before I take my leave, I would like you to know that my conclusion after our discussion is that your work has no scientific credibility whatsoever. It is merely the ramblings of a rather insecure man seeking a place in a world in which he was initially shunned."

STAR-CROSSED FAMILIES

———◆———

And fittingly, we will end this journey through the 1800s with some insights into the family tree of Martha and Margot, who are the main protagonists of this story. Theresa, their mother, was the youngest of the six children born to Siegmund and Martha Nissensohn. Unfortunately, the kaleidoscope has revealed nothing about the early origins of the Nissensohn family—my mechanism for peering into the past is not without its shortcomings! The kaleidoscope, however, did manage to open images from the end of the nineteenth century, and I will use these to continue my story.

A vague image appears, the year is around 1888 maybe 1889. A marriage is being celebrated. I see a very formally dressed young man wearing a kittel[28] standing next to his heavily veiled bride under a marriage canopy, a chuppah. He is lifting the veil and I see a rather demure, slight young woman shyly looking up at the man who is now her husband. The groom is Siegmund Nissensohn, the bride Martha Tannenburg. The image fades and is gone.

---

[28] A long white garment worn by the bridegroom in a traditional Jewish wedding ceremony. Symbolizing purity, it is also the shroud used to clothe the body of Jews prior to burial.

Turning and turning the kaleidoscope and at last colours coalesce and an image appears. It is the 6th August 1890, I am outside the Israelite Hospital of Hamburg. Looking at the building I recall it was officially opened in 1843 constructed from funds donated by the Jewish banker Salamon Heine, father of Henry now Heinrich. After the father died in 1844 Heinrich wrote a poem which he dedicated to the hospital.

> *A hospital for Jews who are sick and needy,*
> *For those unhappy threefold sons of sorrow*
> *afflicted by the three most dire misfortunes,*
> *of poverty, disease, and Judaism*[29]

The kaleidoscope image changes, I am in a room where a tiny infant swaddled in blankets and crying lustily is being handed over to its exhausted mother who is propped up in a bed. I look a little closer and realise that the woman now gingerly accepting the noisy bundle is Martha Nissensohn. Looking at the child Martha says, more to herself than the hovering midwife, "A girl, she is so beautiful, I hope Siegmund will not be disappointed, he was so sure this baby would be a boy. He even spoke to the mohel[30] last week and afterwards we talked about who to invite to the bris milah. He is a very good man, I love him dearly, but when I suggested we may have a girl he just shook his head and said, 'Marta, it will be a boy.' We have been

---

[29] The dedication was written in German, this translation is by Edgar Alfred Browning.
[30] The Hebrew name of the person performing the traditional circumcision ceremony, the bris milah, for Jewish male babies on the eighth day after birth.

married for little more than a year and I have learned not to argue with him when a particular idea enters his head."

Martha's unease is short lived; the midwife who is quite experienced in dealing with preconceived male perceptions regarding the sex of their newly arrived progeny has quietly left the room in order to ambush Martha's husband before he bursts into the delivery room. "Herr Nissensohn," she says excitedly to Siegmund as he comes rushing down the corridor, "mazal tov, you have a beautiful baby daughter. Your wife did splendidly and the child is very healthy, you can hear how powerfully she is crying."

Siegmund is then ushered into the room by the midwife and immediately takes the little bundle out of his wife's arms, smiling broadly. "Her name in Yiddish will be Shaindel," he says, as he looks down at the baby cradled in his arms. "I will name her in the synagogue tomorrow morning."

The Hamburg city records reveal that when Siegmund registered his daughter on the official population register the name given was Selma.

The kaleidoscope spins, I find myself in the same room eleven months later. To be exact it is the 27th July 1891. The midwife is once more carrying a bundle swathed in blankets to Martha Nissensohn. This time the congratulatory message delivered with a broad smile is, "Mazal tov, Frau Nissensohn, you have a healthy son." As she places the baby in its Mutti's arms an excited Siegmund bursts into the room exclaiming, "Nu, what do we have?" "Our prayers have been granted, we have a son," says Martha, bursting into tears. Normally composed, but also prone to giving vent to outbursts of emotion, Siegmund shouts, "With thanks to God," and is careful to wipe the tears running down his cheek on the wrapping around his son as he lifts the baby from the arms of his wife.

"We will organize the bris in the synagogue. It will be held on a Monday, already a good omen for this child because on that day we read from the Torah. I will ask the rabbi to be the sandak, you know who that is Martha, the person honoured to hold the baby on his lap while the mohel performs the bris. I should go and see the rabbi immediately, if he accepts our son will be truly blessed." He places the baby back into the arms of a smiling mother and rushes out of the room excitedly telling everyone he encounters, "Mazal tov, I have a son."

The rabbi accepts the honour, immediately reflecting the high regard in which the Nissensohns are held within their synagogue and their community. Siegmund had left school when he was sixteen and became apprenticed to one of the many Hebrew printing companies in Hamburg. After leaving the yeshivah[31] where he completed his initial education, he never missed a morning service at his local synagogue. When he started his own printing business Siegmund printed the weekly synagogue newsletter as a donation to the community.

Eight days later, in front of the congregation, the mohel performs the bris. As the child cries out in pain, behind the division which separates the men's and women's sections of the synagogue his mother draws in a breath and tries to suppress the tears that are beginning to well. While she is being comforted loudly by the women a chain of "shooshes" burst out from the men downstairs. In the resulting silence Martha hears the mohel ask Siegmund, "Nu, what is the name?" In a voice

---

[31] A school in which the students concentrate their studies on Jewish religious texts.

filled with emotion Siegmund responds, "His name will be Baruch ben Shmaryahu; in this month of Tammuz, we fasted to commemorate the breaching of the walls of our holy temple in Jerusalem. Tomorrow we will pray for the welfare of the Jewish people as we begin the new month of Av. May my son turn away the bad decree and like our father Abraham be a blessing to his parents, his family, his community and all of the nation of Israel."

Martha is now openly sobbing while being simultaneously comforted and congratulated with loud exclamations of "Mazal tov!" Her stoic reserve had been severely tested when the baby cried out in pain and then finally broke down after she heard the emotion in the voice of her usually reserved husband.

After the bris Siegmund registers the birth of his newborn son with the civil authorities, recording the name as Bruno Nissensohn. The boy had been born with a shock of dark brown hair and in old high German the name Bruno meant brown.

After the birth of Bruno, Martha, who is not a physically strong person, struggles to cope with the competing demands from two babies both under twelve months of age. Little Selma is forced to deal with her first rite of passage when she is abruptly displaced from her mother's breast by a demanding brother. The disturbing political climate that is evolving around them does not prevent the Nissensohns from growing their family. Martha's life is about to become more challenging when the third baby in just over twenty-four months arrives less than fourteen months later, on the 16th September 1892. The normally reserved Siegmund is nevertheless known to give vent to the occasional emotional outburst. As he walks into the room to greet his new son who is swaddled in blankets and lying within the cocoon of his mother's arms, Siegmund exclaims loudly, "The bris will be on the second day of Rosh Hashanah,[32] an honour for us, and for this new child."

Once more the bris is held in the synagogue, it takes place immediately after the Rosh Hashanah service. The president is the sandak and the majority of the congregants attend. After naming the boy Aharon ben Shmaryahu, Siegmund expresses the hope that his second son will follow the example set by Aharon the brother of Moses and become a peacemaker, a person who would bring peace to a troubled world and reconciliation between the Jewish and non-Jewish citizens of "our beloved Germany". Aharon ben Shmaryahu is registered with the civil authorities as Arthur Nissensohn.

On the 19th June 1894 the Nissensohn family celebrates the birth of another daughter, their fourth child. It is Sunday, the day after a special Sabbath known as Nachamu, a Sabbath of comfort following the twenty-four hour fast commemorating the destruction of the first and second temples in Jerusalem occurring on the ninth day of the Hebrew month of Av. The baby had been expected to arrive one month later, and the midwife tells Siegmund they had struggled to get that vital first breath after the birth. As Siegmund looks at the tiny body cradled in Martha's protective arms, he feels a surge of compassion for the little girl who has battled against the odds to survive. "Martha my dear, we need to give extra charity in gratitude for the survival of this baby. I was learning a text with our rabbi some weeks ago and he was talking about the way a name expresses the character of a human being. It was destiny maybe," he continues, "that we spoke about the name Mathilde

---

[32] Jewish New Year.

which the rabbi told us can mean powerful or mighty in battle. Our baby came into this world fighting to be alive, we will name her Mathilde."

In the midst of the welling up of anti-Jewish sentiment all over Germany, and five months after Mathilde's birth, Martha falls pregnant again. On the 11th October 1895 she and Siegmund welcome their third daughter and fifth child in five years. The baby is born on the 23rd of the Hebrew month Tishrei, one day after the holiday known as Simchat Torah, the rejoicing over the Torah. The Hebrew month of Tishrei is replete with holidays and festivals and Martha is exhausted after having to prepare fourteen festive meals in addition to the usual Sabbath fare. She goes into labour a few hours after the festival ends and has a very difficult time during the birth. When Siegmund enters the room to view his latest child Martha tearfully tells him that if it wasn't for the exceptional care provided by one of the midwives, she would not have had the strength to get through the labour. Siegmund pats his wife on the shoulder and tells her he was positive the God of Israel was also present. "Good people," he says, "should always be remembered, so we will give this child the Hebrew name of Puah, one of the brave midwives who refused to murder the male babies born to Israelite families in Egypt." He squeezes Martha's hand, tickles the tiny baby on the cheek, then rushes off to the Saturday afternoon prayer service to name his latest daughter. After the short naming ceremony, Siegmund announces to the small congregation present that his wish for the child is that the Jewish people should be brought to ultimate redemption through her good deeds. This baby is registered in the civic records with the name Paula.

On Friday 21st May 1897 the Nissensohn family celebrates the birth of their youngest child, another daughter. It is the 19th day of the Hebrew month Iyar; fifty-one years later the Jewish state of Israel will be declared on the 5th of this month. Siegmund is thirty-four years old and we assume his wife maybe a little younger. The baby enters a family where the oldest child, Selma Shaindel, is nearly seven, the two boys Bruno Baruch, and Arthur Aharon, six and five respectively, Mathilde nearly three, and Paula Puah seventeen months. Martha arrives in the hospital desperately trying to push aside the anxiety welling up in her. She pictures herself walking into their small apartment as the new baby in her arms begins crying, while at the same time trying to fend off Matilda who is not quite weaned and wants the breast. As this struggle is taking place the two boys who have both missed their mother terribly while she was away giving birth come running in and began pulling her dress demanding attention. Seven-year-old Selma is nowhere to be seen; she is sulking in a bedroom because she feels totally rejected. The birth is very difficult and the midwives in attendance decide that a doctor should be present. When the baby finally emerges after a long labour, Martha has difficulty in framing a question about the baby's sex and its health. The doctor comes up to her and says quietly, "Mrs. Nissensohn, you should not have any more children; your health will not cope with another pregnancy." Summoning up the strength Martha replies, "Please tell my husband that."

Siegmund breezes into the room oblivious of the drama that has taken place and eager to inspect his latest child. Before he can approach the bed, the doctor pulls him aside and quietly informs him that his wife is not strong enough to go through another pregnancy. A chastened Siegmund approaches the bed, looks down at this wife who is very pale and lying prone with eyes closed. Next to her the baby is moving its lips and wriggling gently in the wrapping blanket. Feeling her husband's presence Martha slowly opens her eyes and gives him a wan smile of welcome. He pats her cheek gently and says, "My dear, I understand this has been a very difficult time for you, we will listen to the doctor, she will be our youngest and our delight. Tomorrow in the synagogue we will name her Tirza, our delight." In the civil records the baby is named Theresa.

By the end of the 1800s the Nissensohn family have moved into their new home at Neuer Steinweg 76, in Hamburg. Siegmund's business, The Nissensohn German-Hebrew Lithographic & Book Printing Company, is by this time also firmly established and operated out of Bruderstrasse 2, which today is near Grossneumarkt.

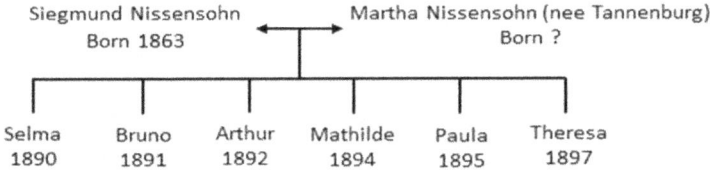

The kaleidoscope was particularly uncooperative when it came to revealing images about Martha's father's family, the Brauns. Try as I might nothing would come into focus and all I could find were a number of scattered and rather vague images. From these I was able to develop the following picture.

Daniel Braun, the youngest child of Joachim and Minna Braun is born on the 3rd January 1893, the 15th day of the

Hebrew month Tevet. Five days before his birth, devout Jews in Germany and elsewhere had observed a day of fasting and prayer to remember the day Nebuchadnezzar first laid siege to Jerusalem, two thousand two hundred and sixty-four years before. Daniel has seven brothers and sisters: Morris, Isadore, Max, Leo, Sally, Sofie, and Emilia. He will marry Theresa, the youngest child of Siegmund and Martha Nissensohn. Unlike Siegmund, Joachim Braun, Daniel's father, is not an observant Jew but he has an affectionate affinity for the enjoyable traditions like Sabbath and festival meals. Joachim never refers to the Hebrew calendar and is unaware that the tenth day of Tevet is a fast day; his social milieu does not include the devout, strictly Orthodox members of the Altona Jewish community.

    Joachim's traditional approach to his Jewish inheritance brings the family together for a Friday night Sabbath meal although he sees no point in observing all the Sabbath restrictions Jewish law demands. Joachim earns his living as a cabinet maker and rather than spending his Saturday morning in the synagogue he uses the time to apply finishing touches to the pieces due for delivery in the coming week. Through his business connections Joachim has a large and diverse circle of acquaintances both in Altona and in Hamburg. He prides himself on having both Jewish and non-Jewish friends and although no intellectual, his wide range of experiences exposes him to many of the ideas swirling around the Germany he considers home. The distasteful innuendos and at times raw hatred about Jews expressed within earshot do not particularly worry him, he is inclined to shrug them off as aberrations in a usually tolerant society. The upsurge of anti-Jewish rhetoric coming from mainstream political parties and politicians, however, disturbs him greatly and his views about this and a general concern for the future are often the main topics of conversation around the family dinner table on a Friday night. Daniel, together with his brothers and sisters, was brought up to be aware of the inherent dangers lurking within the toxic antisemitic environment building up around them.

The seeds of a virulent antisemitism were already firmly planted into the social fabric of their Germany, the country they called home. These seeds would later burst out and morph into something alien, a voracious inhuman beast that wiped out centuries of Jewish civilization in Germany and in Europe.

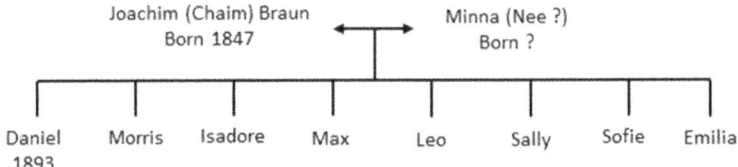

BOOK TWO

1900-1918

The Great War and the Jews in Germany

The Path to War

---◆---

It is generally accepted by historians that the origins of World War II are embedded within the peace treaty that ended World War I. For that reason, dear reader, I decided to prepare this introduction to Book Two—it is a brief summary of the events leading to the outbreak of the Great War. World War I is also a major event within the historical timeline of our story.

What is fascinating, and somewhat disturbing, is how often personal agendas and massive personal egos lie at the core of strategies supposedly formulated and executed to protect the national interest!

When the war between France and Germany we know as the Franco-Prussian War ended with the defeat of France in 1871, the peace terms were incorporated into a treaty known as the Treaty of Versailles. The terms of the treaty not only required France to pay a war indemnity of five billion francs to Germany, a huge amount at today's prices so you can just imagine how much it represented back in 1871. The treaty terms also provided that the German army would continue to occupy parts of France until the payment was complete, and the final knife thrust into the belly of France was the loss of its territories Alsace and Lorraine which were to be ceded to Germany. The Treaty of Versailles therefore imposed onerous penalties on the

French nation and severely impacted on national pride. It also left the French with a determination to get back the territory lost and to restore the glory of France.

At the peace negotiations the Prussian ruler, Kaiser Wilhelm I, was represented by Otto von Bismarck who after the conference succeeded in getting most of the German states to come together and become a united Germany. For the next seventeen years, Bismarck, who was appointed Chancellor of the newly unified Germany, proceeded to negotiate a complex web of defensive international alliances and agreements to bring security to Germany and to isolate France. He was given free rein to implement his strategic program by the Kaiser. In 1882 Bismarck facilitated the formation of a Triple Alliance between Germany, Italy and the Austro-Hungarian Empire. The agreement obligated each member to provide mutual support in the event of an attack by any other great power.

Kaiser William I died in 1888, aged ninety-one, and was succeeded by his son Frederick William who ascended the throne as Frederick III. The new Kaiser, who had cancer of the larynx, died at the age of fifty-six after only a ninety-nine-day reign. He was succeeded by his son who became Kaiser Wilhelm II in June 1888. Wilhelm II has been described as intelligent but emotionally unstable. An accident at birth had left him with a withered arm which never grew to a size beyond that of a small child. His force of will enabled him to overcome the disability but apparently left him with an acute inferiority complex.

The new Kaiser had no time for the conservatism of his Chancellor and was jealous of the power and prestige Bismarck enjoyed in the international arena. Their disagreements also represented a clash between the old landed Germany nobility who tried to maintain moderation for reasons of conservatism, and the new imperialist Germany, which did not see itself restrained by that moderation. Bismarck was unable to find support in his struggle against the wilful Kaiser and was ultimately also opposed by the army. On March 18, 1890, he was forced to resign.

Bismarck's strategy to isolate France and protect German security began to unravel as the nineteenth century drew to a close. France, looking to recover both national pride and the territories of Alsace and Lorraine, concluded a secret agreement with Russia in 1894. The agreement obligated each to come to the other's aid if attacked by Germany or a German-supported Italy, the exact scenario Bismarck had tried to prevent.

The majority of Europe's rulers belonged to the same family, grandchildren and great children of Britain's Queen Victoria. Ironically the petty jealousies and bitter rivalries driving the relationships between them contributed greatly to tensions that ultimately led to World War I. Of particular note was the rivalry between the Kaiser and his uncle, King Edward VII of England. A significant expression of this rivalry was the Kaiser's determination to have a bigger navy than his uncle, possibly one manifestation of the German ruler's inferiority complex.

Britain's policy of splendid isolation, the foundation for its foreign policy during the last decades of the nineteenth century, ended in 1902. The island nation feared being starved into submission should it be drawn into a conflict where its navy no longer controlled the sea lanes. It therefore viewed the strengthening of the German navy as a significant threat to national security. To safeguard its empire and supply lines in the far east, Britain entered into an alliance with Japan in 1902. The terms of the alliance obligated both to remain neutral should either party go to war. It also provided that should either Britain or Japan be attacked by two or more nations the other would come to its aid.

As the first decade of the new century unfolded Germany found itself to be more and more isolated. In 1904 Britain and France entered into an *Entente Cordiale* which was not a formal alliance but the "understandings" embedded within the terms brought Britain and France closer together. The Kaiser tried to break the Entente Cordiale but his efforts only strengthened the relationship. German isolation deepened in 1906 when Britain negotiated a further entente with Russia in 1906. *Europe's future would now be determined by the leaders of two opposing sides, that of Germany, Austria-Hungary, and Italy, who were facing off against Great Britain, France, and Russia.*

Germany began planning an invasion of France because the Kaiser and his advisers believed that the French were recovering too quickly from the punitive peace terms imposed in 1871. The mood in France on the other hand was xenophobic, the French yearned to avenge their loss of national pride and wanted to get back its lost territories. Germany also perceived itself to be isolated and encircled, and to complicate matters its foreign policy aspirations were driven by a Kaiser who aspired to be more powerful and influential than other members of his extended family. Both Germany and France had already drawn up battle plans before the heir to the Austrian throne, Archduke Ferdinand, was assassinated by Gavrilo Princip, a Serbian national, in Sarajevo on 28th June of 1914. The assassination triggered a series of events that culminated with Austria-

Hungary declaring war on Serbia on the 28th July 1914, bringing Russia into the conflict when it came to the defence of its ally Serbia. Four days later, on the 1st August, Germany, coming to the defence of its Triple Alliance partner, declared itself to be at war with Russia. *So, the agreements binding Germany to Austria-Hungary, and those binding Britain and France to Russia, pitted the Triple Alliance against the Triple Entente and the civilized world plunged headlong into a conflict that would end with the loss of thirty million lives.*

The Triple Entente binding France to Russia now gave Germany the pretext for unleashing its pre-planned invasion of France bringing both France and Britain into the war. Neither side was able to deliver the knockout blows envisaged by their respective battle plans, and a war of attrition resulted with opposing armies dug into trenches facing each other across a neutral space called "no-man's land".

When Germany declared war on Russia a huge patriotic demonstration took place in Munich's Odeonplatz on the 1st August 1914. An emotional crowd belted out "Die Wacht Am Rhein" (Who Will Defend Our Rhine), and their national anthem, "Deutschland Uber Alles". In the middle of the throng stood a twenty-five-year-old man joyfully caught up in the patriotism and commitment of the moment. A social dropout rejected by society, a man with minimal talent who aspired to be both celebrated artist and architect, but was capable of neither, "a nonentity who was angry at a world which, in his mind, had rejected him".[33] The war offered "a cause, a commit-

---

[33] Ian Kershaw, *Hitler: An Autobiography.* W. W. Norton and Company, 2008, page 51.

ment, comradeship, a sense of belonging".[34] That man was Adolf Hitler.

Prior to World War I, the German army had avoided promoting non-converted Jews to officer positions. Jews also found it difficult to gain admission to German military academies and were excluded from certain prestige regiments. All that changed when the Great War broke out. Jewish soldiers, sailors, and airmen, fought alongside their non-Jewish countrymen, and against other Jews fighting on the opposite side. In Germany, the Jewish community joined the patriotic fervour sweeping the country when hostilities began. They identified with the propaganda line that Germany had been dragged into the war against its will and was now engaged in a struggle to defend Western European culture against Russia, Britain, and France. German Jews also saw the war as an opportunity to strike a blow against the virulent antisemitism in Russia which had afflicted Jewish life under the Czars for so many years.

When war broke out the Jewish population of Germany was around six hundred thousand. Jews immediately enlisted in the war effort providing communal support by involving themselves in the collection and distribution of donations, assisting refugees, and engaging in a number of social work projects. One hundred thousand German Jewish men would serve in their country's armed forces of which around ten thousand were volunteers. When hostilities ended in November of 1918, twelve thousand had either died in the fighting or were declared missing in action. Over twenty thousand Jews were promoted, two thousand rose to officer ranks, thirty thousand

---

[34] Ibid.

were decorated, many, more than once. One thousand Jewish soldiers were awarded the Iron Cross first degree, and seventeen thousand the Iron Cross second degree. Around eighteen percent of the Jewish population served their country in the Great War, a percentage no different to that of their non-Jewish fellow citizens. Eighty percent served on the front lines, on the battlefields, and for years endured the hell that was the trenches.

Among the first Jewish volunteers to sign up were Dr Ludwig Franck, a member of the Social Democratic Party, and Dr Ludwig Hass, a member of the Progressive Faction in the Reichstag. Franck enlisted in the army and fell in battle three days after arriving at the front. Hass also enlisted in the army, was cited for bravery and decorated with the Iron Cross. After serving on the front for nearly a year, he was appointed to head the military government in Warsaw.

These are important facts and statistics to remember when our story timeline takes us to the period in between the first and second world wars. A conspiracy theory asserting that the Jews had not only avoided military service but had in fact profited from the war became a popularly accepted reason for ordinary Germans to hate their Jewish neighbours!

Daniel Braun Goes to War

———◆———

Twirling the kaleidoscope to detect images about Jewish participation in the Great War I see a young man in Hamburg saying farewell to his parents—a handshake with the father, a brief embrace with the mother. It is Daniel Braun and he is twenty-one years old. The image fades and another appears, a group of young German soldiers in uniform. Daniel is with them obviously enjoying the moment with his fellow soldiers. The group are about to board the army truck I see in the background. They are young men filled with a spirit of adventure and believe they are about to go into a short battle that will end in victory for their Fatherland!

  The image fades and my interest piques. Did Daniel keep a diary? Surely, he wrote to his parents? What would he have told them, I wonder, what would he have recorded in that diary? I am after all a teller of stories and I thought, you know, Daniel's diary and the letters to and from his parents would make really interesting reading. His words could also provide an intimate understanding of what German Jewish soldiers had to contend with in the Great war. He was after all a decorated soldier, Iron Cross no less!

1st October 1914

Liebe Mutter und Vater,

I have just completed my training and we are about to be sent to the front. I don't know where we are going and even if I did, we were warned not to put that in our letters. I am not the only Jewish soldier in my company but I am not too sure how many of us there are. Last week we had a visit by a Rabbiner and our Hauptleute[35] ordered all Jewish soldiers to meet with him. Not all did though, I don't know why. The Rabbiner's name is Leo Baeck[36] and he was very nice. He did not look like a Rabbiner with his uniform and the gun slung on his shoulders. A Christian priest also visited our company. It was quite funny because the priest and the Rabbiner had the same uniform but the Rabbiner wore a gold chain around his neck and on it there was a Mogen Dovid[37] and something that was supposed to be a copy of the tablets on which the ten commandments were originally written. I was quite proud of myself because many of the other Jewish soldiers asked me what was on the gold chain and I was able to tell them. I will send you another letter as soon as I can. Mutti please don't worry about me; I am sure this will be over very soon and our Fatherland will be victorious. Keep up the good work you are doing to provide warm clothing for our soldiers.

Your son Daniel

---

[35] Captain.
[36] Leo Baeck was a prominent rabbi, leader of the Reform movement in Germany and renowned internationally.
[37] Star of David.

Diary note, 30ᵗʰ October 1914

    Finally, after five days with almost no sleep I am back at base camp. It is in Belgium near a place called Ypres. We have been at the front for six days and now have some rest before going back. I can't forget the sight which confronted us when we first came here, it was horrible. There is a huge battle going on, day and night you can hear the big guns. There are many tents with red crosses painted on the outside; the screams coming from inside are terrible to hear, all around are unburied bodies lying under canvas because the burial parties are unable to keep up. All the time stretchers carrying screaming, crying soldiers are flanking our column. We were marched to a place and ordered to dig trenches, three meters deep, and two meters wide. I was lucky to be spared the digging, the ground is hard and the cold makes it difficult to hold a shovel. When we arrived our Korporaal asked for anyone with carpentry skills to come forward and I immediately volunteered. For five days and nights I measured and cut boards that were then used to make a solid floor at the bottom of the trenches. Other soldiers are making sandbags to line the sides of the trenches. I don't really see how this will keep out the mud when the rain starts. It is so good to be eating hot soup and I am looking forward to a cot in a tent, something soft to sleep on tonight not the hard cold ground.

Diary note, 4ᵗʰ November 1914

    A very bad day today. Someone confronted me when we were lining up for food, shouting in a loud voice so that everyone could hear, "You should be ashamed of yourself avoiding the real work while your companions dig trenches.

You are cutting wood, that is easy work." I tried to explain that this was not easy work. All day you are crouching in a small place trying your best to fashion the boards with tools that are totally inadequate. He then became very angry and began shouting, "Just like a Jew, you not only find a way to get out of hard work, you also make excuses." Some of his friends told him to stop and one even came to me later to say sorry. I never thought that my being Jewish would matter in this place where possibly next week most of us will join the many bodies I see lying under canvas.

5th November 1914

Liebe Mutter und Vater,

I am writing this short letter to tell you I am fine. We are preparing to move to another location and I may not be able to write for some time. Vater, you will be very pleased to know that my job as a carpenter has proved to be very useful and I am working very hard to fortify our positions here on the front lines. I very much hope to be home with you soon.

Dein liebender Sohn
Daniel

Diary note, 30th November 1914

I didn't want to write about the things I have seen, what I have been through. But in the end, I had to write it down, maybe by doing so it will remove the emptiness in the pit of my stomach that has become my new reality. On the 10th November our company was ordered to get ready for departure with full battle gear. I had managed to get hold of a really good wood saw but the Hauptleute told me, "Braun, you don't need that, you need your gun." We marched overnight to a heavily wooded area and then spread out in three lines about 100 meters long. I was in the second line. I looked at my watch, a present from Vater on my bar mitzvah. It was 6am, still dark, the air very cold. We were crouching there shivering, it was not only because of the cold. Our Leutnante came down the rows speaking quietly to the men as he passed by. "Men, the enemy is in retreat, you are going into battle to make sure they continue to retreat. In a short time, our artillery will begin firing behind us, it will go on for around two and a half hours. When it stops, we attack; be brave, be strong, for the Fatherland. We will prevail today, prepare yourselves, our cause is just, our Lord Jesus will be with us." Dawn was beginning to break but it was difficult to see because of the heavy mist. And then I remember falling on my face, covering my ears as the sound of artillery exploded into action somewhere behind us. It went on and on. In front of me the dawn sky turned orange. I remember thinking please let the artillery go on and on because when it stops, I will have to run into that sea of orange in front of me and I don't want to go there. Suddenly the artillery guns fell silent, thirty seconds of relief, and then the order, "fix bayonets" another thirty seconds, "charge". I ran, I didn't know where I was going, my companions on either side and in front were falling, many screaming, others collapsing without a sound. I remember jumping over my friend Willie and when I looked back saw him lying on his back clutching his chest. I wanted to stop but the third line coming up behind pushed me forward. Then, I saw the face of my enemy, he was aiming his rifle and it was straight at me. The shot never came, I don't know why, maybe he was as frightened as me, maybe his gun jammed, but then my bayonet was piercing his chest and blood came spurting from his mouth and I was screaming like a mad person. I twisted the bayonet to release it and looked down at the man who would have killed me. His helmet had been knocked off when he fell, I saw the face of a young boy, maybe eighteen, a contorted face, fixed in a grimace of death. Something ripped the arm of my uniform, I felt a stab of pain and looked down. The bullet had grazed my left arm. Shocked into action I began running again, screaming once more, looking frantically ahead to detect those who would kill me before I could kill them. My companions were running next to me also screaming. Suddenly my knees gave way and I found myself in a kneeling position shooting blindly at who knows what and once again panic forced me to get up and I madly built a pile of bodies, crouched behind them trying to recover some sense of what to do. And then, explosions all around, it was as if the shells we had sent over were now being returned. All around a macabre ballet, bodies leaping in time to the music of exploding shells. I don't know how long it went on and then, somehow in that chaos, an order to retreat, back to the shelter of the trees. Those of us still living found ourselves in a thick wooded area I now know to be Nonne Bosschen, many were sobbing, many were bleeding, some were on the ground writhing in pain while medical orderlies tried to stabilize injuries. And then another shouted order, "retreat back to our lines" and as we began moving suddenly the sound of gun fire, bullets whistling passed, many finding bodies to rip apart. Those of us who could still manage to walk somehow got up and ran, yes, we ran to the safety of our own lines. I don't know how many of us died that day, we could not bring ourselves to count the faces that were missing.

20th November 1914

Liebe Mutter und Vater

I want you to know I am fine; it is difficult to write letters at the moment. I am sure that you visited Willie's family. If you see them, please pass on this message, "Your son was a very brave man, a true son of our Fatherland." I miss him so much. These are difficult times. I am trying to adjust to this new life.

Your son
Daniel

Diary note, 31st December 1914

I must write to my dear parents, there has been very little time and I don't really know what to tell them. Three days after the battle of Nonne Bosschen, that is what everyone is now calling it, we were moved to another area and told to dig trenches. This time I was told to dig and also to make boards so I had a double duty. I was too afraid to complain. It was very cold and rained for days, we had to toil day and night in the cold, rain, and mud. The soil became sticky and thick like the dough used for making bread. Thankfully this hard labour lasts only four or five day stretches and then another group relieves you. Today it snowed, I am fortunate to be out of the trenches. I am also happy to have been in the trench on the 25th December, the Jewish soldiers had to deal with some very difficult moments when the Christmas celebrations began. I think this was caused by the appearance of a Rabbiner on the 11th December who brought candles for the Jewish soldiers to light on Chanukah which he told us would begin on the 12th. I actually forgot the date and never lit the candles; I was in the trenches at the time. Tomorrow is New Year 1915; we all pray for this to end.

1st January 1915

Liebe Mutter und Vater

Thank you for your letter which I received a few days ago. I am glad to hear that everyone is well. Mutti, it would be very strange if I were to receive one of the scarves you are knitting for our soldiers. Have you had any news from Morris, Isadore, Max and Leo? It is very difficult when some members of our family are living in the country of the enemy who wishes to destroy our beloved Germany. I wanted to be with you all to celebrate the new year but it was not to be. The next best thing is to send you a letter. I don't know when you will get this but hope it arrives soon.

Your son
Daniel

Diary note, 25th March 1915

My home has become a trench. We have done everything possible to make it liveable but the reality is that I now live in a narrow passage with three-meter-high walls on either side of me. In the daylight hours you would not dare to climb out because your head would be blown off by a sniper on the other side. We have our snipers too. The rain and snow seeps through the boards that I helped to make, the boards sink and mud oozes through the cracks. Some pumps arrived last week to assist in removing the water. You cannot get rid of the mud. There are three rows of trenches on our side. The first row looks over a large expanse of land on which barbed wire is strewn, they call this no man's land. Our enemy are also in trenches, about 500 yards away. Behind our front line trench is a second row and behind that a third row. We occupy the three trench lines in rotation, six days in each row, eighteen days in total, then a short break in the rear where there are showers. I never believed that a shower would be something you longed for day after day. Not being able to shower is only one problem, there is nowhere to wash clothes in the trenches, for eighteen days you live in what you have. How wonderful is that nineteenth day when you receive fresh clothing and stand under water removing mud from your pores and every other bodily orifice. The trenches smell very bad, you get used to it and only realise how sickening the smell is when you leave. The latrines are supposed to be far away from the living spaces but in many of the trenches they are just open buckets that must be constantly emptied. Many people are becoming very ill and then there are the rats, they eat anything and everything. At times you pick up your ration bag and out jumps at least one rat. Some of the men are organizing competitions to see who kills the most in a day. A real problem that has begun to make life even more difficult is trenchfoot. Our feet are always wet from the mud and the rain, and although we have a few spare pairs of socks it is almost impossible to dry them. The doctors told us that constantly wearing tight boots with wet socks could cause gangrene. I heard that some soldiers have already lost toes, feet, even legs because of this. The worst times are the six days in the front trench. You live every day with the threat of having to go over the top. It is suicide, you charge into a hailstorm of bullets, many thudding into your companions running to the left, right and front, expecting any moment to feel a momentary stab of agony before darkness finally blots out the madness. I thank God I have not been involved in any of the current actions. Periodically the enemy artillery blasts shells over to our side and they explode in or close to the trenches. The lucky ones die immediately, for the unlucky ones the injuries are horrible. At night, groups of soldiers are ordered to sneak quietly out of the trench to repair gaps in the barbed wire. Most of the time however there is nothing to do in the trenches and like a rat you just crawl into a hole cut into the dirt walls and wallow in misery, praying for the end of your tour in the front line trenches. There is no glory here, just mud, rain, rats, the sickening smells of death, human waste, and unwashed bodies.

15th April 1915

Liebe Mutter und Vater,

A big surprise for the Jewish soldiers in our company last month. A Rabbiner came to the camp bringing matzos, grape juice, and a few Pesach Haggodos[38] so that we could hold a seder.[39] He told us the first night was Sunday March 28th. I was very lucky to be in the camp at that time. There were about seven Jewish soldiers in the camp that night and we tried as best as we could to have some sort of seder. One of the Jewish soldiers, Walter Goldberg who comes from Berlin, had some knowledge about the service and led it. Most of us were very quiet, we missed our homes terribly and were wondering how our families would be celebrating the holiday.

Your son Daniel

---

[38] The prayer book used on the Passover festival.
[39] The name for the festive meal on the Passover festival.

2nd June 1915

As always, your letters and news from home are very appreciated. I have some good news at last. The army has now created a special engineering unit responsible for building and looking after our trenches. It is called the Pionier unit. I will explain what this means when I see you. Our Hauptleute sent my name to the unit and I got orders yesterday to report for duty beginning of July. The even better news is that I have been given a fourteen-day pass to return home before joining the new unit. I will be home on the 2nd July. I am so excited.

Dein liebender Sohn
Daniel

Diary note, 20th August 1915

Five months since I wrote anything in this notebook, no time, no desire. The trenches are becoming permanent and constant repair is needed which puts great pressure on us. Sometimes the shelling is so bad that whole sections need to be rebuilt. Being rushed to do quick repairs is the worst, we often arrive while broken bleeding bodies are being removed from the rubble. You don't get used to that. We do try to make things as comfortable as possible for the men in the trenches, even try to make up some tables from board cut offs. We were told not to show our heads above the parapet when working in the trench because of the snipers, they would get us if we did. In the trenches you are always nervous, shells are exploding, and often both sides are exchanging rifle and machine gun fire. I keep repeating to myself, I am only here for a short time and if I can't stand it, how does anyone do this for a week and then have to come back again two weeks later. I don't want to remember too much about my home visit. Mutti, you looked so tired, the bubbling energy which kept our family moving seemed to have left you. I asked if you were ill, you just gave me a weak smile. I never visited Willie's family despite your requests. I suppose my excuse that I had no time was stupid, you just stopped asking. When I thought of going to Willie's apartment the image of him lying there, blood spurting through the fingers fruitlessly covering the hole in his chest, and his eyes, his eyes looking at me, pleading, for what, I could do nothing. What would I say to his parents, that I was a witness to the last seconds of their son's life? I just couldn't. We thought all of this would be over very quickly, I think it will go on forever.

Diary note, 15th September 1915.

A Feldrabbiner visited our Pionier group to tell us that the Jewish new year was 10th September. There are only five Jewish soldiers in our unit, the Rabbiner said we should get together and talk about what the new year could bring for us. We should also remember to fast on Yom Kippur[40] which will be 18th September. He gave us two Hebrew prayer books printed by the Nissensohn German-Hebrew Lithographic and Book Printing company in Altona, so strange, I remember passing the printing works which is at Bruderstrasse 2. On the 10th we were working in the trenches, I don't think I am interested in fasting. The prayer book contained a page in which all the dates of the holidays from new year to Simchas Toyra[41]

---

[40] The day of atonement, holiest day in the Jewish calendar. Jews traditionally fast for twenty-four hours from nightfall to nightfall.
[41] The day on which Jews celebrate the end of the annual cycle during which the reading of the Old Testament written on a Torah scroll is completed and immediately recommenced.

were listed. I don't see anyone dancing with a Torah scroll here in this hell, strange how I never appreciated the holiday when I was able to celebrate it.

Diary note, 10ᵗʰ December 1915
    Everyone is talking about Xmas and how they wished they were home. Even two of the Jewish soldiers are complaining that they will not be home for Xmas, one told me his family always celebrated this holiday with a tree and everything. I remember that our family always celebrated Chanukah[42] this time of the year, we never had a visit from a Feldrabbiner this time so I don't know when it is or was. Yesterday there was something going on at lunch when I walked in, everyone stopped talking. I heard some comment about Juden but am not sure what it was about. I spoke to a non-Jewish friend about it, he was a bit embarrassed, told me the talk around is that the Jews are to blame for the war not being over quickly. He said that the families at home were having difficult times and Jewish profiteers were being blamed for taking all the money out of the country.

20ᵗʰ May 1916

Liebe Vater,
    I wish I could be with you now. It must be so hard without our beloved Mutti. I too am having a very hard time here, on my own, with no family to share my grief. When she passed and I was allowed special leave to attend the funeral I remember

---

[42] The annual Jewish holiday celebrated over eight days commemorating the rededication of the Temple in Jerusalem by the Maccabees which occurred in the year 164 BCE.

wishing it was just a trick you all arranged to get me home. When she was not at the train station and I saw your faces, I knew that it was no trick. Just before Passover I was so hoping I would be able to come home, and then I was told that I was being granted compassionate leave. I wish it never would have happened. It was some comfort to hear all the things people said about her, a truly wonderful woman, generous and caring. I never knew she was doing so much to help our soldiers, the people she worked with were so generous in how they praised her. These are times when it does not matter if you are a Jew or a Christian, everyone is working together and I am sure this will be our new future when the war is finally won. I have a Christian friend here and told him everything that was said about Mutti. Have you had any more letters from my brothers, it was very painful not having them with us. Please write and tell me how you are doing. I sit on my own and think that Mutti will never be able to celebrate the end of the war, will not be there when I marry, will never see my children.

Dein liebender Sohn
Daniel

Diary note, 16th July 1916

I have been at the front for months now. There are two very big battles going on, our unit is here in France near Verdun where the one battle is taking place, I am told the other one is near the river Somme. We are building fortifications behind our lines. All day thousands of injured men are being sent to the hospitals in the rear. I am told that thousands are dying every day. We are working day and night with little rest I don't know when I will be able to write anything again. I do not even have time to send a letter to my poor father. Will I ever see him and my sisters again? I don't think I will ever see my brothers again. After all this bloodshed will we Germans ever be able to travel to England or the English visit our country? Something is really worrying me and I have to be very careful what I write here in case someone who does not wish us well sees it. There are so many mutterings about Juden going on all the time. I hear that some sort of investigation has begun aiming to find out how many Jews are in our army; I heard one of the officers talking about a Judenzaehlung.[43] I don't know what that means but it has changed the way our fellow soldiers look at us.

18th September 1916

Liebe Vater

I am sure you know about the big battles going on now. Please don't worry about me I am fine and working very hard to build the fortifications that will protect our Fatherland from invasion by the enemies trying to destroy us. I was hoping to receive a pass to return home but all leave has been cancelled at the moment. We had a visit from our unit's Feldrabbiner yesterday and he brought us some provisions to celebrate the Jewish new year which I understand is on the 27th September. It is going to be a difficult time for you and although we were never what you would call an observant family these holidays were always very special when everyone was together. I am sure that my sisters will be looking after you and helping you through. There is some talk here about a sort of census being

---

[43] Jewish census organised to determine how many Jews were actually serving in the German armed forces.

taken about Jews in our armed forces. Have you heard anything about this at home?

I will be thinking of you when the new year arrives.

Dein liebender Sohn

Daniel

Diary note, 20th December 1916

I think that things are not going well for us. The front is not moving forward, we were talking amongst ourselves yesterday, it seems like we are moving backwards. There are only three Jews now in our unit, we were five. Two were killed this year, one by sniper fire, the other by a shell that exploded in the place he was working. I am a bit nervous about the approach of Xmas, I don't understand why but many of my fellow soldiers are accusing the Jews of not committing themselves to the Fatherland because they are always looking to be excused from serving. I just pray that none of these people know that my brothers are in England. So far, I have not been attacked personally but at one time I walked into a tent and heard some very horrible things being said about Jews; one of my friends who was there quickly said, "But Dani, we are not talking about you, you are ein guter Jude."[44] In my father's last letter, he mentioned that things are becoming difficult for the family but he never explained what these difficult things were. On Xmas we are collectively found to be guilty of deicide, I asked for leave to go home but it was denied.

Diary note, 1st March 1917

---

[44] A good Jew.

At last, one month leave granted, I will be home for Passover.

Diary note, 30th April 1917

This war has been going on for two and a half years, no one seems to have any idea of when it will end. I am grateful that I am still alive and suppose that should wipe away any other thoughts going through my mind. My home leave was very distressing. Being with family after so many months should have brought relief but the man who was my dear Vater is no longer there. He is in his seventieth year and sadly seems to have lost the desire to be alive. The loss of Mutti was a big blow, but there was something else weighing heavily on him. It had sent him into a dark place where no one else could visit. We are not a family that talks about these things but I was so concerned that I confronted my sister Emilia, challenging her to tell me what was going on. She immediately started to cry and finally told me that our father was a broken man. Many of his customers had stopped buying from him because they accused him of being a Jew who was making money over the dead bodies of German soldiers. It did not help when he spoke about me because the only thing the accusers were interested in was that three of his sons had left the Fatherland and were living with the enemy. Most of his non-Jewish friends and acquaintances would no longer have anything to do with him and even those who knew the accusations were lies had stopped meeting him because they did not want to be branded Jüdischer Liebhaber.[45] I tried to talk to Vater but he became angry and stormed out of the room. Other little bits of information also made me very sad.

---

[45] Jew-lover.

The rumours of the Jew Count are apparently true, a census was taken to find out how many of us were serving the Fatherland. No results have been published, I wondered how Willie's family were dealing with this! Why are they singling out the Jews and taking such a census? I met an old school friend in Hamburg, he told me about a rumour that Herr General Ludendorff, the second in command of our German army, had publicly stated the Jews were pacifists and socialists who were undermining the strength of the army. This was too much, I told him not to spread such rumours because they could not be true, the General would know that we Jews are in the trenches, in the front line dying like everyone else. My time at home away from the fighting never gave me peace, it just increased the numb feeling I walk around with every day.

Diary note, 15th July 1917

Our unit has returned to a place near Ypres in Belgium, it is very strange to be back in the place where for me this horror began. Our unit is building a long line of new fortifications close to a village called Passchendaele. The talk among the men is that there is going to be a big offensive very soon. I just pray that I am far away from the front. I don't think I could stand being in the trenches. Things must be getting very desperate, for the first time I have heard some talk about deserters.

Diary note, 12th August 1917

The attack came at the end of July. It was ferocious, the deaths and injuries on our side have been enormous, the procession of bodies and injured soldiers being transported to our rear never stops. They pass replacement troops moving to the front, their turn to be slaughtered. We are working day and night on the fortifications to block the enemy from breaking through. I am just so exhausted and so numb, sometimes I just pray for a shell to end this for me.

Diary note, 8ᵗʰ September 1917

Our unit Feldrabbiner visited last week, there are only two of us now. Walther was too close to a shell, he was sent to the rear without his legs. The Rabbiner asked me how I was. I am so ashamed, I began crying and the story about my Vater, who does not write anymore, poured out of me. I even told him about some of the horrible things I had heard my fellow soldiers saying about Jews. He let me talk and when I recovered said, "Daniel, the words of a few are not the views of our country. In every age there have been those who seek to harm the Jewish people and yet we survive." He then told me a story about a Jewish aviator, Willie Rosenstein, who also confronted a very ugly anti-Jewish incident. His direct superior, Hermann Goering, one of Germany's most decorated flyers called Willie a Jewish pig in front of the whole squadron. To annoy Goering one of the other aviators, a man called Adolf Auer who is not Jewish, painted the Jewish Star of David on his aircraft in support of Willie Rosenstein. The strangest part of this story is that Willie immediately requested a transfer to another flying corps and Goering, who had insulted him, wrote a letter of recommendation saying Willie was one of the best pilots in the squadron. The Rabbiner shook my hand and told me I should be grateful that there are more Adolf Auers than Hermann Goerings. His words did not offer me any comfort, nor do I think they would have been a replacement for Walther's legs.

Diary note, 9th December 1917

The battle is over. I think it stopped because everyone is so tired and empty, they just don't care anymore. I have been here for three years. I asked if I could have extended leave, I am not sure I can carry on much longer. It was turned down.

Diary note, 3rd March 1918

The Russians are beaten, they signed a peace agreement today. Great celebration all around. Maybe that means the end is about to come here as well. There is talk of another big offensive. I don't think that I will survive another one.

Diary note, 10th March 1918

I am being sent home. Apparently, I had some sort of fainting attack and was carried to the infirmary. The doctor examined me and declared that I was no longer fit for active service. How do I feel? There is an emptiness inside and I really feel nothing. I even have no joy in the Iron Cross I was awarded, it cannot bring Willie back and will not return Walther's legs to him.

AND SO, IT HAD ALL BEEN IN VAIN

---·◆·---

In October 1914 Adolf Hitler was sent to a military hospital after being caught up in a mustard gas attack. The glorious future promised by that outpouring of patriotic fervour in the Odeon Platz in Munich four years previously was not to be. For a man whose life before 1914 was just a succession of ignominious failures the war had offered redemption and now the cause he had so eagerly embraced became the shame of defeat.

Later Hitler was to write in his memoir *Mein Kampf,* "And so, it had all been in vain…did all this happen only so that a gang of wretched criminals could lay hands on the Fatherland." In his mind and in the mind of many others this gang of wretched criminals was made up from members of the German Reichstag together with "the Communists and the Socialists". The ultimate criminals, however, had to be the people who were behind them all, the Jews in Germany who were allied with the secret international Jewish conspiracy, the master puppeteers who pulled all the strings, that shadowy cabal plotting and scheming to destroy the German volk and ultimately to take over the whole world.

BOOK THREE

1918-1926

A noxious growth emerges from
fertile ground

ARMISTICES AND PEACE TREATIES

———◆———

The exit of Russia from the war in 1917 released German manpower and material deployed on its eastern front, enabling the high command to reassign resources to the west. A battle plan was formulated, the objective being to exert enormous pressure on the allied forces, forcing them to retreat and finally tipping advantage on the battlefield to the German army. On the 21st March 1918, eleven days after Daniel's last diary entry, Germany launched Operation Michael, its final major offensive in the Great War.

The operation began with a massive artillery barrage supported by mustard gas, smoke, and infantry. The opposing forces, weakened after years of unrelenting trench warfare, initially buckled under the pressure and the German offensive achieved unprecedented gains measured in miles rather than yards. But the British and French forces slowly rallied and by the summer had managed to dig in and halt the German advance. The German army suffered enormous losses over the ensuing months in a campaign that came to be known as the Spring Offensives.

On the 8th August a combined British, French, and American force launched a counter offensive at Amiens and by the end of October, the German army had been pushed back to the battlefields of 1914 and was in full retreat. German casualties were high and the Spanish flu epidemic was impacting heavily on the availability of additional manpower. Morale on the home front was also very low as the population struggled to cope with severe shortages of food and basic necessities. It became clear that it was all over; the war was lost.

In September 1918, the German high command advised both the emperor Wilhelm II, and the Imperial Chancellor Count Georg von Hertling, that the military situation was becoming hopeless. In a very shrewd move that was to have significant political and social implications for Germany after the war, General Erich Ludendorff recommended one, acceptance of US president Woodrow Wilson's Fourteen Points for an armistice, and two, that the Imperial German government be switched to a democratic footing. *This move effectively would place responsibility for capitulation and its consequences squarely into the hands of the democratic parties and the parliament, enabling the army to save face and place blame for defeat squarely on the shoulders of "peacemakers" who became known as the November Criminals.*

Ludendorff's suggestion was adopted and in early October the Imperial Chancellor was replaced, transferring responsibility for negotiating terms to end the conflict into the hands of a new chancellor, who came from the liberal faction, and the parliament. A month of negotiation followed with progress being blocked by the German military who stridently complained that the terms being demanded were unacceptable. Between the 29th October and the 9th November 1918, however, two significant events occurred which ultimately forced the

German negotiators to accept an armistice which in time became a formal peace treaty signed in 1920.

The first was a revolt by sailors in the German navy that began in the naval port of Wilhelmshaven on the 29th October and then spread across the whole country. It was clear that the influence of the Bolshevik revolution was beginning to infiltrate into German society. Another example of this was a push from the ranks to form "Soldiers' Councils", which then challenged the authority of the officer corps.

The second was the abdication of the Kaiser on 9th November 1918 following a proclamation from the Reichstag that Germany was to become a republic. The incoming chancellor was a member the Social Democrats who were well represented in the imperial Reichstag but had never been an influential political force. The Social Democrats had been calling for a negotiated peace since 1917 and now its members became a prominent force driving the peace negotiations.

It became obvious as the negotiations commenced that the German delegation had very little leverage and it was ultimately forced to accept the terms as presented to them. After three days of discussion the parties concluded their negotiations at 5:00 a.m. on 11 November and the armistice itself came into effect at 11:00 am on the eleventh hour of the eleventh day of the eleventh month. Finally, the guns were silent.

Some of the harsh provisions embodied within the formal peace deal that was finally ratified in France at the Palace of Versailles on the 28th June 1919 became a symbol of national shame for Germany. Forced to accept that it had been the aggressor and initiator of hostilities, Germany also had to give up around ten percent of its territory, including the overseas colonies. The provisions imposed limitations on the size of the German army and the country was forced to pay reparations assessed at the time to be the equivalent of four hundred and forty-two billion United States dollars.

Even from the middle of 1916 there were moves to find scapegoats to blame for the inability of the German army to achieve a glorious victory. After Versailles, when Germans were forced to confront the destruction of the second German Reich, the need for scapegoats become more imperative. Out of the cacophony of disinformation and rumour surging through all levels of German society a conspiracy theory emerged. This theory claimed that the war had not actually been lost, that Germany was betrayed by a group of traitors. These traitors were known as the November Criminals, a cabal made up from communists and socialists backed by the traitorous, all-powerful international Jewish conspiracy. These bloodsuckers, the theory went, had not only profited from the war but were now profiting from the peace. The perception that Jews were the bloodsuckers in society was ironically reinforced by non-publication of the outrageous "Jew Count", a census which set out to prove that Germany's Jews were avoiding military service. The results actually proved the opposite, around one hundred thousand Jewish men had answered the call to serve in their country's military and twelve thousand had paid with their lives. Non-disclosure gave antisemitic individuals and organisations a golden opportunity to fabricate outcomes and spread a lie that Jews had deliberately avoided military service, leaving their non-Jewish neighbours to shoulder the burden.

Richter Der Geschichte

———•◆•———

The kaleidoscope spins, images appear and disappear, the whole period is very confusing. I need a guide to navigate me through this maze, someone who can find the stories embedded within the confusing images that are post-1918 Germany.

The kaleidoscope brings me to the door of a small nondescript residential building on a quiet street. I look around and discover I am in Munich. Below the door knocker I notice a name, Richter Der Geschichtenerzähler. The humour of the situation does not escape me. I, Korim Seforim, a reader of books, am about to meet Richter Der Geschichtenerzähler, whose name means "teller of stories that end up in books". The door knocker is itself a story, an elaborate contraption about twenty centimetres in height shaped in the image of Father Time bearing a scythe on his shoulder. The knocking mechanism, I eventually determine, is the scythe, which I now push down repeatedly with two fingers.

When the door opens, I immediately understand the reason for the unusual door knocker; it is a replica of the apparition in front of me. Thankfully this apparition is not bearing a large scythe over its shoulder because I might have had second thoughts about accepting the softly spoken invitation to enter. "Herr Korim Seforim, willkommen, I have been expecting you, kommen Sie bitte herein." Readers, please take note, when you enter a kaleidoscope world the unexpected becomes the norm, so I merely express my thanks and step over the threshold. It is like walking into a vast museum, endless galleries open up in front of me, there appears to be no end, each hall morphs into another and into another. It is like a myriad of mirrors stretching into infinity.

"Aha, Herr Korim Seforim, I see you are a little overwhelmed, welcome to my little museum of times that have passed. My museum can be a very confusing place and I caution you not to enter these galleries without a guide, the past will swallow you up you see. But now bitte, tell me what it is you wish to understand and I will guide you and bring my version of the past back into the present. Understand, however, from me you will not get history, from me you will get stories, for that is what I am; just a storyteller. Visitors to my little museum must decide for themselves what is true and what is not. There is nothing wrong with that, is there, truth is relative is it not, mein Herr?"

I nod my head in agreement and reply, "Herr Richter Der Geschichtenerzähler, I am looking for a guide to help me understand events in Germany between 1918 and 1939. Some time ago I heard a story about a young Jewish girl and her sister, who were put on a train in Hamburg on the 21st May 1939 and sent away from their family. They went to England, and in that year so did ten thousand other children. I want to know why."

"Herr Korim Seforim, first of all please call me Richter Der Geschichte, my full name is very difficult especially for non-

German speakers. Second, your request is complicated, you are asking about stories that are really parts of other stories, but come let us try to find an answer for you." He takes my arm and leads me into a gallery with a very odd sign emblazoned over the entrance, "*A tired stray looking for a master*".

GALLERY 1:
THE EVOLUTION OF A STRAY DOG

---•---

My guide leads me into a small circular well-lit gallery explaining all the while that the exhibit begins to our left and is viewed by walking around the room in a clockwise direction. This ultimately brings you back to the entrance which also doubles as an exit. On the walls are a series of photographs, the first being a man with a large head whose face I can only describe as bipolar. The eyes are intense and seem to bore into you while the lower part of the face, dominated by a dark handlebar moustache with turned up ends covering the upper lip, appears to be frozen into a permanent smirk.

"This man," explains Richter, "is the person I call the twentieth century Doctor Frankenstein. His name is General Staff Officer Karl Mayr, head of the Education and Propaganda department in the Reichswehr, which is what the German army was named during the interwar years. And why, you may ask, did I name him Dr Frankenstein? Because, mein Herr, he was the one who initiated the process that turned Adolf Hitler into a monster. You look a little sceptical I see, humour me, allow the story to unfold."

He then moves to the second photograph, a man with a round face on which is perched a high military cap. The bristle moustache just above the upper lip and a scar on the bridge of the nose should have been a giveaway but with a questioning look I turn to my guide and ask, "Who is this?"

"If he had been in his Nazi uniform, I am sure you would not have asked that question, look again."

With a start I realize it is a photo of a young Ernst Rohm who uncharacteristically is displaying a hint of a smile. Rohm who created the Stormabteilung,[46] Hitler's private army which numbered around one million by 1931; Rohm who was appointed Reichsleiter[47] in 1933, the highest rank in the Nazi party, second only to Hitler himself; Rohm who was imprisoned and executed in 1934 after Hitler purged the party of any potential rivals. What is his photograph doing here, I ask myself.

We move on and stop in front of the next photograph, beady eyes peer through round spectacle frames, the unsmiling moustached man in the photo looks a little untidy although he is wearing a suit, a waistcoat, and a necktie. To me he looks a little bit like the owner of a dingy haberdashery store. "This is Anton Drexler," says my guide with a bit of a flourish, "the founder of a political party called the German Workers Party. It became the National Socialist German Workers Party which you, mein Herr, would know as the Nazi party, Der Nationalsozialistische Deutsche Arbeiterpartei. A very ordinary man this Drexler, a fitter and locksmith by trade, he did not even serve in the German army during World War I because he was considered to be physically unfit for duty."

---

[46] Storm Division.
[47] Reich Leader.

Richter then takes me by the arm and brings me to the last photograph in the gallery. I am looking at a young man with hooded eyes beneath bushy eyebrows whose untidy hair is hanging down in an uneven fringe on the left side of the forehead. The face seems to portray the hint of underlying anger; an impression enhanced by the big bushy moustache which spreads down from the nose to the lower cheek bones. "Adolf Hitler in 1919," says Richter with a shrug and walks off towards the gallery exit. He stops in front of a large flat TV screen and motions me to stand in front of it. "Look into the past, mein Herr, I will be with you, we will travel together to the time and the place where our story can be told, it is what we do in my museum of the past; here however we require a tool a lot more powerful than the kaleidoscope which brought you to me."

The first images appear, they are both familiar and shocking, the interior of a barracks in a concentration camp. The image sharpens, focusing on one of the bunks from which four gaunt unshaven faces are peering out talking to a frail looking man in an ill-fitting prison uniform. He is apparently quite unsteady because he is supporting himself by leaning on one of the wooden uprights. I notice that all five have red triangles sewn on their prison jackets; the barracks we are visiting is for German political prisoners. Richter whispers, "Buchenwald, second February 1945, the man standing is Karl Mayr, one week before he was shot; the dog eventually turned on its master!"

The gaunt stooped figure that I now know to be General Staff Officer Karl Mayr looks like a stick man over which clothing had been draped, totally unrecognizable from the photograph I had seen earlier in Richter's gallery. He is saying something to his three companions and Richter motions me to move closer.

"Ernst Rohm wasn't a nobody, you know; he was Chief of Staff to the leader of the Freikorps[48] in Munich; how could I know he was a deviant and a thug. It was Rohm, you see, who recommended I recruit Hitler as an informer for my unit. I had huge responsibilities; my task was to gather intelligence and wherever necessary take action using propaganda and indoctrination to remove dangerous attitudes inside the German army. As for Hitler, I can tell you, when I first met him, he was like a tired stray dog looking for a master, just someone who would throw in his lot with anyone who would show him kindness. I tell you this, he was totally unconcerned about the German people and their destinies. Anyway, as I said before, on Rohm's recommendation I recruited Hitler and sent him for a course to the university in Munich. There we discovered he had a natural talent for public speaking, probably his only talent. Further training brought out this raw ability and unknown to all of us we unwittingly converted a stray dog into a pit bull. I then made one of the biggest blunders of my life, one that probably brought me to this place, I sent Hitler to a meeting of an obscure political party that held its meetings at Der Sterneckerbrau brewery in Munich. His task was simply to report back to me but, Hitler being Hitler could not contain himself could he, he had to join in, spout his views. The chairman of this totally irrelevant little group of misfits, Anton Drexler, was so impressed that he asked

---

[48] An armed right-wing group of former German World War I soldiers who found common cause through their rejection of the terms Germany accepted in the peace treaty that ended the war.

Hitler to join their pitiful little party and invited him to attend the next meeting."

Richter pulls me away, smiles wryly and says, "The rest, mein Herr, as they say is history. And oh, about Herr Mayr, ja, unfortunately for him one week later he was shot. Yes, the dog turned on its master!"

We are back in the gallery in front of the screen which lights up once more and with a theatrical flourish of his hand Richter says, "Sterneckbrau, the date is January 1920." The picture on the screen is that of a large crowd, in fact a packed house, all are focused on the speaker, it is Hitler. "Der Juden, they are part of a race not a religion," he is shouting, "the aim must be the removal of the Jews altogether," and the image fades once more leaving a blank screen.

"Yes, mein Herr, here we are in 1920 and he is demanding that all the Jews be expelled, these people who are Germany's misfortune. It is interesting to note that in the year Hitler became leader of the German Workers Party, 1921, a German Jew named Albert Einstein was awarded the Nobel prize for physics. And now I would like us to visit one more venue before we leave this gallery."

The screen again flickers into life and I am provided with a bird's eye view of a circular structure on which sits another circular structure. It looks a little bit like a flying saucer with the cabin for its alien occupants sitting on top!

"Der Zircus Krone," says Richter, once more with that flourish of hands I had noticed previously. "Originally the home of the Munich circus because the building could seat around six thousand people. After the first world war it also became a venue for hosting large political rallies and famous speakers.

Come, let us go inside, it is January 1923 and the French have just occupied the Ruhr Valley territory that had been Germany's before 1914. We are going to attend one of the largest meetings yet addressed by Hitler, his speech that day even has a title, *'Down with the November Criminals'*; this became one of his popular slogans."

As we enter the building, I immediately feel a change in temperature. The warmth exuded by thousands of bodies in an enclosed space significantly blunts the bitter cold of the Munich winter. Hitler is speaking and clearly stirring up the emotions of the crowd. His message is simple and to the point. Germany was a strong and proud country; it has been made into a weakling by those cowards and traitors, those November Criminals who betrayed, yes betrayed, the Fatherland. We lost the war because of this betrayal. And who were these November Criminals who betrayed our Fatherland, the communists, revolutionary socialists, international financiers and we all know who they are, the Jew, the Jews are behind all of this. To make the betrayal even worse we have been forced into an ignominious treaty, they call it a peace treaty, this treaty of Versailles is no peace treaty it is the way the French and English have chosen to finally destroy our Fatherland; it is not a peace; it is a badge of shame, an instrument forcing us Germans into a state of slavery; our Fatherland is now run by a bunch of Jews and their criminal associates; their government is corrupt, it is bringing economic misery on all of us ordinary Germans, we the Herrenvolk belong in this country, the Jews have no place here; we the Herrenvolk have to fight this alien criminal race who seek to destroy us.; we must build up our strength and crush these exploiters, move them out of our midst into camps so we become separated from them and stop them from undermining the strength and spirit of our people.

His shouting and ranting are clearly striking a nerve, time and time again Hitler stands back pausing while the crowd applauds and shouts, clearly in agreement with his conspiracy theories and odious racial views. The image of a Roman amphitheatre hosting blood sports crosses my mind, however, in this case, although the lions are in the arena their hapless victims are absent, still going about their daily lives believing in a future.

Richter takes my arm and leads me out of the gallery. "Come, mein Herr, let us now leave this gallery we still have much to see and the hour is late."

Gallery 2:
Prayers During Wartime, Celebrations During Peacetime

———◆———

The gallery Richter now leads me into is brightly lit with a number of exhibits in glass-topped cabinets arranged around the room. "So, mein Herr," Richter begins, "while Hitler was ranting about November Criminals and Jews, the Jewish community in Germany was trying to recover from the losses it sustained in the Great War. You know, of course, that around one hundred thousand Jewish men served in the German armed forces, twelve thousand died, and when those fortunate to survive returned from the front, many were broken in both body and spirit. There was no recognition of PTSD[49] in those days, you came back and got on with living however you could."

Richter then stops in front of a cabinet in which there are two medals resting on a white velvet cushion. The medal on the right is attached to a black ribbon that has two thin black and white bands running down its borders, the medal on the left is attached to a red ribbon also with black and white bands on both borders. The inscription on the information card in the cabinet

---

[49] Post-traumatic stress disorder.

explains that these are Iron Cross medals first and second class, Germany's highest military awards that are given either for exceptional bravery or for outstanding contributions in a battlefield environment. In bold print I read that eighteen thousand Jewish servicemen were awarded Iron Crosses during World War I.

"Why is this here?" Herr Richter is saying. "Daniel Braun, the father of the girls, was one of the eighteen thousand Jewish servicemen awarded an Iron Cross in the Great War. It never helped him when the Nazi party took over Germany in 1933 however, but let us return to the main story. In this gallery, mein Herr, we are going to discover the sequence of events that set in motion a cycle of circumstances ultimately leading to the birth of Martha and Margot Braun."

Richter steers me to a second cabinet and there under the glass is a very old and rather badly worn copy of a Hebrew prayer book. The name emblazoned on the front page says *'Prayers During Wartime: for our Jewish Soldiers'*. I read the inscription on the information card and it telld me that the prayer books were printed in 1915 by the Nissensohn German-Hebrew Lithographic and Book Printing company and were handed out to Jewish troops by Feldrabbiner on their visits to the front lines.

Moving to the last cabinet, and once more with that customary flourish Richter points to the photograph it contains and announces, "Daniel Braun and Theresa Nissensohn." This is my first sighting of Martha and Marjorie's parents and I eagerly bend over the cabinet to see more closely the photographs on display. I am immediately drawn to the photograph of Daniel; he is looking at me sideways, a gentle smile playing on his lips. The eyes are the giveaway, they are kind, warm, and compassionate, I immediately feel that they extend an invitation, "welcome", they are saying, "I would like you to become part of my personal space." Turning to the photograph of Theresa, I find myself looking at someone who I think was a lot more private. A shy smile plays around her lips but there is a lot of reserve in her facial expression and the eyes, which are gentle, say, "I need to know you before I will invite you in."

Accompanied by that now familiar flourish of the hands Richter says, "And so, mein Herr, circumstance or fate brought a Feldrabbiner to visit Jewish soldiers at the front during the Great War. He gave Daniel Braun a copy of this prayer book, later this prayer book brought Daniel Braun to Theresa Braun, they married and had two little girls named Martha and Margot. Come, let us go to the time travelling screen in this gallery and we will plunge into the past to discover how a prayer book in wartime became the trigger for a celebration in peacetime."

The screen flickers and in front of us is a narrow beach. The light brown sand forms the bank of a river whose tiny wavelets lap gently at its edge. Behind the beach, a picturesque cluster of small shops and cafes stretches out to the left and right. The early hour and morning chill are obviously deterring patronage and only a few of the tables along the promenade are occupied. Richter takes me by the arm, steers me to a table in front of a café and then motions that I should sit on one of the chairs around a small round table facing the river. "This is the River Elbe in Altona," says Richter. "Look to the left, mein Herr, and see who is sitting there." About two meters away I recognise Daniel Braun slumped in a chair, a beer stein in hand.

Opposite him sits an older woman with a rather anxious look on her face. Daniel looks troubled; this is not the face with the gentle smile I had seen in the photograph in the gallery. "His companion is Emilia Braun," continues Richter, "one of Daniel's older sisters. As you know he was the youngest child in a rather large family, five sons and three daughters to be precise. It is quiet, the air is crisp and clear, listen carefully and we will be able to hear what they are saying."

"Dani, Liebling, you must pull yourself together; be positive, why not think about what you have achieved since those terrible years in the war. Our Fatherland recognised your bravery, you came home with an Iron Cross."

"Yes, and now," Daniel interjects, "now they are saying that Jews were cowards, that they hid away, that all they did was make money while the real Germans fought and died."

"Don't listen to the words of a small number of trouble makers, Dani. I was talking to one of my neighbours about this last week, you know her, old Mrs. Becker, and she said that she knows many Altona Jews were soldiers, some also died she told me. But Dani, let's not talk about the war, it has been nearly two years since you came back, thanks be to God you did come back. And, look what you have done in those two years. So many young men were not able to find work and are still wandering the streets. You worked almost immediately, yes, I know just a decorator, a nice word for a painter. But you never accepted it, you managed to improve yourself, becoming a cabinet maker rather than just a plain carpenter; just like papa. That is really an achievement."

Daniel looks at her with a resigned expression and says quietly, "But Emi, you don't see what I see every morning when

I wake up after a very troubled night; I see broken bodies lying in mud with rats gnawing at exposed flesh; most of all I see Willie clutching his chest blood spurting from between his fingers. I left him there, Emi, left him where he died alone and in agony. I see a young soldier, like me, just in a different uniform; he is screaming in agony as my bayonet rips into him; I see him lying on his back, I see his pleading eyes, Emi, as I pull out the bayonet; I left him there in the dirt you know, never found out whether he lived or died. That is what I see in my dreams and think about in the morning, Emi, not what I have achieved since coming home. And what about Mutti, Emi, I never even got to say…"

His remaining words are inaudible and merge into a choked sob.

Emilia Braun pleads with her brother who is staring with unseeing eyes at the wavelets lapping gently on the sand at the water's edge. "Dani, I know I can't see these horrible things but please we cannot bear to see you this way, you have to somehow get past this."

"I am trying, Emi, do you know I even thought of going to synagogue, I found this with some of the things that I had never unpacked after coming home."

Daniel pulls a rather tattered looking book out of the satchel lying on the table next to his beer stein and after handing it to Emilia says, "It was given to us in the early days of the war by a Feldrabbiner, I don't even remember his name, but do you see who printed it, Emi?"

Emilia examines the book she is now holding gingerly in her hands and says, "What a coincidence, I know this printer, when I got married, he made special little books for us containing the blessings you normally say after a wedding celebration, it's the Nissensohn printer in Hamburg."

"Yes," replies Daniel, "it was very strange, Emi, most of us up there were not particularly observant but having this little book somehow became a comfort. I had this hope that it would possibly bring some sort of comfort again when I found it a few weeks ago but that was not to be. Anyway, maybe I will go and find the Nissensohn printing works when I am next in Hamburg, tell him that I have his prayer book and how we appreciated receiving it at the front. But now, Emi, I thank you for meeting and listening to me this morning. Please do not think of me as ungrateful, and yes, I will try to get out from under this black cloud which follows me by day and by night. Now, I must leave, or I will be late for my shift."

As the two siblings stand up and embrace, the surroundings fade and I find myself back in the gallery. Thinking that we have now completed our tour I start to move towards the exit but Richter pulls me back. "Wait, mein Herr, this story has only begun, the screen holds another tale it wishes to tell us." The screen lights up, we are standing on a narrow street, five-story buildings on either side, their facades embedded with rows of small windows aligned horizontally and vertically; I think of a never-ending chequer board made up from transparent squares. We slowly walk down the street following a gradual curve to the right that brings us towards an intersection. I read a street sign which tells me we are on the corner of Bruderstrasse and Wexstrasse. Noticing my inquisitive look Richter says, "Hamburg, and look who is there just in front of us." A man is standing at one of the setback entrances to the last building on our left before Bruderstrasse ends and enters

Wexstrasse. It is Daniel Braun, the number above the entrance says 2 Bruderstrasse and underneath in bold type *The Nissensohn German-Hebrew Lithographic and Book Printing Company.*

Daniel is standing in the street looking up at the sign over the entrance, seemingly unsure of his next move. After a minute of indecision, he pulls a book out of his satchel, walks purposely up to the door of number 2, opens it, and walks in. Richter motions me forward and we follow Daniel into the twilight interior, the single window for the tiny reception area lets in very little light. The desk in front of us together with one rather uncomfortable looking chair appear to be the only items of furniture in the room. The desk itself is free of clutter, on one side is an old lamp, on the other, one of those bells you strike with a little hammer. Daniel has approached the desk and is about to pick up the hammer when a door opens, allowing light to flood in against which the figure of a woman is silhouetted. "A moment, mein Herr," the figure says in a soft voice, "I will just switch on this table lamp." She leans over the desk and flicks a switch which allows a rather subdued light to enter the room. With a start I recognise a younger version of the Theresa Nissensohn I had seen in the photograph in the gallery. Although she has some sort of covering over her hair and is dressed in what is obviously working attire, her very attractive features are still clearly apparent and Daniel is definitely taking note.

"How can I help you; we do not see many customers coming into our premises, my father normally visits them. If you will be so kind and provide me with your name and address, I will ask him to make arrangements to see you."

A little flustered, Daniel looks at her and stammers, "Oh, nein, I am not a customer I...I came to thank you for this, I mean not you, whoever sent it," and shows her the little prayer book he had been holding when he walked in.

Theresa takes the book from him and says, "Oh I have heard Papa speak about this, I saw an old copy on one of the shelves in our workshop when we were cleaning up some time ago. When did you receive this?"

"It was in the war, somewhere in France, there were a few of us Jewish men there, a Feldrabbiner brought it to the front one day, as I recall it was before..." he was about to say "a Jewish holiday" and then realises he is speaking with someone who understands and says "Rosh Hashona".[50]

"It was a great comfort for us and I just wanted to thank whoever had prepared and sent it for doing such a kind thing, for thinking of us there on the front, and actually doing something to show us that people at home cared," continues Daniel.

"I am so sorry he is not here, mein Herr. The person who prepared these prayer books is my Papa, Herr Siegmund Nissensohn, he would have been so grateful to meet you. The Feldrabbiner who brought the books is now Uber Rebbe of Hamburg, Rabbi Carlebach. If you would like to provide me with your name and the place where you live, I am sure my father would be very pleased to visit you and talk with you about your experiences."

"No, no," interjects Daniel quickly, "that really would not be necessary, and anyway I live in Altona not Hamburg, but," a little haltingly he continues, "maybe you can tell me when he

---

[50] New Year.

will be here and I will return, and you can introduce me to him, that is of course if you are also here."

"Oh, I am not here all that much," replies Theresa, "only when my Mutti is unable to come in and she is unfortunately not all that well these days so I have been here a lot more than normal. But maybe if I give you our home address you will visit my father there," says Theresa, "after all your need is not for doing any business, it is a personal matter that would be of importance for my Papa."

Theresa was later to say to her sister, "I have no idea why I offered that, but I saw a man with a kind face and kind eyes and he seemed a little troubled so I thought maybe it would be interesting to find out more about him."

Daniel, who has got past his first appraising glance of the woman in front of him and is making a more circumspect inspection says, maybe a little too eagerly, "Yes, yes, I would certainly like to do that, if you could please, that would be very good. What is the best time to visit you, I mean Herr Nissensohn?"

"He is at home most nights, here is the address," says Theresa, and writes on a sheet of Nissensohn stationery lying on the desk, *Neuer Steinweg 76, Hamburg*. "Oh, and I am also at home most nights now, as I said my Mama requires some care and I help Papa. I would be able to introduce you to Papa, my name is Theresa but my family and friends call me Resi."

A little shyly Daniel accepts the paper and tucks it into his satchel. "I am Daniel," he says, "Daniel Braun. Thank you for your assistance. I would be very honoured to meet your father and to be able to thank him personally for what he did to help the Jewish soldiers in those terrible times. Einen schönen

Nachmittag wünsche ich dir,"[51] says Daniel, and after a slight delay adds, "Resi," smiling shyly, then turns away, and walks slowly out into the street.

Again, the scene around us begins breaking up and once more I find myself standing next to Richter in Gallery Two.

"My sources for dating these past events have not proved reliable with regard to that little meeting, mein Herr," says Richter with a shrug. "What I have been able to determine is that it probably occurred either in 1922 or 1923. And yes, Daniel returned to Hamburg, he visited Siegmund in his home and the two spoke at length which Daniel later told his sister Emilia had been a real comfort, so much so, that he asked Siegmund if he could visit again. There is an interesting twist to this story, mein Herr, what I did find out was that when Theresa was showing Daniel to the door after his second visit, she looked at him and with a cheeky smile said, 'Daniel are you visiting my papa or are you visiting me?' I understand Daniel coloured bright red and was about to mumble something unintelligible when he decided this was a moment of truth and said, 'Actually, Resi, I am visiting both of you,' and their romance began from there."

I find the story about the meeting between Theresa and Daniel very touching and say as much to Richter. He smiles, looks at me somewhat roguishly and says, "Mein Herr, you are totally aware of who I am, I am Richter Der Geschichte, I tell stories. So, are the stories true or are they just stories? It is up to you to make the conclusions and that, mein Herr, is why I am such a fascinating companion and the reason you sought me out.

---

[51] I wish you a nice afternoon.

But now, I have one other tale to tell before we leave this gallery, come."

Once more Richter's screen lights up and I recognise the little reception area in the premises of the Nissensohn printing shop. An elderly man with a trim goatee beard, protruding ears, and very pleasant but rather impish face is sitting in the chair facing Theresa who is behind the desk. "Meet Herr Siegmund Nissensohn," says Richter, and yes, it is said with the customary Richter der Geschichte flourish!

"But Resi," Siegmund is saying, "although I too have found him to be a very pleasant and responsible young man, he does not maintain our traditions like we do. I was very disturbed last week when he arrived on shabbes[52] morning, never mind he had travelled here with the train but to make matters worse, he was then asking you to come and spend the day on the Elbe with him. He does not understand that we are a family who keep the shabbes, that it is a sacred day, and now you are telling me he is going to ask if he can marry you. And not only this, you tell me you want to marry him! Resi, you were not brought up this way, and yes, I know we have had our disagreements about the things you do, this ice-skating and gymnastics, about many of the friends you bring home, but marriage to a man who does not observe, he will take you away from us, from our family, from our thousands of years of tradition, how can I agree to this."

"Papa, you are not being fair to Daniel, he loves coming to our home on Friday night, enjoys the way we celebrate shabbes. He told me when he was growing up that his family also had a special Friday night, it only stopped during the war years after his Mama died. His poor father is still not over that

---

[52] Sabbath.

loss and there is no woman in the house doing exactly what you have told me a wife does to keep our traditions. You should also know that Daniel was a very troubled man before he started visiting. Talking to you, Papa, helped him, he told me that he was having difficulty facing every day before that. What happened to him in the war was horrible, he told me some of the stories and I am sure that I helped him too. And, what is more, Papa, please do not do this to me, you always told me time and time again that it is the mother who keeps the traditions, maintains a kosher home, lights the shabbes candles, prepares a special meal to keep the family together on one special day. What you are telling me, Papa, is that you do not have confidence in your own daughter, that you believe I will just discard everything you taught me, that I will just give you a *pootch in poonim*,[53] that I will not be the woman in the home who keeps the tradition and the family together."

Theresa sounds quite emotional, however a closer examination would reveal that behind the emotion is a definite stiffening in her demeanour towards her father.

Richter turns to me and whispers, "Do you see that stiffening; it is a danger sign her father immediately recognises. Look at him, he is not responding to her accusations. What I know and you do not, mein Herr, is that Siegmund is stubborn, at times volatile, but he has a very soft spot for his youngest child, secretly she is his favourite although he would never admit that out loud to anyone, not even to Martha his wife. That she is accusing him of having no confidence in her is like a knife to the heart, and although he feels deeply about the reasons for rejecting the marriage, he also knows instinctively that she

---

[53] Yiddish for "slap in the face".

made a very powerful point and to pursue his objection to the union would potentially drive them both down a direction from which there would be no retreat. I can tell you that based on his experiences with previous altercations over some of Theresa's more outlandish exploits he knows how stubborn she can be. When Theresa decides on a course of action, she becomes an immovable object, that I can tell you!"

"Well then fine," shouts Siegmund, more to maintain dignity and parental authority than in anger, "tell your young man to come and talk to me and I will question him myself about how he intends to live his life as the husband of my daughter and as a member of this family," whereupon he stalks out of the front door, slams it shut, and disappears into Bruderstrasse without a backward glance. Theresa meanwhile leans over to switch off the lamp and as she does so I notice a small smile playing over her lips. She knows she has won over her father and that marriage to Daniel is now a certainty.

The image fades and Richter and I are back in the gallery. "The marriage took place about six months later and that, mein Herr, is the story of how prayers during wartime brought celebrations during peacetime. Come, let us leave this gallery and move on to the next part of our story."

Friday Night Dinner at the Nissensohns – Scene One

---◆---

The sign over the entrance to the next gallery is a quote from the Hebrew Bible, "Remember the Sabbath day to keep it holy." We enter and a light rises upwards from the floor revealing a large rectangular table around which a number of chairs are arranged. As we watch the image begins to change, the table is suddenly bedecked with a white cloth and at one end there appears two ornate silver candlesticks standing on a silver tray. On the table in front of each chair silver cutlery appears, knife fork, and spoon, the handles engraved with the initials SN.

"Stands for Siegmund Nissensohn," says Richter. "Today is the thirteenth April 1923, one week after the end of the Passover festival. And so, Herr Korim Seforim, welcome to the Nissensohn home. It is Friday evening, Siegmund has gone to the synagogue, his wife Martha and daughter Theresa who is still living with her parents have just set the table in preparation for the festive Friday night meal. They are about to light the Sabbath candles."

The image flickers, changes, Martha and Theresa come into view; they are standing in front of the candlesticks. Martha uses a match to light the two candles in the candelabra, turns to Theresa and says, "God willing, soon I will be in front of the candles in your home." The two women then cover their eyes with their hands and begin intoning the blessing for the lighting of the Sabbath candles, embrace and exchange the traditional Sabbath greeting "ein guten shabbes".[54] Martha appears to be a little unsteady and Theresa gently guides her to one of the chairs in the adjacent sitting room. "Mutti, you need to rest, sit there and let me deal with the rest of the meal. Daniel promised he would arrive before Tatti returns from synagogue, Bruno will be late as always, he knows this upsets Papa and yet he continues to do it, I just don't understand him; Herbert is with Tatti and Paula will be here shortly. There is nothing for you to do right now."

The image fades and reappears. Daniel is in the room holding a large bunch of flowers, he appears to be in high spirits and is talking animatedly with Martha. Another woman I don't recognise appears, she is holding a dish covered with a cloth and calls out, "Theresa, here is the gefilte fish[55] where do you want me to put it?" Resi[56] reappears and after giving Daniel's proffered hand a squeeze turns to the lady with the dish saying, "Paula, you can put it in in the kitchen on the counter next to the blech."[57]

---

[54] The literal translation is "a good sabbath". It is the traditional greeting exchanged by Jews on the Sabbath day, which begins at nightfall on Friday and ends with nightfall on Saturday.

[55] Translated as "filled fish" in its traditional form it was stuffed carp fish. Today it is usually minced fish that is either made into balls or a log and then boiled in a broth.

[56] Many members of the family call Theresa Resi. It is a term of endearment.

[57] Jewish law does not allow cooking on the Sabbath but you are allowed to keep food warm. A blech is a metal covering placed over a stove top which then heats up and enables food placed on top of it to retain warmth.

"Meet Paula, formerly Nissensohn now Friedberg, and married to Herbert," Richter tells me quietly.

The image fades and reappears. This time we see Siegmund dressed in a fine suit standing at the head of the table. To his left is Martha, standing, but holding on to the side of the table. Paula is to her right, one hand poised in case it is needed to support her mother. The man to Paula's right is staring at Daniel who is standing on the other side of the table next to Theresa. I assume this to be Paula's husband, Herbert Frieberg, because next to Daniel is an empty chair clearly set aside for the absent and always late Bruno.

The family is singing the last verse of a song traditionally sung in a Jewish home before the Friday evening meal, "Go in peace, angels from the supreme King of Kings, the Holy One, blessed be He."

Siegmund then proceeds to pour wine into an ornate silver goblet that is resting on a silver tray on the dinner table in front of him. Arrayed around the goblet are five small silver cups. Lifting the silver goblet, Siegmund begins to recite the kiddush, the prayers that by tradition sanctify the Friday evening meal of the Jewish Sabbath. He is not reading from a prayer book; the ritual is etched into his DNA inscribed there from his earliest childhood memories.

As Siegmund ends with the words ברוך אתה יהוה מקדש השבת "Blessed are you, our God, who sanctifies the Sabbath," everyone around the table responds, "Amen."

A lengthy ritual then follows. Siegmund lowers himself into his chair, the only one with handrests on each side. This is a signal for everyone to sit and they watch silently as he carefully pours wine from the goblet into the five little cups on the silver tray. After filling each cup Siegmund sips a little wine from the goblet and passes it carefully to Martha who also takes a small sip and hands the goblet back to her husband. Replacing the goblet on the tray, Siegmund slowly, one by one, hands Theresa the four little silver cups. She gives the first to Daniel, the second to Paula, and the third to Herbert; the fourth, she keeps for herself, swiftly drains the contents, and puts the empty cup back on the silver tray. After receiving his cup Daniel has copied Martha and taken one small sip, however, when he sees Theresa drain her glass, he does the same wincing a little.

"The wine is very sweet," whispers Richter, "he is not used to it."

While this is going on Siegmund is loudly complaining about the behaviour of his absent son. "Bruno is not only late, but has the chutzpah[58] to let us know two hours before the start of shabbes that he is coming for dinner, what is the matter with this boy. Theresa, please put the tray with his cup of wine on the sideboard. If he still honours his father, he will make kiddush before he drinks it."

He then stands up abruptly and commands, "Bitte alle waschen."[59]

With a scraping of chairs on the wooden floor everyone stands up, and follows Siegmund to a little table on the side of the room on which stands a large pitcher of water next to a small basin. They wait respectfully while he pours water from the pitcher into a strange looking cup with handles on each side. With his hand over the basin Siegmund begins tipping water

---

[58] The cheek.
[59] "Please, everyone should wash." The washing of hands prior to eating bread goes back to the time when the Temple stood in Jerusalem and is an act of ensuring ritual purity.

from this cup on to one hand three times, repeats the process with the other hand, then wipes his hands on one of the little towels folded neatly in a small pile behind the pitcher. After he has returned to his seat each member of the family goes through their own hand washing ritual with Theresa manoeuvring herself so as to be behind Daniel. As he approaches the basin, she whispers a few instructions in his ear before he picks up the two-handled cup then hovers behind him nervously as he awkwardly goes through ritual hand washing process.

When the company is seated once more, Siegmund removes the cloth that has been covering two impressive braided bread loaves, chants a blessing, cuts a slice from one of them that he dips in a small dish containing salt, takes a bite, places the rest on the plate in front of him, cuts another slice, dips it into the salt and hands it to Martha. He then proceeds to cut the rest of the loaf and carefully arranges each slice on a silver tray handed to him by Martha. As he is sprinkling salt over the bread in the tray Daniel suddenly calls out, "Herr Nissensohn, why does—" stopping in mid-sentence with a quiet "ouch" after receiving a kick on the shin from Theresa. Siegmund in the meantime has given the tray to Theresa and without a trace of annoyance responds, "Daniel, we do not speak between washing the hands and eating the challah,[60] I will explain the reason to you later."

As the silver tray proceeds around the table conversation breaks out while Theresa disappears into the adjoining kitchen and returns with the gefilte fish prepared by Paula.

---

[60] The name given to the braided loaves of bread specially baked for the Sabbath meal.

"I am so happy to be eating bread again," Herbert begins, "my stomach does not do very well with matzos."[61]

"I quite enjoy the matzos," replies Daniel, "especially since I remember what it was like at the front when we could not get any. Anyway, after what happened in Munich last month, I think that matzos are not really a problem for the Jews in Germany right now; I worry about our future here."

"What are you talking about, Daniel?" says Siegmund, a trifle snappily. "Jews have been part of German life for over five hundred years. The Jews in Germany will never forget how many of us lost their lives defending the Fatherland and neither, I might add, will our non-Jewish fellow Germans forget the sacrifices we made."

"What I am talking about, Herr Nissensohn, is that when the French took the Ruhr Valley away from us in January, Herr Hitler announced that it was the fault of a shady group he referred to as the November Criminals. He claims this group is made up of Marxists, Socialists, and also some parliamentarians who are against the Fatherland. He also keeps repeating that Germany lost the war because of the actions of these people. Now, what disturbs me greatly, Herr Nissensohn, is Hitler's claim that the Jews are the movers and shakers behind these people, which is totally untrue."

"Hitler, augh," spits out Herbert, his mouth full of gefilte fish. "Why worry about that ridiculous little man. I saw a photograph of him giving a stupid salute just like that gangster Mussolini now running Italy. The problem with people like Hitler and Mussolini is they believe the war has not ended and that the real fight is still to come. Besides, all that talk about

---

[61] The unleavened bread eaten by Jews during the seven days of Passover.

November Criminals, Daniel, it's all happening in Munich not in Hamburg; it was a speech in the Circus Krone. And really the place was not that full of people, it was a small number if you ask me. Theresa, meine liebe, another piece of gefilte fish please. Paula, you have outdone yourself tonight."

"Herbert, please don't talk with your mouth full of fish," scolds Paula who is smiling bashfully in response to the compliment. "And Daniel," she continues, "why worry about this Hitler and his party they call Nazi, they are just one of many groups of disaffected people who are struggling to cope with the great problems our Fatherland is experiencing. What we now pay every day for necessities is a bigger problem than Herr Hitler. I want everyone to know, and Tatti I am not asking for any money from you, the karpfen[62] I bought this morning for the gefilte fish cost me almost twice as much as it did a year ago. I really don't know where all this is going, it is very frightening."

Daniel is clearly becoming agitated but before he can respond the front door opens and in strides a rather short thickset man I assume to be the missing, late arriving, Bruno. He walks straight to his mother, pecks her on the forehead, bows slightly to his father, walks to the place set for him and sits down. Looking around at what people have on the plates in front of them he says gleefully, "Aha, gefilte fish, just what I feel like. Resi, please put some on my plate, here it is," and hands the plate to Daniel who is sitting to his right.

"Bruno," calls out his father sternly, "you do not eat until you have made kiddush and washed, please."

---

[62] The carp fish used to make the gefilte fish.

Bruno is about to say something but fortunately catches the warning look on his mother's face. Without a word he gets up, goes to the sideboard, picks up the little silver cup, makes a brief blessing over the wine and walks to the wash stand. Seeing that her husband is about to protest because of the abbreviated "kiddush," Martha tugs his sleeve and whispers "Siegmund, not now please."

Bruno reaches for a slice of challah, mumbles something, stuffs the challah into his mouth, lifts his plate and says, "Resi, gefilte fish please." He then turns to Paula and continues, "So Paula, what were you saying when I came in the room, something about troubles in the Fatherland."

"I was talking about how much everything costs, and Daniel was telling us he has a problem with Herr Hitler."

"Hitler, that clown with the little moustache, I wouldn't worry about him, Daniel, and anyway it is a Munich issue, nothing to do with us here in Hamburg."

"Bruno, Hitler is spreading Jew hatred; it is not only a Munich problem, there are also Jews living here in Hamburg, you know."

"Everyone, enough of this talk, it is not for shabbes," quickly cuts in Theresa. "And now, who is for soup, Mutti made it even though she was not feeling her best today."

"Mutti's chicken soup," exclaims Bruno, "now that is exactly what this country needs. Daniel, I promise you if we were to ask Mutti to cook up a huge barrel of her soup and feed it to all Hitler's followers, they would soon start loving us Jews."

The image begins to break up and then in an instant disappears, leaving me with Richter in what is now an empty room.

Friday Night Dinner at the Nissensohns – Scene Two

———◆———

I have already turned away looking for the exit when once more a light rises up from the floor, gradually forming itself into the now familiar image of the Nissensohn family seated around their dining room table. There are more people this time, a quick count reveals nine adults and a young child, a girl with a mop of thick black curls seated next to Martha.

"So, Herr Korim Seforim, let me introduce you to other members of the Nissensohn family. You already know Siegmund, yes? There he is, seated at the head of the table. Moving from his left, we see Theresa, and next to her is Bruno. Aah yes, I will preempt your question; why is Daniel not sitting at the table? Well, we are visiting the Nissensohn home on a very special Sabbath, Daniel and Theresa are to be married in the week to come. Under strict orthodox Jewish tradition bride and groom are not allowed to meet each other for a full week before the wedding and so Daniel is with his family tonight. Continuing around the table to Bruno's left is Sorka, a daughter-inlaw to Siegmund and Martha. She is, as you see, very obviously pregnant with child, her first. Next to Sorka is her husband Arthur, the third child of Siegmund and Martha. Then comes Mathilda, the fourth Nissensohn offspring. She is married to

Max Reiszfusz, there he is on the other side of the table sitting opposite her. Selma, Siegmund and Martha's first born, is at the foot of the table together with her husband Josef Bierman. I will let you into a little secret, Selma is also pregnant, expecting her second child. Ruthie, the little girl with the mop of curly black hair sitting next to Martha, is their first born. Now where are we, aah yes, the only two I have not mentioned are Herbert and Paula whom you met previously. There they are, between Max and Ruthie."

He looks at me and says with a wink, "It should be an interesting evening, no," waves his hand, and the static image in front of us immediately animates.

"I am very glad we insisted the wedding must be in Hamburg," Selma is saying to no one in particular. "Altona is so provincial and Tatti has status in our Schule;[63] the Rabbiner is sure to mention how important our family is. Daniel is very fortunate to be marrying into our family."

Theresa interjects a trifle angrily, "Selma, please don't start this nonsense all over again. Daniel's family is very well known in Altona, his father Joachim is well respected and, as you very well know, had his own cabinet making business. Daniel agreed that we should have the wedding in Hamburg because it would be very difficult for Mutti to travel to Altona. Daniel, in fact, discussed that very point with me shortly after we decided to marry."

"Well, I don't understand why you couldn't wait until the spring, it is so cold in October, not the time to have a wedding," responds Selma.

---

[63] Synagogue.

Deciding that Selma's last comment is not worth answering, Theresa looks across the table at Ruthie and says, "Liebling, do you like the pretty dress Oma[64] made for you? You are very important; Tante Resi can't get married without you being there."

Ruthie buries her face in her Oma's lap and tearfully proclaims, "I don't want to be important, I don't want to carry flowers, and I don't want to walk on my own in the Schule where everyone will be looking at me."

"There, there, mein liebling," says Martha and puts her arm protectively around the little girl who is beginning to sob loudly, "you can walk with Oma and Opa, you and I will hold the flowers together." Mollified, Ruthie sits up, lifts her spoon and scoops some soup into her mouth with a loud slurp. This evokes an immediate reprimand from Selma who is shushed by Arthur with the injunction, "Leave her be, Selma, this is not the time."

Bruno looks up from the wine glass he has been studying intently and says, "It's a pity Daniel is not here, I would have liked to ask him about his current opinion regarding that idiot Herr Hitler and his party of misfits after their failed revolt everyone now jokingly calls the Beer Hall Putsch. For his trouble Hitler will be going to jail and that," he announces with a flourish, "is the end of him and his bunch of troublemakers."

There is a brief silence as everyone around the table turns to look at Theresa.

"Bruno, you can ask Daniel for his views when you see him but now, I have some important news for everyone. Daniel applied for a job as a cabinet maker with Otto Nagel in Altona

---

[64] Oma and Opa are German for granny and grandpa

and I am so proud of him because he was successful and will be starting to work there soon after our marriage. Otto Nagel is a very prestigious company, one of the most important in Altona. The foreman who gave Daniel the job also told him that Otto Nagel workers are guaranteed a long and secure future with the company. And so, Daniel and I are going to be living in Altona after our marriage for two reasons. The first, it is close to Daniel's work place, the second, Daniel's father Joachim is not well, in fact, he is now finding it very difficult to live alone; so, he is moving in with us."

This provokes a cacophony of responses. Arthur raises his wine glass shouting "mazal tov". Selma, Mathilde, and Paula attack Theresa in shrill voices: "What, how can you do this, who will be here to help Mutti, you know how tired she gets, she relies on you. And who is going to help Tatti in the business, you know we don't have the time. You have always been selfish Resi, thinking only of yourself, and this, this is the most selfish thing you have ever done."

At this point Bruno decides the best course of action is to pour himself another glass of wine, and Josef begins shouting at Selma, ordering her to not raise her voice because Ruthie will start crying again. Max, on the other hand, appears rather embarrassed by the antics of his wife who is gesticulating wildly to emphasize what she is saying, and Herbert decides to study the food on his plate rather than becoming involved in the family fracas.

Suddenly Siegmund, who is a short man, stands up, shouts, "Enough, I will not have this in my house and at my shabbes table," then promptly sits down and says in a loud voice, "Resi has already spoken to me and to your Mama about her move to Altona. I gave her my blessing and, what is more, I have my own announcement to make. The Nissensohn German-Hebrew Lithographic and Book Printing Company will be shutting its doors before Chanukah[65] for many reasons, which we can talk about another time. For now, just know I am unable to continue with the business. And this raises another matter which we will also be discussing at another time. Your Mama and I will require assistance from all of our children, not only Resi. I did not want to bring this up now, it is a time for joy, we will soon be celebrating the marriage of Resi and Daniel, but Paula and Mathilde, you left me with no choice. Resi will no longer be required to assist me in the printing business so her moving to Altona does not affect the Nissensohn printing company; it will be no more."

Just as the light had risen from the empty floor revealing the Nissensohn shabbat table and the seated family, it fades away taking the table and the family with it. I protest loudly—a really important piece of information has just been communicated and I want more. Wheeling around abruptly I confront my guide, my arms spread out in a gesture of exasperation, "Herr Richter, please bring the image back, what we have just heard is a vital piece in the puzzle I am trying to piece together about Martha's family history."

"Ahh mein Herr, if we were to spend hours chasing every small incident in the history of this family, we will never leave this place. But be placated by what I am about to tell you. Shortly after Theresa and Daniel married, Martha Nissensohn died. She had not enjoyed good health for many years. After her

---

[65] An eight-day Jewish holiday that commemorates the victory of the Jewish Maccabee family over the Seleucid King Antiochus in 164 BCE.

death Siegmund left the family home at Neuer Steinweg 76, and moved into a residence at Dillstrasse 15. The building was named *The Zacharias und Ranette Hesse und Mathilde und Simon Hesse Stiftung*; it was owned by a charitable foundation. Siegmund's very modest annual living expenses were covered by the five Nissensohn children. After Theresa and Daniel married, they took up residence at 21 Grune Street in Altona. Daniel's father Joachim, who was also in poor health, moved in with them. And so, my dear Korim Seforim, come let us visit the Braun family also on Friday night, this gallery is after all called Oneg[66] Shabbat, is it not?

---

[66] Sabbath delight.

Friday Night Dinner at the Brauns

---◆---

With a flourish Richter spreads his arms in a grand gesture towards the centre of the gallery. He then turns to me and says quietly, "We are going to Grune Strasse 21 Altona; the Jewish cemetery is actually on the opposite side of the road on Koningstrasse. The apartment we are visiting is on the ground floor, Daniel and Theresa rented it when they married. You know of course from the discussion we were privy to in the Nissensohn home that Daniel's father is now living with the young couple."

Light rises from the floor, gradually consolidating to produce the image of a rather small room. A table in the centre of the room is bedecked with a beautiful white cloth on which knives, forks, and spoons have been carefully arranged in preparation for the evening meal. The single electrical globe illuminating the room is not particularly bright and as a result the image in front of us is subdued. The available light is enhanced by the dancing radiance from two candles set into a pair of beautiful silver candlesticks that are standing on top of a small sideboard, the only other furniture in the room.

The silence is broken by a woman's voice I immediately recognise to be Theresa. Preempting my question, Richter whispers in my ear, "Yes, Theresa Nissensohn is now Theresa

Braun. Look carefully on the wall above the sideboard and you will see a photograph of bride and groom taken on their wedding day."

Slowly, at the periphery of our vision, the image of Theresa supporting a rather frail old man comes into view. "Come, Tatti Chaim, let me help you sit down at the table. Dani will be home soon and we can have dinner. I have prepared your favourite food, chicken soup with kreplach[67] followed by gebratenes[68] done exactly how you like it, soft, well cooked with sauerbrauten on the side."

Theresa slowly steers Joachim to the head of the table and holding one arm under his elbow helps the old man to slowly sink into a chair. She then moves over to the sideboard and is busily removing various objects from the drawers when another image appears: Daniel, in his work clothes and holding a large bunch of flowers which he ceremoniously hands to Theresa accompanied by a small bow. After kissing her lightly on the check he walks over to his father saying cheerfully, "How are you, Vater, I hope you had a restful day."

In response Joachim offers a peremptory greeting that takes the form of a slow raising of the left hand.

"Dani, please wash up and let us eat, your Tatti Chaim has not had a good day; isn't that right?" she asks, turning to her father-in-law. "He has not eaten much and I am sure he is now hungry."

Daniel smiles and turning to his father says, "Vater, did anyone ever call you Chaim?"

---

[67] A type of dumpling usually filled with minced meat, served in soup.
[68] Roasted meat,

The images of both Daniel and Theresa move out of the circle of light leaving Joachim slumped glumly in his chair, head down, studying the place setting on the table in front of him. Theresa reappears holding two challah breads and a bottle of wine which she sets down on the table in front of the chair on the side of the table facing Joachim. Turning again to the sideboard she opens one of the drawers and pulls out a silver beaker which she admires briefly before placing it on the table next to the wine. Speaking more to herself than to the old man in front of her she remarks, "It is very beautiful, isn't it, a present for our wedding from my Tatti's synagogue. But oh, you know that, I seem to mention it every week don't I."

Daniel reappears now out of his work clothes wearing black slacks and a clean white shirt. "You see, Liebchen, your husband is not such a rough diamond, look how I clean up for shabbes." Theresa laughs, punches him lovingly on his upper arm and says, "No more self-praise until after you have made kiddush."

Moving to his place at the table Daniel pours wine into the silver beaker and addressing his father says jokingly, "So Vater, did you think you would ever see your youngest son saying a prayer on a Friday night—Morris and Isadore, yes, but me?!"

Joachim looks up, smiles briefly and responds with something that sounds like, "Well at least I lived long enough to see it."

After picking up a prayer book Daniel haltingly chants the Sabbath sanctification then pours a small quantity of wine into a glass which he hands to his father. He then drinks deeply from the silver beaker in his hand and gives it to Theresa. As she is sipping tentatively from the cup, he turns to her with a questioning look and says, "Resi, do we have to go and wash hands now? I know that it is the custom in your father's house but we never did that in ours."

"Make the brocha, and cut the challah so we can eat, Dani. We talked about this before we married. We agreed that although our home will be a kosher Jewish home, I will not compel you to keep all the observances that would make it a religious home."

With a smile Daniel picks up the large bread knife that is next to the challah, intones the blessing over the challah breads and proceeds to cut three slices. He gives one to Theresa, another to Joachim then sticks the third in his mouth while proceeding to slice the rest of the loaf.

"Forgot something Liebchen," reproaches Theresa with a smile. "Ach, salt," says Daniel and knocks the base of his palm on his forehead.

"Don't worry Dani, you will remember next time," says Theresa and disappears from view, returning a half minute later with a steaming soup tureen which she places on the table and begins ladling out large helpings that are handed in turn to Joachim then to Daniel and finally to herself.

After announcing that he is starving Daniel immediately attacks the contents of the bowl in front of him, murmuring approvals as he devours the soup and kreplach. With an empty plate in front of him he leans back into his chair and with a sigh, compliments his new wife on her culinary prowess then says to his father, "Vater, I suppose you have heard that this troublemaker Herr Hitler will now be going to jail because of his part in the act of treason the papers are referring to as 'the beer hall putsch'. It is a scandal that the sentence was imprisonment, he should be shot; that is my opinion and I know many others think exactly the same. What do you think, Vater?"

Joachim has been concentrating on the seemingly complex motions necessary for spooning soup into his mouth. He pauses briefly, looks up at Daniel and says, "Your brothers knew something, they left here and went to England, we should have all gone with them."

"Tatti Chaim, please, you should not say that. We have a good life here; Dani has a wonderful future at Otto Nagel and I know stupid people like Herr Hitler say horrible things about Jews but they are just a small group who don't like us for some reason. I can tell you I have many friends at the ice rink who are not Jewish and we all get on so nicely together; nobody says anything nasty about me being Jewish, we don't even talk about it. Now finish your soup and Daniel will bring the gebratenes and cut some nice slices for you to enjoy."

She turns to Daniel, gives him a warning look, and then says cheerfully, "Dani, please no more politics, let us enjoy our Friday night together in our own home. Now, go to the kitchen and bring the gebratenes to the table, it is on the blech with the sauerkraut; I already have the carving knife here."

"Liebchen, I will do as you ask but I want to say one thing to my Tatti. Vater, we need to always remember that my brothers found homes somewhere else, and because of this we will always have a place to go should the need arise."

As Daniel rises from the table the scene in front of us gradually dissipates leaving bare floor boards and a feeling of loss behind it.

ENDINGS AND BEGINNINGS

———•◆•———

"My dear Korim Seforim, our journey into the past is about to come to an end but before we take our leave I have one more surprise for you. Come, let us go to the last of my galleries that are relevant to your story."

I am disappointed to hear that my visit to the *Richter Der Geschichtenerzähler Museum of Times That Have Passed* is coming to an end but make no comment and follow my guide out of an exit door into the next gallery. The sign over the entrance reads 'Endings and Beginnings'.

"Before I show you the exhibits in this gallery, my dear Korim Seforim, I must provide you with some background. In the year 1925 Daniel and Theresa went through the bipolar experience so typical of Jewish life. On the one hand, there was the joy of marriage, the excitement that comes from beginning a new life together. But—and there is frequently a but, not so, Herr Korim Seforim?—the newly married couple had to cope with grief when Theresa's mother Martha and Daniel's father Joachim both died in that year. But now we will leave 1925 and visit Altona one year later, to be exact the 26th July 1926."

Richter steers me to a screen mounted on one of the gallery walls and stops in front of it. "Now watch carefully and you will be privy to the beginning of Martha Braun's story."

Our surroundings fade and morph into a hospital ward. In the bed I can see Theresa cuddling a bundle swathed in blankets. She is telling Daniel to be gentle, not to tug at the covering, but to move it away from the baby's face very gently. As Daniel moves the blanket aside a tiny face under a shock of black hair comes into view.

"It is so tiny," he whispers to his wife, "I am scared to hold it."

"Dani, not it; it is a little girl. And this little girl has a name, we decided on the name after Mutti passed away. This little girl is Martha, a precious bundle, our very own daughter."

"It is hard to believe that I am a father, Liebchen, and yet there she is in your arms. I can't wait to take her swimming with me; of course I will have to teach her first. We have the wonderful Bismark baths in Altona we will go there to learn. Maybe she will also become a top gymnast, or an ice-skating champion like her Mama, I mean she will have a wonderful teacher, not so Leibchen? Just imagine, maybe we have another Lily Henoch[69] here. But more than anything, Leibchen, I have to tell you at this very moment I am certain that this little girl is the antidote for my black moods and a huge consolation after the death of our parents. I really believe that the future is ours to now take in our own hands."

Theresa is about to say something when Siegmund bursts into the room. "Where is she, where is my granddaughter?" he fusses as he comes over to the bed and takes the bundle out of Theresa's protective embrace. "Let me see her, yes, she is very

---

[69] Lily Henoch was a German Jewish track and field athlete who set a number of world records.

beautiful and Risa surely you are going to name her after your Mama."

Theresa sighs and responds, "Yes Tatti, her name will be Martha, Dani and I had already decided to name our first child Martha if it was a girl."

"Wonderful, I am sure that somehow your Mama is here with us and is so happy that her name is now continued into the next generation. Daniel, will you allow me to name this little girl in my synagogue on Thursday? She entered this world less than a week after our people afflicted themselves by fasting for twenty-four hours in commemoration of the destruction of the holy temple in Jerusalem. She, however, has chosen to arrive not in a time of sorrow, but in a time when we renew our hope for the future of the Jewish people."

"Of course, Papa Siegmund, please do this for us we would be greatly honoured," responds Daniel enthusiastically, while inwardly heaving a sigh of relief that this duty does not have to fall on him.

"Very good, my boy, and I expect you there as well when we drink a l'chaim[70] in gratitude for the arrival of this child. I will let you know what time to be there," is the rather stern response after which Siegmund hands the bundle back to Theresa and departs.

Abruptly the image fades and we are back in the little gallery.

"There is a postscript to this story, Herr Korim Seforim. On the 18th December 1927, just seventeen months later, the Brauns returned to this hospital where Theresa gave birth to a second child, also a girl who they named Margot. The Hebrew

---

[70] To life.

date was the 24th day of the Hebrew month Kislev, it was the day before Chanukah. Siegmund of course was able to weave a wonderful story about the significance of Margot's timing and he expounded on this at length in his synagogue when the baby was named."

At this my guide bows and motions me to follow him. We walk through a doorway and I find myself in the street looking at Richter standing in the doorway at the entrance to the Richter der Geschichte Museum. I thank him profusely and a little awkwardly suggest that possibly some small gratuity may be appropriate. He looks at me quizzically and responds, "Herr Korim Seforim, we are in the universe of stories, it is a place of both reality and fantasy; you will have to decide to which category I belong." He shuts the door and I find myself in the street looking at Father Time sculpted on the door knocker of a nondescript building on a Munich street. The name Richter Der Geschichtenerzähler inscribed underneath the elaborate door knocker, that I had viewed when I first stood in front of this building, is no longer there.

BOOK FOUR

1926-1939

Martha tells her story

Prologue

―――♦―――

Stories are fascinating are they not, you never know what is fact, what is fiction, what is truth, and what is fantasy. It is a conundrum that contributes a great deal to the fascination we humans have with storytelling. In the preceding pages we heard from different storytellers, some who were protagonists themselves, members of Martha's closely knit German family which disintegrated on an ordinary Sunday morning on the 21st May 1939.

It was late spring, a lazy day, perfect for a picnic at the family's favourite spot on the banks of the River Elbe. It was also Theresa Braun's birthday, her forty-second. In normal times two excited giggling girls would have burst into their parents' bedroom holding the birthday greeting cards they had secretly been preparing for their mother all of the previous week. It was not to be, instead of celebrating, a heartbroken Theresa said goodbye to her two precious daughters at the Hamburg railway station and never saw them again.

What was family life like for the Brauns before the morning on which it was abruptly obliterated? To find out we can dispense with time warps, kaleidoscopes, and time travellers as we introduce Martha, who will now tell us her own story.

Before Martha begins however, it is important to turn the spotlight on the proverbial elephant lurking in the room because it will be the force behind her story.

Adolf Hitler was released from Landsberg Prison in December 1924 after serving only nine months of a five-year sentence for his part in the notorious 1923 Munich Beer Hall Putsch. While in prison he wrote *Mein Kampf*, a rambling, poorly-written manuscript in which he set out his personal ideology and political agenda. The book, replete with anti-semitism and racist ideology, contained many ominous pointers to what the Jews in Germany faced if Hitler was successful in his quest to gain power.

After the failure of the Munich putsch Hitler decided that the path to gaining political power was not through insurrection but through the ballot box. Initially, however, the Nazi party was not that successful and by the year 1928 they had only managed to secure a mere 2.6% of the common vote for the Reichstag, the German parliament. In 1929, however, the party received an incredible gift, the crash on Wall Street. The impact this had on the German economy and on the political alignments in the country was significant, and the resultant social upheaval thrust the conservative movement to the forefront. Josef Goebbels, the Nazi propaganda specialist, skilfully manipulated public opinion in favour of the Nazi party and in the 1930 election it received just under twenty percent of the vote with one hundred and seven seats in the Reichstag.

In 1932 Hitler ran for president against Field Marshal Paul Ludwig Hans Anton von Beneckendorff und von Hindenburg, the incumbent. A totally unmatched contest, you would think—Adolf Hitler, the upstart corporal up against one of

Germany's most respected military figures? But, although he lost the election, Hitler polled surprisingly well, gaining just over one-third of the vote, not that far behind the fifty-three percent gained by Hindenburg. Hitler and the Nazi party were now clearly a force to be reckoned with and when elections were held for the Reichstag in July 1932 they emerged as the largest party with two hundred and thirty seats. Hitler's strategy for achieving power utilising the democratic process had paid off.

When Martha Braun celebrated her sixth birthday in July 1932 the elephant in the room was seven months away from becoming the most powerful man in Germany.

My Early Life in Altona

———•———

I don't have many memories about my early childhood but I do remember that our house in Altona was on Grune Strasse 11. It was an old-fashioned red brick building of three levels situated among rows of similar buildings all around. There was a cast iron stove in the living room with a metal chimney coming out the top that went up into the roof. My sister Margot and I shared a bedroom; we didn't have much furniture, just a cupboard and two metal beds that were like baby cots, they had bars all around them.

I went to a kindergarten before starting school. It was more of a day care centre and I really don't remember much about it. The kindergarten was very convenient for my parents because it was on Grune Strasse 5, just a few doors away from our house. We were very close to the river, I remember going for walks there, holding hands with the other children and the teachers, then sitting down to eat our lunches watching little boats sailing by.

I guess most of my memories about my early life in Altona start from the time when I first went to school, I was six years old.

We lived in the centre of Jewish life in Altona, the Great Synagogue was nearby, also Jewish schools and the shops where my Mutti would buy all our needs. She kept our home strictly kosher, you know, kosher meat and all, and we did go the synagogue but only on holidays.

I remember going with my Mutti to the kosher butcher shop on Friday mornings, that day must have been the meeting place for all the ladies in the neighbourhood. There were three men working in the shop, they wore big black yarmulkes[71] on their heads and had long beards; they must have been rabbis. Behind them uncut meat hung on huge metal hooks. Where we all stood waiting to be served there was sawdust on the floor and I remember the shop had like a meaty smell of blood; but I didn't mind it because I loved meat.

It was very noisy in that shop, the ladies waiting to be helped by the bearded men seemed to know each other and all around conversations were going on. Occasionally a lady talking to Mutti would lean down and say to me, "Mein Gott, look how Martha has grown, Theresa, she is such a beautiful child." And I would smile at her, feeling very important.

Mutti always seemed to be waiting for the same bearded man to serve her; I don't know how she recognised him because they all looked the same to me. Now that I think of it, she never called him by name, he was always "mein Herr". When he finally turned his attention to us, he smiled and said, "Frau Braun, I have for you today wunderbares fleisch, also chicken wings, perfect for your soup." On Friday night my Mutti would always cook gebratenes, it was roasted meat that she prepared in her own secret way. Gebratenes was my father's favourite dish and Mutti told me that Opa Joachim had also loved it. For years Mutti bought the meat for the shabbes meal meat on a Friday

---

[71] Also known as a skullcap.

morning; she would go to the store during the week to buy meat for other days. Later I realized it was because we did not have a refrigerator when we lived in Altona.

After the butcher shop our next stop was the bakery. There were many of these in our area but Mutti always went to the same one. She bought challah for Friday night and either an apfelstrudel or steuselkuchen,[72] our treat on the Sabbath. Sometimes the lady who owned the shop—I remember she was very large and always had her hair tied up with something that looked like a scarf—would walk over and with a smile give me a little cake called a schneken. It was a bun rolled up like a snail filled with sugar raisins and nuts. I so loved those days shopping with Mutti, they were marvellous.

Across from our street was Konigstrasse where the Jewish cemetery in Altona was situated. Tatti always joked that we lived in the middle of both Jewish life and death in Altona.

There was a big church nearby, the Trinitatiskirche of Altona, a huge building with a tall spire on one side sitting in a beautiful expanse of green lawns and pretty gardens, very different to the congestion of red brick buildings where we lived on Grune Strasse. Mutti always told me not to go and play on those lawns; she never gave me a reason, just a vague comment that "we are Jewish and don't go to a church". Father did not seem to have the same views but he never corrected Mutti. I remember when I was older and made friends with many of the non-Jewish children in our neighbourhood we would often run to the church and play on the lawn until someone came and chased us away. I never told Mutti about these adventures.

---

[72] This would be equivalent to a crumb cake which is made from a yeast dough and covered with a sweet crumb topping

On the other side of Grune Strasse was the River Elbe, it was not very far, we could easily walk there. It was one of my father's favourite places and on Sunday when he was not working and the weather was sunny Mutti packed a delicious lunch and we walked to the river for a picnic. The best thing was that on the other side of the river there was a big sandbank, it was like a seaside beach; Tatti would arrange for a small boat to take us across and we would sit on the sandbank and swim in the river.

My grandfather, Opa Siegmund, lived in Hamburg, on Dillstrasse 15. Mutti would take us to visit him, always on a Sunday, we never went on Saturday. I remember asking my Mutti why we never went to visit family in Hamburg on Saturday, my Mutti had sisters and brothers there. She always said Opa Siegmund is very religious and does not like us to travel on Saturday to see him. I was not quite sure what Saturday had to do with travelling but later we moved in with Opa Siegmund so the question disappeared. But that is another story.

I am not sure when it was but sometime before I went to kindergarten my Auntie Selma and her husband Josef and their three children also moved into Dillstrasse. Their youngest child Marion has a big story to tell but more about that later. My uncle Arthur also moved into Dillstrasse with his wife Sorka and son Joachim and then when I was nine my family also moved in there. It really became the whole Nissensohn family home and when I think about it now I realise we really were a very happy extended family in Hamburg.

I was very fond of my Opa, he would break into a big smile when we walked into his apartment and hold out his arms, inviting us to run into a big hug as soon as he saw us. He always had a big black yarmulke on his head when he was at home, just like the men in the butcher shop. Come to think of it, when he left his apartment, he always put on one of the hats hanging from the wall in the entrance to his apartment.

Tatti had a very important job at Otto Nagel in Altona, it was a very big factory that made furniture. And how do I know his job was important? Tatti told me he was the person responsible for ringing the bell that regulated work time and off time; I guess he was like a foreman. I know that fourteen men worked for him; they must have liked him a lot because he often brought us sweets that his workers had given him to take home for us.

Mutti was very athletic; she did gymnastics and was very good at it. She also encouraged us to do gymnastics and once a week we went for classes in the gymnasium of the Talmud Torah School. I was an excellent gymnast, but Margot never did much in the class. Mutti was also a marvellous ice-skater; it was her favourite sport. The skating rink was in Hamburg not in Altona and when I asked her to take me with her, she would say, "Martha, wait until you are ten and then I will take you." But that is also another story for later.

Tatti was a wonderful father, he did so many things that most fathers never did. He made us clothes, a swing, a sandbox, and was always buying new toys for us to play with, he even made us a dollhouse and some small pieces of furniture to put in it. Tatti had a beautiful singing voice and sang in a choir. I was his favourite, you know; my sister Margot was Mummy's girl and I was Daddy's.

I don't really remember when my sister Margot arrived, for me she was always there. She was born seventeen months after me, on the 18th December 1928. We were very close sisters always but Margot was different, very quiet, never caught on to things quickly.

I have wonderful memories of my early childhood. Nothing you can do about it, can you, that life is gone.

I Learn How to Swim

———◆———

You don't usually remember much about the time you were four but a very important thing happened to me just after my fourth birthday: I learned how to swim. One Sunday after we had finished breakfast Tatti announced, "Come, we are all going to the Bismarck Bad, I arranged for Martha to start swimming lessons." Mutti was not happy and started arguing with Tatti, complaining that I was too young and that it was definitely not the place to be taking Margot who had not had her third birthday yet. What happened between them I don't really know but in the end, I went with him to the swimming pool and Mutti remained at home with Margot. I do recall him calling out as we left, "Risa, you know what I told you after Marchendam and now is the time." As we were walking away, I will never forget that he turned to me, knelt down, and said, "I want you to go swimming, I'm going to take you to the baths so you can have lessons. I had to save two little girls who didn't know how to swim and that is not going to happen to you."

I did not know the story about the two little girls until many years later, we were already living in Hamburg. I was nagging Mutti to take me to the ice rink with her to learn skating and her response was, "Martha, you are still too young, I will take you after you turn ten." I was a very argumentative young girl and immediately put my hands on my hips, looked at her and said, "But Tatti took me to learn how to swim when I was four and now you can see what a good swimmer I am. And, I am also such a good gymnast, best in my class at school, so why not now?"

Mutti looked at me, trying to hide the smile on her face which she quickly changed into a rather stern expression and said, "Martha, that was a very different reason, Tatti was scared for your safety when you were near water and as you know we do spend a lot of time at the river." After I pressed her to explain why he was so concerned, she told me this story.

Before I was born Tatti and Mutti were walking together near the sandbank on the river. It was a Sunday afternoon, not many people about, they often came here towards the end of the day. I think it was one of Tatti's favourite places in all of Altona. He once told me that it was important to him because after the war when he did not always feel happy, he would come here and sit for hours at a table outside one of the little cafes just watching all the people go by. Anyway, this one afternoon all of a sudden, they heard a woman scream "my baby". Tatti had very good reflexes, he said it was something he learned in the war, and immediately ran down to the bank of the river where a lady was standing and shouting. She was pointing to a spot not far away and when Tatti looked, he saw a little head in the water. Realising that a child had gone too far out and was caught up in the current, he immediately pulled off his boots and rushed into the water. Because he was a very strong swimmer, he managed to reach the spot where he had seen the child and began to dive under the water looking for her. With a shock he saw two children, little ones, probably around four years of age. It was not only the child of the lady who had shouted, there was also a friend with her. The water was not very deep at this spot and Tatti managed to grab both girls and bring them to the shore. Fortunately, they had not taken much water into their lungs and after a short spell of coughing in between crying they appeared to be none the worse for their escapade.

When Tatti came back to Mutti, he looked at her and said, "Risa, when I have children, they are going to learn swimming."

My Tatti was a real hero in so many ways. Do you know he was awarded an Iron Cross in the war, he never said anything about it. I only found out when I saw it in one of his cupboard drawers one day and asked Mutti what it was. Didn't help him, though, when the Nazis came, did it!

Well, when I arrived at that pool, I just loved it, in three months I could swim perfectly. Tatti was very proud of me and would often say to Mutti as I ran off to jump into the river or the pool, "You see, Risa, she was not too young."

Sadly, it was not the same for my sister Margot. When she turned four Tatti also took her to the Bismarck Bad for private lessons, but she was frightened of the water and would not get in. Tatti tried to take her a few times, even took me with to show her that she should not be frightened, but it did not help. In the end he gave up; so, she could never swim.

My Three Years of School in Altona Before Moving to Hamburg

———◆———

As I think back it is quite strange for me to realise that I only had three years of school in Altona because we moved to Hamburg when I was nine. Opa Nissensohn was unable to manage on his own so we had to move in with him, but that is another story for later. I always regard Altona as my home but really, it was only my home for nine years. Come to think of it, my whole life in Germany only lasted for twelve years!

If things had been normal, I would probably have been there all my life but that was not to be, was it. In 1932 I started school. I didn't know then that in all my life I would only have six years of schooling.

The school I went to in Altona was a Jewish school, it was only a short ten-minute walk from our house on Grune Strasse. Mutti would walk with me in the morning but after a short time she trusted me to come home by myself after school finished at 12.30. In 1932 Hitler wasn't Chancellor yet, so it was still safe for Jewish children to walk home by themselves after school!

Ruth Carlebach was my best friend in Altona. Her father, Rabbi Carlebach, was very well known and respected in

Germany, he was an Uber Rebbe.⁷³ The Carlebach family had a very big house in Altona, well, he had nine children, I suppose they needed the space. Ruth would often sleep over at our house and I would sleep at hers, we were very close. Someone once said to me it was strange Rabbi Carlebach allowed Ruth to sleep over in our house because although we kept kosher and all that, we never went to the synagogue except when it was holidays. I never understood why the person said that because I knew we were Jewish, I mean we went to a Jewish school and all.

I did have other friends besides Ruth, even non-Jewish ones. There were around eight or nine non-Jewish children who lived close to our house and we would play together in the street because most families didn't have gardens.

Rabbi Carlebach and his family moved to Hamburg and that was where he became known as the Uber Rebbe. I still saw Ruth when we were both living in Hamburg but it was not like in Altona. Rabbi Carlebach's wife was the one who took us from Hamburg to London but that is another story for later.

I remember going to our synagogue on Grune Strasse when we were living in Altona. I couldn't really follow the service but I enjoyed going there because I was able to meet up with my school friends. I could say the "Shema Yisrael"⁷⁴ though, we learned that at school. Mutti would make me sit next to her if there was an empty seat and she would try and help me follow the service in the prayer book. She knew that book very well and could follow without a problem, it must have been what she learned from my Opa Siegmund who was a very

---

⁷³ Very important rabbi.
⁷⁴ "Hear Israel," a daily prayer in Hebrew said in the morning and at night. It consists of three excerpts taken verbatim from the Old Testament.

religious man. I have a very strange memory about one time I was sitting next to Mutti, I remember thinking, "I am so glad Mutti is alive and not dead." Why did I think this? I just don't know.

When my sister and I went to synagogue Mutti dressed us very smartly. Our dresses were the same, had little aprons in the front, and on our heads, white linen hats. Tatti was not able to make this kind of clothing for us and Mutti could not sew, so she bought everything. Oh, I remember how excited we were when she said, "Girls, we are going to the shop to buy you new clothes."

I never told you about our Friday night dinners in Altona, they were wonderful. Mutti always made a special meal, most often it was chicken soup followed by gebratenes but sometimes she would make this beautiful roast chicken and a potato pudding she called kugel. The table cloth was white and we had a beautiful silver candelabra which she always set up and lit before Tatti came home. Mutti would put a scarf on her head and call me and my sister to stand with her and say the blessing over the candles. Afterwards she set the table and I remember our challah was always covered with one of several beautiful specially made cloth covers that were kept in a special drawer together with the white tablecloths. Mutti told me that these covers and the tablecloths were presents she and Tatti received when they got married.

Every Friday night Mutti would tell us that the candelabra belonged to Oma Minna, Tatti's Mutti. Margot and I would look at each other and whisper, "She already told us that hundreds of times." I remember looking at the challah covers and thinking that maybe I would also get presents like that when I married. When Margot was not around Mutti would sometimes look at the candelabra and say, "Martha, you are our oldest daughter, maybe one day you will be lighting this silver candelabra at your own shabbes table." Of course, that was not to be. I often wonder what happened to that candelabra, I suppose the Nazis stole it.

Very soon after the candles had been lit Tatti arrived home, it was never a quiet arrival. He called out, "Risa, kinderlach,[75] I am home!" After hanging his coat on a hook in the hallway he walked into the room, gave Mutti a hug, and then turned to Margot and me and said, "What do you think I have in my pockets?" That was a signal for us to rush up to him and go through his pockets to retrieve the sweets hidden there. As we were doing this, he gave each of us a hug. Oh these were wonderful times, he was such a wonderful father, I don't think anyone had a father like that, he was marvellous.

Tatti would make a blessing over the wine and after we sat down to eat, he would first ask us to tell him everything about our week in school and then we would talk about what we were going to do for the weekend. I loved summer time specially because we would often spend our days at the sandbank on the river. Winter could also be a fun time because Tatti made little snow sleds for us and if there was soft snow on the ground and the weather was fine, he would take us to a place where there was a gentle hill and watch, laughing, as we slid down on our sleds. These were such wonderful times; we had a pram for our dolls and Tatti even built a swing for us to play on in the doorway of our house. Tatti also loved having photographs taken of our family. When I left Hamburg Mutti packed many

---

[75] The Yiddish word for children.

of them in my suitcase; it was important you see, it's all that Margot and I have from our childhood.

Mutti and Tatti never shouted at each other, you know; they were the happiest couple. Margot and me were never smacked if we were naughty, never got shouted at, I have never seen parents like that. I was the naughty one, though, Margot was always a quiet sweet child hanging on to Mutti all the time. Our parents were very cuddly and warm, they always kissed us if we had to say goodbye and go somewhere especially when we went to school in the morning.

I remember there were times though when Mutti got upset about things Tatti was saying and she would quickly tell him, "Dani, nit ein front fin di kinder,"[76] it was in Yiddish, she thought I did not understand. I had often heard Mutti talking to Opa Siegmund in Yiddish and I slowly worked out what some of the words meant. I was very good at languages, you know, even managed to learn some English quite soon after we came to Manchester.

One of the things that always caused Mutti to warn Tatti not to speak in front of us was when he started complaining about the Nazis, about Hitler, and when he started talking about what they were doing to Germany. I sometimes overheard them talking in the kitchen when Margot and I were supposed to be asleep. Tatti would talk about his brother Morris in England, telling Mutti we should go there, that Morris had written to say he could find Tatti a job in a furniture factory. When he started talking this way, sometimes very loudly, Mutti immediately asked him to stop saying she would never leave Opa Siegmund and her family in Hamburg. I never heard the whole conver-

---

[76] Not in front of the children.

sation because they always seemed to close the kitchen door when Tatti began talking about leaving for England.

There was one person I hated in Altona: the dentist. I am really a coward, you see. Until my eighth birthday we would have to go there every three months; Mutti and Tatti were very strict about our teeth. They made sure every night that we brushed, it was a kind of before-going-to-sleep ritual. That all changed when the Nazis came, of course, but that is a story for another time.

The Beginning of the End

When I think back to my life in Altona, I realise our family was short of nothing until Hitler became Chancellor in 1933. After that it all started.

It was a Sunday in July about two weeks before my birthday. Margot and I were playing in the street with children in the neighbourhood, I don't remember their names but I know some of them were not Jewish because they were the ones we would go to the church lawns with. I heard loud shouting and also screaming. We stopped our game and looked down Grune Strasse to see what was happening. I will never forget the panic that gripped me when I realized the shouting came from hundreds of men marching down the street holding big red and black Nazi flags; the screams were from women who happened to be in the street and were being attacked and beaten. I remember holding Margot's hand, unable to move, I was like frozen. And then, Tatti was picking us up and running into the house. As we were being carried inside, I remember the men shouting, "Jews, out, we will get you!"

When Tatti brought us into our house and closed the door I was crying and shaking. We had a big settee in our living room and I remember dropping to the floor and trying to crawl under it to hide away from the horror outside. For some reason I was unable to move. I looked back to see what was holding my legs and saw it was Tatti, who was saying "Liebchen, you don't have to hide under there, I am here to protect you." There was a reason he did not want me to go under the sofa, do you know why? When I tell you why, you will really understand how wonderful my Tatti was. He had both made and bought a whole lot of toys for my birthday and hidden them under the sofa. In that terrible moment my Tatti did not want to spoil my birthday surprise!

When I spoke to other children in our street after that terrible day many told me that the marchers were banging on doors and sometimes even smashing them open, taking people out and beating them. We were lucky this never happened to us, but we were terrified to go out of the house and never went to school all of the next week.

From that day our happy life in our happy street was never the same again, nor were our lives in Altona.

From that day, when we Jewish children came out of our houses and into the street, the non-Jewish children we thought were our friends shouted, "Jews, we don't play with Jews!" They even started throwing stones at us.

From that day, our parents never let us walk anywhere on our own, even to school. Anyway, I didn't want to be on my own, I was too frightened. Thinking back on this time I have another strange memory—we stopped going to the dentist regularly, I don't know why. Maybe the dentist was not Jewish and would no longer treat Jewish patients because he was not allowed to, maybe he didn't want to, I just don't know.

The biggest blow to our family happened sometime after my ninth birthday, I don't know exactly when it happened. Tatti was no longer allowed to work at Otto Nagel. Oh, this was a terrible, terrible day, it was the only time that I ever saw him in tears. It was a Friday; Tatti came home early long before Mutti lit the Sabbath candles. I heard him at the door and remember shouting "Tatti is home", Margot was with me in the dining room we were setting the table for Friday night dinner. I remember that we stopped what we were doing and turned to the door expectantly looking forward to a hug, and a hunt for sweets in his pocket. But Tatti never came into the dining room, we heard him go into our parents' bedroom and close the door. Mutti called out from the kitchen, "Dani, why are you home so early", and came into the dining room expecting to see him. She looked at us with a puzzled expression and said "where is Tatti?" We both pointed to the bedroom.

She immediately walked out and we heard her open the bedroom door and close it. I remember feeling abandoned; our parents had never closed the door on us during the day. Margot looked at me and was about to cry but I took her hand and said, "Mutti and Tatti must be talking about leaving Germany, they always close the door when they do that."

At least fifteen minutes passed and then we heard the door open. Mutti went to the kitchen and Tatti came into the dining room, I saw tears in his eyes, I could not believe it. "Tatti," I said, "what is the matter, are you sick, are you hurting somewhere?"

He looked at me and said quickly, "No, Liebchen, I am not sick and not hurting, at least not the way you know. Something happened today at work that made me very sad but we will talk about it another time. Come let me help you get ready for our Friday shabbes meal, it's not every day I am home at this time."

The meal that night was very strange. Mutti did not ask Tatti about his day at work, she was not very talkative at all. She also seemed to be squeezing Tatti on the shoulder whenever she was near him. After we had cleaned up and us girls sent to bed, I pretended to be asleep hoping I could hear what Tatti and Mutti were talking about. I was a little panicked but I admit to also feeling some excitement—did this mean we were about to leave Altona and go to England? That would be a real adventure.

I heard Tatti come to our bedroom door and stop for a short moment to check if we were sleeping, then I heard him walk away and go into the kitchen. I slipped out of bed and moved silently to the door, hoping to hear what they were saying.

"Risa," Tatti was saying, "we have to leave and leave now, these Nazis don't allow Jews to work anymore, how do I feed my family? Do you know what the Direktor said to me today, he said, 'Herr Braun, I am sorry you cannot work here anymore.' I looked at him, in shock I think, and said something like, 'Herr Direktor, I have been here for nearly ten years, you have never had any questions about my work, about my honesty, and about the way I managed my department. Always you compliment me and my men on the quality of our work. What have I done that you now come and tell me I cannot work here anymore?'

"Do you know what he said to me, he said, 'I am sorry, Herr Braun, but we work under new rules, Jews are not allowed to work here anymore.'

"I lost my temper, Risa, started shouting, "Oh, I see I am a Jew, but let me tell you, Herr Direktor, this Jew was fighting in the trenches for three years. This Jew received an Iron Cross. And you, you were here, hiding in the Otto Nagel factory.'

"Then, I turned around and walked out, never said another word to him. I passed some of my work friends as I walked through the factory to pick up everything in my locker. They never looked at me, just kept their eyes down, pretending to be concentrating on their work."

Mutti said something I could not hear and I heard Tatti say, loudly, even in anger, "Theresa, don't you understand, no one will employ me anymore, racial reasons, I am a Jew. We have to go, to get out, we are finished here. I am going to write to Morris and tell him to make the arrangements that will allow us to go to England. Many of our friends are talking about leaving, we are not the only ones."

I heard Tatti leaving the kitchen and quickly jumped back into bed pretending to be asleep. My mind was racing—what did Tatti say, racial reasons, is this what they now call Jews? I remembered the day I tried to hide under the settee when the Nazis were marching outside and although I was scared, Tatti was there to protect us. I lay there unable to sleep. Did this new thing mean that Tatti could not protect us anymore?

WE MOVE TO HAMBURG

When I think back now, I realise that our wonderful happy life in Altona ended in 1933. My non-Jewish friends did not want to play with us anymore, they called us names and sometimes threw stones at us. Nazis had marched down our street beating people and shouting Juden Rauss, *"Jews get out"*. Mutti and Tatti would not allow us to walk to school on our own, and that happy Grune street community feeling was gone. And then, in 1935, Tatti lost his job, I know after that he tried to be the same wonderful father he had always been, but there were times I saw him sitting on his own on our settee staring, not wanting to talk. I don't know where our money came from after Tatti lost his job, Mutti still worked teaching gymnastics and Tatti would get odd jobs but not all the week. Sometimes they must have involved very hard work because when he came home his clothes were very dirty and I heard Mutti complaining that she had to boil his overalls to get them clean. Discussion about moving to England no longer happened behind closed doors, Tatti spoke about it often saying he was waiting for a letter from Uncle Morris and when this came, we would leave Germany.

And then the final break, our family left Altona and went to live with Opa Siegmund in Hamburg. I don't know if we moved because Tatti wanted to get out of the place that had turned on him, or if Opa Siegmund needed assistance, or whether this helped my parents to survive without a regular income from Tatti. I don't remember much about that move, it all happened very quickly. I was sad to leave my friends, my school, the street I had lived in all my life and the people I saw there every day. But I was happy to be leaving the non-Jewish friends who now spat out "Jew" whenever they saw us. Also, Ruth Carlebach and her family had moved to Hamburg and I was looking forward to being with her again.

Opa Siegmund's apartment was on the first floor of a building on Dillstrasse 15 in the Grindel quarter of Hamburg, a very Jewish area. It was quite large and we seemed to be able to fit in there without any difficulties, at least I don't remember any. Margot and I shared a room, and here the beds we slept in were normal, without any bars around them. My Auntie Selma Bierman also lived in Dillstrasse 15, as did my uncle Arthur Nissensohn, so I had four cousins now living right next to me, Ruth, Werner, and Marion Bierman, and Joachim Nissensohn. I was very happy and have good memories of the three years Margot and I lived in Dillstrasse 15; we were like one big happy family. Opa Siegmund loved to play games and he taught me and Margot to play draughts. On Friday nights when the table was cleared, he would bring the board, set it up and say, "Who is going to try and beat me tonight?"

I do have some very bad memories of our times there; it was not all good. When I was nearly eleven, I reminded Mutti she had promised to take me to the ice rink with her after I turned ten. I was desperate to learn how to skate—I was such a good gymnast, top of my gymnastics class in school, I just knew

I would also be a good ice-skater. Anyway, she finally agreed and this one afternoon after we came home from school; oh, not sure I mentioned it, it was a Jewish school and I was very good at Hebrew, you know. Anyway, that afternoon Mutti said, "Martha, don't hang up your coat, put away your school bag and come with me, we are going to the ice rink." I was so happy that I jumped up and down in excitement. Margot never came with us but we could leave her at home because Opa Nissensohn was there. I took Mutti's hand and together we walked off to the Hamburg Ice Rink, I think that I must have skipped alongside her all the way there. We arrived at the ice rink and Mutti walked up to the place where you bought tickets. She must have known the lady sitting there because she called out cheerily, "Inge hallo!" I will never forget what happened then. The lady, Inge, said to Mutti, "You're Jewish, no Jews are allowed to skate here, I can't let you in, you have to leave."

"But Inge," Mutti stammered, "I have been coming here since I was a little girl, I teach people to skate, you know me." Inge turned away without a word to look after another family who had just walked up, obviously they weren't Jewish.

I saw the tears in her eyes as Mutti took my hand and we walked away. She looked at me and said, "Liebchen, I came last week and they allowed me in, I would never have brought you if I knew this would happen, I am so sorry you had to hear this. Tatti is right, it looks like we will have to leave Germany if we are ever to have a normal life again. Come Liebchen, I will buy you an ice cream and we will go home. Please don't say anything to Opa, it will upset him so much." So, I didn't go ice-skating, that was the end of that. I eventually did learn to skate and was very good at it, Mutti would have been proud of me.

After that visit to the ice rink, I began to notice signs in many shops that said "no Jews allowed". I never told Opa Siegmund about what happened but I am sure he would have seen those signs in the shops when he left our apartment to go the synagogue. Everybody knew him, well at least everyone who lived around us. He was very religious you know, put on tefillin[77] every morning and never missed going to the synagogue on Friday night and Saturday morning. The synagogue was a very small place close to our apartment. Mutti, Margot and I sometimes went with him on a holiday. Mutti told me when Opa was younger, he would go every morning and afternoon, but now found it too difficult because of his health. This tefillin business was a very new experience for Margot and me because our Tatti never put them on, I don't even know if he had any. If we were home when Opa was praying with tefillin we would creep up to his door and watch him. I am sure he knew we were there but always pretended he didn't.

While we were living in Hamburg Jewish holidays were more enjoyable than in Altona because we had so many family members around us. We would celebrate meals together; oh, it was wonderful. I loved paysach,[78] we enjoyed big family seders[79] that Opa Siegmund always led. When it came to saying the mah nishtanah[80] Opa would always look up and say, "Martha, you are so good at Hebrew, why don't you sing for us?" I think I was

---

[77] Phylacteries.
[78] Passover in the Yiddish vernacular.
[79] The meal celebrated during the first two days of the Passover festival. Before the meal a special book is recited which tells about the origins of the Jewish people and the exodus from Egypt.
[80] A segment at the start of the Passover seder that poses four questions traditionally sung by the youngest child at the table. The adults then answer the four questions.

his favourite because I was the grandchild with my Oma's name. The holiday us children would never miss going to synagogue with Opa was the one when everyone danced with the Torah.[81] We had a wonderful time everyone was so happy and the signs saying "no Jews allowed" seemed to have been forgotten. We always came home with so many sweets on that holiday, they lasted us for days.

Margot and I went to the Jewish school on Karolinenstrasse when we first arrived in Hamburg. Our school day started on Sunday and finished on Friday. I had a lot of difficulty adjusting to this; in Altona Sunday had always been our special family day, now it was gone. Saturday was very different because Opa Siegmund was very religious and never allowed us to do normal things on that day, he also did not like it if we were not at home for Saturday lunch, so our wonderful days at the beach in Altona were a thing of the past.

As the months passed it became more and more difficult and dangerous for Jews to walk around freely and so my parents were very careful where we went, and where they could take us. One of the really horrible things about going to school on Sunday was that people knew you were Jewish because the non-Jewish children did not have school. I remember feeling ashamed and also frightened so I stopped taking a satchel to make sure I looked like just another child walking in the street.

My school in Karolinenstrasse included gymnastics as a subject and I was top of the class. I was also very good at Hebrew; I think I told you that before. I made new friends at the

---

[81] This holiday is called Simchat Torah, celebration of the Torah. The Torah is the five books of the Old Testament written on parchment rolled into the form of a very large scroll.

school but it was very different to Altona where we all came home and played in the street. In Hamburg Jews were afraid to be in the streets, you stayed inside your apartment or in your own garden so it was a lot more difficult to spend time with friends. I was very fortunate that Ruth Carlebach was in my school and we were able to spend a lot of time together.

In 1937, when I was eleven, the Nissensohn family celebrated the Bar Mitzvah of my cousin Joachim; he was the only child of Onkel Arthur and Tante Sorka. I have a photograph taken at around a quarter past twelve midnight, with Opa Siegmund in the middle of the whole family. Me and Margot are not in the photograph because we had already been sent to bed. When I look at that photo now, I still find it hard to understand that, except for Tante Paula, Onkel Herbert, and cousin Carmen Friedberg, all the other thirty-three people in that photograph were dead by 1945, merely eight years later. It was probably the last photograph taken of my family because after 1937 things became very bad very quickly.

1938 TO 1939, TWO YEARS THAT DESTROYED MY FAMILY

———◆———

In January 1938 the Nazis forced my Tatti and around thirty other Jewish men to leave Hamburg and go to Buxtehude where they were forced to dig canals. They were like slaves, not allowed to come home for two months and then given one weekend with their families. I don't know much about what happened in that place because when I asked Mutti where Tatti was and what he was doing there all she said was, "He is working in Buxtehude." Any further discussion was cut off by, "You are too young to hear about things like that."

I can tell you one thing, my Tatti had three gold teeth and they pulled them out, those Nazis, pulled them out so they could take the gold. Who does that?

Exactly what happened in Buxtehude was a behind-closed-doors conversation between my parents on the two nights every two months when Tatti was home. It was a lot more difficult for me to sneak up to the door and listen in because Opa Siegmund always seemed to be in sight of that closed door. I am sure that things were terrible in Buxtehude because every time Tatti came home, he looked thinner and thinner. All the wonderful energy and life he always brought with him into a room was gone. I do know that he had to live in the house of some couple who were not Jewish, that he had no bed, and had to sleep on the floor.

Things were now very hard for Mutti, she had to do everything on her own, look after the house, do the shopping and look after Opa; he was always asking her to do things. By this time so many shops had signs on their doors or windows that said, "no Jews served here", I don't know how she managed to find any food at all. And of course, like Margot and me, she missed Tatti so much. Many times, when I couldn't sleep, I would hear her in her room crying quietly. I also cried for the Tatti I loved but I didn't want to upset Mutti so never let her see or hear me crying.

The one thing Tatti always spoke about when he came home on those weekends was Onkle Morris in England. He would tell us over and over that we shouldn't be sad because he knew all the bad times would end as soon as we got our permission to go to England. Tatti would pick up a couple of books he had bought about England and show us pictures of Manchester, the town where Onkle Morris lived. In September 1938 Onkle Morris had a heart attack on a bus and died, that was the end of that. Mutti had to send a message to Tatti who was in Buxtehude when the telegram was received. The Tatti who came home the first weekend after Mutti received that telegram was no longer the Tatti I knew.

I don't want to say any more about that whole story, it is too painful.

Sometime near the end of 1938, I think it was in October, Tante Selma and her whole family were sent to Poland. I will never forget that day. My cousin Marion was in the same school as me, only two years younger. Well on this day the Nazis came to the school and demanded to know where Marion Bierman was. They marched her out of school, put her on top of this wagon, then took her away; she must have been scared stiff, I saw that she was crying when they stuck her on top of that wagon. I don't know what I would have done if it had been me or Margot who was taken away. Anyway, Mutti told us that they brought her to our house and then took her and Tante Selma's family away, all five of them. Mutti said that they had been sent to Poland because Onkle Josef was born there. Made no sense to me because Tante Selma and my cousins were all born in Hamburg.

Well, you can just imagine how this affected our family in Dillstrasse. I heard Mutti telling a friend that Opa Siegmund started shouting at the Nazis, "Leave my daughter and grandchildren alone, how can you do this, they are Germans, they were born here in Hamburg!" She made Opa stop and took him inside the apartment. My poor Mutti, first Tatti was forced to go away and now her sister and family as well. I remember her packing up some of Tante Selma's things and trying to send them to Poland, I don't know if the parcel ever reached them. That was that, I never saw them again. It got worse though. Very soon after the Biermans were taken away, they came for Tante Mathilde and her husband Max who was also born in in Poland. And so, all that was left of our large happy family living in Dillstrasse was Opa Siegmund, Mutti, Margot, and me.

I don't seem to remember much about the night of 9th November, Kristallnacht. I think it must be because not very much happened on our street. Many synagogues were burned down but not our big synagogue in Hamburg called the Bornplatz. Opa Siegmund's synagogue was also not burned down maybe because it was so small the Nazis never knew it was there. I remember what happened afterwards though—six months later Margot and I were sent away.

Just after Kristallnacht Mutti's brother Onkle Arthur was arrested and sent to a concentration camp, a place called Sachsenhausen. He was kept there until the end of December. I was shocked, to me it was like he had done something wrong and been taken away to jail. When Tatti came home after Onkle Arthur was arrested I asked him, "Tatti, what did Onkle do, why was he arrested and taken away?" Tatti looked at me and said, "Liebchen, he did nothing, he could not help it that when he was born the blood in his veins was Jewish blood."

Onkle Herbert, who was married to Mutti's sister Paula, was also sent to a concentration camp, but this is a good story. He and his family managed to escape from Hamburg and go to Brazil. Carmen, their daughter, was working in a solicitor's office when all this happened, she was learning how to type and I suppose how to be a secretary in a law office. Her boss who wasn't Jewish really liked her and when he heard that Herbert had been arrested, he called her in and said, "Carmen, I am very fond of you, I know your father is in a concentration camp, I'll see what I can do for you, I'll try and get him out. If you are able, would you and your Mutti go to Brazil?"

"Oh yes," she said, "we will go anywhere, to get out."

So, he did, he got them out. Paula and Carmen went to Sao Paulo in Brazil and afterwards this man managed to get Herbert out of the camp and he was able to follow his family to Brazil.

Everything got worse the next year, 1939. In April the Nazis kicked all the Jewish girls out of the Jewish school and we had to go to the boys' Talmud Torah which was nearby. I never realized that when this happened it was the beginning of the end for my whole school life.

And then, on the 21st May 1939, my Mutti's birthday, Margot and I were put on a train and sent away to England. But that is another story.

READ BETWEEN THE LINES

———•◆•———

For Margot and me, our fates were determined just after Passover 1939. We got to live. It all started with a knock on our door in the early afternoon. That knock set off a brief moment of uncertainty and fear because we were not expecting anyone and, in those times, you never knew who may be knocking on your door. Mutti was home with Margot and me, she put her hands on her lips signalling silence, went to the front door and called out, "Wer ist da?" There was no reply, but the mail slot in the door opened and an envelope was pushed through and dropped to the floor. Mutti picked it up, stared at the envelope for a short while, then abruptly walked to her bedroom and shut the door. I was very aware that shut doors immediately signalled secrets to be kept from Margot and me, and seeing the look on Mutti's face when she picked up the envelope was enough to tell me it contained a big secret.

My first thought was, something happened to Tatti. When the door opened and Mutti came out with the letter in her hand, I was very fearful but she looked at me and said, "Liebchen, I have wonderful news, you and Margot are going to England. Until Tatti and I also get permission to leave Hamburg you and Margot will be living with cousins, Onkle Isadore's children. The letter I just received is from England, it gives permission for you both to travel there, it's good news, you should be excited. Martha, please don't say anything to Opa, he was very sad when Tante Selma, Onkle Arthur, and their families had to go and live in Poland; and then, Tante Paula also left and went to Brazil. He will be very upset when he finds out you and Margot are going to England. I need to explain to him that we will only be apart for a short time because Tatti and I will eventually get permission to join you there and bring Opa with us."

I don't really remember how I felt, probably a bit numb, but I do remember that I looked up at her and said, "I am not going, I am not going without you and Tatti, and that's that." I was very stubborn.

She took me by the hand, walked back into the bedroom with me, closed the door, and said, "Liebchen, you have to go, you and Margot, it's no longer safe for us to live here in Germany, we have to leave. You and Margot are the first part of our family to go. But just think how exciting it will be, it is a big adventure. Think of all the stories you will be able to tell Tatti, me, and Opa when we get there. I also have some other good news; you will be travelling with many other children and Mrs. Carlebach is going to be with you all the way on the journey to England. Mrs. Carlebach and her husband, the Uber Rebbe, helped me to make the application for you and Margot, we have a lot to thank her for, you should always remember that Martha, promise me. Now let's go and tell Margot before Opa comes home."

Ignoring the promise, my first response was to ask if my friend Ruth Carlebach would also be going to England. I was not happy when the answer was no. It was some comfort that

Mrs. Carlebach would be with us on the journey, I knew her as a kind, warm person, who always made me feel like one of her own children when I was in the Carlebach house visiting Ruth.

When Mutti told my sister that she and I were being sent to England, Margot rushed up to Mutti, grabbed her dress, and started crying. It was a very hard moment for her. I told you before she was Mummy's girl and I am sure in Margot's mind Mummy was telling her, "I don't want you with me anymore." It was always very hard for Margot to understand things.

Well, we never spoke about this again for a few weeks because Mutti had not said anything to Opa Siegmund. Then, she got another letter, Margot and me were going to England on the 21st May.

That second letter must have been like a knife thrust into Mutti's heart, the pain would have been almost unbearable; the 21st May was her birthday, you see, and there was no way we could change that date.

After that second letter everything seemed to happen very quickly. I don't remember the time very clearly at all, I know that we both had to go for injections which was not very nice and I also remember that Mutti and Opa hardly spoke to each other.

Because Tatti was not at home Mutti not only had to do all the shopping and the normal things necessary in our house, she also had to make all the arrangements for our leaving. Something she spent a lot of time doing was to decide what we would take with us. Of course there were our clothes, but Mutti kept saying we should also have things to remind us of home until she, Tatti, and Opa joined us. She would put everything she wanted us to take out on the beds in our room and then pack them all into suitcases to see if they would fit in. One time, after packing the suitcases she picked them up and said, "They are too heavy, you will not be able to carry them, I must start again."

What were the reminders of home we finally left with? Opa Siegfried and Oma Martha owned a beautiful silver cutlery set. Each piece had the initials "SN" inscribed on the handle. I really don't know if they bought this or were given it as a wedding gift. In normal times the set would have been shared out to all members of the family after Opa Siegmund died, it was a family heirloom you see. So, Mutti decided that Margot and I should both have something from the family heirloom.

This however was not an easy thing to do because we were living in Nazi Germany and Jews were not allowed to take valuables with them when they left. I am not sure who helped Mutti get the permission for us to take some of that cutlery set with us, maybe she did it on her own. Whatever the answer, when I think back now it shows just how resourceful and brave she was during such difficult times.

Mutti chose from the set four spoons, forks and teaspoons, and one knife. She also added a wristwatch, two silver bangles and two silver chains with pendants, and then organised to have the whole package valued by a jeweller in Hamburg, I still have that valuation. After she received the valuation Mutti must have taken all the items and the letter from the jeweller to the Chief Financial Officer in Hamburg and got approval for them to leave Germany. I cannot imagine how stressful this must have been for her because although she got the letter from the jeweller in April, approval for the items to leave Germany was only given on the 19th May, two days before we left Hamburg!

The sad thing for Margot and me was that when Mutti filled our suitcases with the things she thought we needed there was very little space for us to put in the things we wanted. She put in photographs of our family, school books and two storybooks and of course our clothes. I still have the two storybooks, written in German of course. The one was about four eight- or nine-year-old girls who are in a club and they go swimming and skating, it's really a children's book about friendship. The other is called *I Remember When I Was Four*, I haven't read them for a long time. Oh, the other thing Mutti packed for me was my autograph book where my school friends wrote their names, my grandfather and my parents even wrote in it. Sadly, there was no room for our toys, we couldn't even put in a doll or a teddy, nothing.

The suitcases were so heavy we could not carry them ourselves, so very cleverly Mutti came up with a solution. She took the cases to the Gestapo office and asked for them to be sealed and sent straight to the train station in Hamburg. When Margot and me got on that train we had certificates of valuation for what was in our luggage, approval from the Chief Financial Officer in Hamburg to take what was valuable out of Germany and, the Gestapo had sealed the suitcases. I will tell you later why this was so clever and so important.

In those final weeks before we left for England, Opa Siegmund became almost like a tortoise, he just drew into himself, said very little, and seemed to be very angry with Mutti. I don't know if she noticed this change in him, maybe she didn't, she was so busy with packing and everything and just had no time to speak to Opa about what was going on. On the Friday night before we left Mutti tried to be cheerful, talking about the adventure we were going on and how wonderful it was going to be when we were all together again when she, Tatti, and Opa, eventually came to England. Opa said nothing, he made the blessings, ate a piece of challah, and went to bed. To make things worse, Margot was very tearful and Mutti spent a lot of time hugging her, talking about how Martha was there to look after her, and that there was no need to be frightened; she was going to cousins, family, so there was nothing to worry about.

On the day we left Mutti took me aside and said, "Martha, you will have to be the big girl now who looks after her sister. There is something important I must tell you and please never forget it. Tatti and I will send you letters, special letters, where you are only allowed to write twenty-five words. These letters will come to you through the Red Cross. You and Margot will also be able to send us letters, again, through the Red Cross. Twenty-five words is not a lot and I am sure at times we will have many things to tell you. Me and Tatti will also have to be very careful about what we write because I am sure the Gestapo will be looking at the letters. So Liebchen, you will need to be very clever when you read those letters, always read between the lines to see if we are telling you important news that we had to hide inside the twenty-five words."

I never forgot what she told me and I always did read between the lines. One time Mutti sent me a very important message between the lines, but that is a story for later.

The day we left; I will never forget that day. Mutti asked me what I want for breakfast and I said, "I want a boiled egg."

Well, I was sitting at the table in the kitchen eating my egg when Opa Siegmund came into the room, in a real fury he was. He started shouting at Mutti, "Theresa, how can you send your children away without you. You can't send the children to a strange country; you can't do a thing like that. I know they are relations but they don't know them."

Mutti was fighting back tears and shouted back, "I am trying to save their lives", then she stood up, looked at him, and said quietly, "Tatti I've got to send them away, I don't think we can come, there is no way we can get over at the moment, I can't get any permits, but I've got to save the children. Dr Carlebach's wife has offered to take them, and I am going to send them."

Well, he went berserk, shouted and carried on, and then he just stormed out of the kitchen in a temper, banging the door as he left. I never saw him again; it was a terrible morning. And it was Mutti's birthday. Tatti not there, a horrible argument with Opa, Margot and me leaving, it was no birthday at all.

I don't really remember much about what happened after that. Mutti asked me how I wanted to go to the station and I said, taxi, I want to go by taxi, I have never been in a car. We had to be there by 11 o'clock, so she got a taxi. Before we got in the taxi Mutti put these cards around our necks with our names on them, and details about where we were going, "so you can never get lost" she said, and we went off to the Hamburg Hauptbahnhof, it was the biggest train station in the city.

When we arrived, there were lots of other children there, I don't know how many, some say one hundred, others two hundred, all different ages, most were younger than me, under twelve, and there were some who were sixteen. I later found out there was a baby of six months and he wasn't lying in a pram, he was in a suitcase. While we were standing around someone came and told us, "You are not allowed to hug, not allowed to kiss, just go straight to the train and when you sit down do not look out the window, now go and get on the train."

I took Margot's hand, she seemed to be in a bit of a daze, and began walking with the others to the train when I noticed nearly all the children were carrying suitcases and we had none. I turned round and shouted to Mutti, "Our suitcases, our suitcases, we forgot to bring them." I had forgotten that she organised for both to be sent ahead so we would not have to carry them. Mrs. Carlebach who was standing near the entrance to the train carriage walked quickly up to us, put her hand on my shoulder and said quietly, "Martha, don't worry, your suitcases are on the train, your Mutti arranged for them to be brought here, now come along and let's get on." Mrs. Carlebach was in charge of everything.

When I think back to that moment when we boarded the train, I know I wasn't frightened, maybe part of me was looking forward to the exciting adventure Mutti had told us we were going to have. I never thought that I would never see my parents and Opa Siegmund ever again. I had wanted to ask Mutti one or two questions, girl's questions you know, I was twelve years old, but I couldn't, there was no time.

Funny I never thought then about what our leaving did to Mutti and Tatti, but I was twelve and I guess these would not be the concerns of a twelve-year-old child. Many months later I received a letter from Mutti through the Red Cross, it was the first time I had to read between the lines. Mutti wrote that they had gone to Auntie Hennie and were staying there. I knew that by Auntie Hennie she meant friends who lived in Altona, she was Jewish and he was German; they were a wonderful couple with no children of their own, we had known them forever. Auntie Hennie and her husband Karl lived in a very tiny house and the only place Mutti and Tatti could have slept in was a cellar. Many years later when I visited that place, I realised that they preferred to go to that cellar rather than our home with its empty bedroom and accusations from Opa Siegmund. Funny I never thought about how Opa managed to look after himself while they were away, Mutti did everything for him, he never cooked or anything. I suppose he must have managed somehow.

BOOK FIVE

1939-1958

Nineteen years living with a first cousin

Our Journey to Manchester[82]

———•◆•———

When Margot and me got on the train the carriage was already quite full. I took her by the hand and pulled her to seats near a window; she followed me, never spoke, I think she was in a bit of shock. I sat in the seat next to the window and although they told us not to wave or look out the window until we left Hamburg station, I took many quick peeks trying to find Mutti in the large crowd outside. I thought I saw her but when I looked again, she was not there.

We were at the back of the carriage and I stood up to check whether I knew any of the children, there must have been around thirty to forty. Most were sitting quietly, some were crying. I could not see any familiar faces. The nurses with us in the carriage were walking around talking to the children, they were very kind. Mrs. Carlebach came into the carriage and I saw she was carrying our suitcases. She put them on the rack above us, patted Margot on the arm and said, "Girls, you see you did not have to worry, your mama organised everything." It was so comforting to know that someone on that train knew who we were and was looking after us.

---

[82] Martha and Margot travelled from Hamburg to the Hook of Holland by train, then boarded a ship that took them to Harwich; from Harwich they travelled to London and boarded another train to Manchester.

Anyway, when the train started moving, I didn't like it, I began to cry, and when Margot saw me crying, she started. We may have hugged each other then, I don't really remember. I do remember, however, one of the nurses telling us not to worry, we were on a big adventure, going on a train and a ship and all, it was very exciting. We did eventually stop crying, I don't remember why, maybe it was because they brought us something to eat.

So, we left and that was that.

In the beginning the carriage was quiet—unusual when there were so many children together. The children who knew each other began exchanging seats so they could sit next to their friends. I tried talking to Margot but she sat silently not wanting to talk so I gave up in the end and must have fallen asleep. Next thing I know the train had stopped and out the window I saw Nazi soldiers and men with coats and hats. I remembered the day I tried to hide under our sofa while Nazis marched down our street shouting, "Juden Raus", I was terrified. The nurses in our carriage starting walking down the rows of seats telling us to take out our passports and any other travel papers we had. They told us not to be afraid because we were leaving Germany and when you travelled to another country it was necessary to show these papers. Mutti had given me a little bag with our passports and an envelope, she said I should give the envelope to anyone who wanted to open our suitcases during the journey. When I took the papers out of the bag, I think my hand was shaking.

Two men with coats and hats came into the front of our carriage and began asking the children for their papers. They also took the suitcases off the racks and began opening them, pulling things out and leaving them on the floor. As they left a row of seats the nurses helped the children pick up the clothing on the floor and pack it back in the suitcases. When the man checking our side of the carriage came up to Margot and me, I gave him our passports and the letter with a shaking hand. He stared at our passports for quite a long time and then told us both to look at him. I was too scared and he shouted at me to lift my head. He looked at the envelope said quietly, "Was ist das," pulled out the papers inside and began reading. "Where are your suitcases," he snapped at me. I pointed to the rack above our seats. "Take them down," he ordered; I did not know what to do because I was too short to reach the rack. One of our nurses standing behind him came up quickly and took the suitcases down. I saw that there was a paper pasted over the front of each which the man proceeded to study. He finally gave me back the letter and without another word moved on to the next row of seats. The nurse gave us a weak smile and put the suitcases back on the rack.

My heart was pounding, it took a long time for me to feel safe again.

After that nothing much happened, I must have slept most of the time until the next stop which was the end of the first train journey. It was dark outside, the nurses told us we were now in the Netherlands and were going to get on a boat to England. This time we had to carry our suitcases; they were very heavy and Margot could not manage hers. Luckily a nurse saw that she was struggling to walk carrying the suitcase, she came up to us and took it from Margot telling her not to worry, she would look after it. All the nurses were carrying suitcases, I guess for all the younger children. We then spent a very long time in some building before we got on the boat early in the morning, I heard gulls screeching like they did in Hamburg and I wanted my Tatti and Mutti very badly. We went into the inside of the boat and sat on seats; the nurses never allowed us to go anywhere except to the toilet. I never liked the boat journey but I wasn't seasick, some of the children were. All this time Margot refused to speak; when a nurse asked her if she was feeling sick, she just stammered something I could not understand.

The journey took a long time and when we finally got off the boat it was raining. We all got wet as we walked to another building and waited there for a short time before getting on another train which the nurses told us was taking everyone to London. I was so tired and must have slept the whole journey because all I remember is Mrs. Carlebach giving us instructions on what to do when we got off the train in London. She told us to wait in the place we would be taken to with all the other children after arriving in London; that someone would call our names and help us to get on the train for our journey to Manchester.

"Don't worry girls," she said, "the cards around your necks have your names and the place you are travelling to, you can't get lost. Now Martha, listen to me very carefully, there will be no nurses on the train with you, but when you arrive in Manchester your Tatti's brother, Onkle Isadore, will be there to meet you. Two other children are going to Manchester, they are much younger, and so Martha you should look after them and your sister. One other thing, liebchen, remember no one on that train will speak German, everyone here in England speaks English".

She then turned to Margot and said, "Liebchen, you must listen to Martha, she is your big sister and will look after you, understand?" I could see Margot was close to crying but she managed to say "ja" as Mrs. Carlebach squeezed her shoulder and then moved away to speak to the children in front of us. When the train slowed, I saw a long board with a name I couldn't read. I felt panic, wanted to cry, but did not want to alarm Margot, so held it in. Many months later I found out that we had arrived at Liverpool station.

We were taken to a big hall with long benches, told to sit, and after a short time they brought us sandwiches and small bottles of milk to drink. After about half hour a man started calling out names. The children he called walked to the front of the hall where someone met them, sometimes with a hug, but most times without. This went on and on for hours until the only children in the hall were me, Margot, and two other girls who looked to be around five or six. Finally, our names were called and this time a man walked up to us, smiled, and said something I could not understand. Our blank looks must have told him we didn't understand what he had said, so he pointed to his chest, then to us, and made signs we should follow him. Margot could not lift her suitcase nor could the other two children, so I pointed to the suitcases and opened my arms with a shrug trying to explain that they were unable to carry them. He seemed to understand, motioned with his hands we should sit down, walked up to a lady still standing at the front of the hall and brought her back with him. They each picked up two suitcases and motioned all of us to follow.

We had walked a very short distance when I desperately needed a toilet and, in a panic, realised I didn't know how to ask in English. Too embarrassed to ask the man, I quickly caught up with the lady, pulled at her sleeve and whispered in German, "toilette". "Oh my," she said, followed by something I couldn't understand, and after calling out to the man marched us quickly to the toilets. Let me tell you, it was a huge relief for all four of us.

Things then moved quickly, we walked to another part of the station and together with a lot of sign language were helped to get on another train. Our two helpers came on the train with us, found four empty seats that were together and lifted the suitcases onto the racks. When I saw that I felt another surge of panic, and pulled the lady's sleeve trying to explain with arm movements that we would not be able to reach the suitcases to bring them down. "Oh," she said, and after talking to the man they took the suitcases down and put them on the floor in front of the seats. After giving each of us a small paper bag which we found out later contained a sandwich and a bottle of milk, the two smiled and left us alone in the carriage with people we didn't know and couldn't understand. The loneliness and the fear we all felt at that moment broke out into tears and we were all crying softly when the train left the station.

That journey seemed to go on forever—it was actually around five hours—and we arrived in Manchester at eleven o'clock that night. As the train stopped, I opened the window and looked out, hoping I would somehow know who my uncle was. With huge relief I saw someone walking and waving as the train slowly came to a stop. He caught up with our carriage, rushed up to my window shouting in German, "Martha, Martha, it's Uncle Isadore, I am so relieved you are here safely, where is your sister, stay there, I will come and help you to get off the train."

Well, he came on the train, and hugged Margot and me so warmly, I could see tears in his eyes. From that moment I loved Uncle Isadore, he was like a replacement for Tatti and I know if he had not died so soon after we came to Manchester our lives would probably have turned out to be very different. He asked me where our cases were and was about to pick them up, preparing to take us off the train, when I told him that we also had to make sure the two little girls with us were met by their grandparents. Uncle Isadore then spoke to the girls in German telling them not to worry, he would help them to meet up with their grandparents. As we finally got down from the train it was not long before the grandparents rushed up to the two little girls, picked them up and started smothering them with kisses. As they thanked Uncle Isadore and walked off, I remembered Opa Siegmund shouting at Mutti, telling her she should not send us away and slamming the door as he went out the room. I choked up but did not want uncle to see me crying so I did my best to stop the tears.

So, Margot and me were now in Manchester, what happened to us after that can be told through many stories, so let me tell you some of them.

Our Introduction to Manchester

―――♦―――

Uncle Isadore was very talkative as he led us from the train and through the station to a car parked in a street nearby. I don't remember much about what he was saying other than him telling us he was very happy we had arrived safely and he would be taking us to our new homes. But he was sure we were very hungry so we would be having supper first. I must have fallen asleep in the car because the next thing I know we had stopped and Uncle was telling us to come with him to meet the family.

As it turned out we were both going to live in two different places, Margot with one of Uncle Isadore's daughters, Leah, and me with the other daughter, Ella. The house he was leading us into was Leah's.

When we got inside it was all very confusing, there were many people and I only found out much later who they were. There was Leah and her sister Ella, their husbands Morris and Ike, Uncle Isadore's wife who was Russian and I suppose my auntie, Uncle Isadore, Margot and me. The Russian auntie came up to us immediately, said hello and then something in English we couldn't understand. Uncle laughed when he realized this, turned to us and said, "She asks you to tell her your names." I answered very shyly, "Martha," and waited for Margot who looked like she was about to cry. So, I pointed to her and said, "Margot."

Auntie then asked me a question in Yiddish which I understood a little bit because my uncles in Hamburg often spoke Yiddish to each other and to Opa Siegmund. "Maidelach farshteisht ir Yiddish?"[83] to which I replied shyly, "A bissel."[84] "Gut," was her reply, "mir veln redn tsu dir aoyf yiddish biz du vest lernen English, kumen epes essen."[85] With that she motioned us to follow her into another room, sat us down at a large table and put a plate of food in front of us. The food was fish but I was so overcome by the whole situation I just could not eat. I tried to nibble a little bit but it was no use, I think I would have been sick if I ate. Margot, however, was eating her food but dropping bits on the floor because for some reason she would not lift her head. One of the ladies who had followed us into the room sat down next to Margot and said in Yiddish something like, "Margot, my name is Leah, you will be living in this house with me and my family, say hello to my husband Morris." Margot must have understood enough of what was said because she lifted her head and stammered, "H-h-h-hallo" in German. Margot had been silent most of the journey and I knew that she was missing Mutti very badly, she was what you call a mummish girl. I could not understand why she was stuttering; she never did that before. But from that moment she continued to stutter very badly, it took years before she would speak normally. I really don't think my sister ever recovered

---

[83] Girls, do you understand Yiddish?
[84] A little.
[85] We will speak to you in Yiddish until you learn English. Come and eat something.

from being taken away from her mum, she was never altogether alright after we left Hamburg.

The other lady in the room then came up to me and said in Yiddish, "Martha, you will be staying with me and my family, you can call me Auntie Ella and this is my husband Uncle Ivan. We have a little boy Robbie, he is five, you can look after him if you want." She was my first cousin and I had to call her Auntie!

Well, after that a maid came into the room and Uncle explained to Margot in German that the maid, whose name was Mildred, was going to show her where to sleep and to put all her clothes. With that Mildred helped Margot out of the chair, took her by the hand, asked which was her suitcase, picked it up with the other hand and escorted Margot out of the room. I found out later that Margot never had her own bed in the beginning, she slept in the same bed as Mildred. Leah had a spare room with furniture in it that was never used, it was ridiculous. Anyway, eventually the maid went off to the war and Margot got the bed to herself. She lived with Leah for twenty years, my sister. She wasn't happy but did not have the courage or the confidence to move away.

Auntie Ella then said to me we were also leaving, that I should take my suitcase and follow her and Uncle Ivan to their car which was outside. Uncle Isadore gave me a squeeze on the shoulder as I left but I don't think I have ever felt as lonely as I did when I walked in the dark to that car. We drove a short distance to the house where I would be now living without Tatti, without Mutti, and without Opa Siegmund. Our cousins were not poor, they had nice houses, new cars, not second-hand ones. Uncle Ivan had a market stall and Morris a factory which later made uniforms for the army. The house I lived in had three bedrooms and a garden front and back. One thing though, I did have my own room. My Russian auntie and Uncle Isadore lived across the road. I found out later that Auntie Ella never cooked, her mum did it all. Auntie Ella made sandwiches and stuff like that, never cooked a thing.

Well, I found out very quicky what my life was going to be like living there. Auntie Ella was hard, very hard. I came down the stairs in the morning and she was bathing her child. I had been crying and was wiping my eyes as I came down the stairs. She looked at me and said in Yiddish, "What's the matter with you, your eyes, you look as though you've been crying?"

"I miss my Tatti and Mutti," I replied.

"Big baby," she said, "crying because your mum's not here. Look, Ronnie, she is crying for her mommy and daddy, a big girl like you, twelve years old."

That hurt me a lot, I want to cry when I think about it; that was my cousin, no feelings. When her mother died, she was crying all the time but I never said anything, wouldn't have helped, would it.

And then, there was the food. That first day when we sat down to eat, I saw all the food was in the middle of the table and Auntie Ella said to me, "Sit over there, that is where your food is, on the side." I got bread and margarine; they got bread and butter. Eventually I said to them, "My mother never used to do that, when my cousins came, we all had the same." Didn't help, did it. I was always hungry; she didn't give me enough to eat. "I want this for my little boy," she would say, "he's only a baby, only three."

For at least two years I used to pinch a slice before I went to bed, there was sliced bread in the bread bin. Things got better, but in the beginning, I was always hungry. And then they would not allow me to see Margot every day, even though she lived round the corner and I could get there in about three minutes. Ella would not let me out, and Leah would not let her out.

These are horrible memories and I was not a bit happy there. I would have been happy if I had nice people to live with, but they were nasty, that's why I eventually ran away. But that is another story.

LIFE WITH AUNTIE ELLA

Well, I have told you some of the stories about what happened when we arrived in Manchester. Let me tell you about my life with my first cousin who I had to call Auntie Ella.

We arrived in Manchester in the month of May which meant there was still around two months of schooling before the summer holiday. I don't know if it was on Uncle Isadore's insistence but we were both sent to a Church of England school because at that time there were no Jewish schools in Manchester. There were four other Jewish children besides us and when it came time for morning prayers, we were sent out of the room. It was a very difficult time because me and Margot could not speak English and to make it worse the classroom was in fact four different classes in one room. I had never seen anything like that before! Margot had the additional problem of her stutter which had got much worse. I really wanted to go to school to learn English and other things. I was good at languages and gymnastics when I lived with my parents but Auntie Ella had other plans for me, which I soon found out.

When the new school year was about to begin in September, she said to me, "Oh you are not to go to school again, you are going to do housework and help me in the house." She wanted me for the housework, cleaning, and looking after her son.

"I have never cleaned houses before," I told her, "and besides that, I want to learn something, then I can earn a bit of money and pay you back for keeping me."

"I don't need you for a job," she said, "you can stay at home and do housework, I will show you how to do it."

She didn't like housework, you see, always the smart woman with high heels walking around all posh and made up. In the beginning she never gave me any money for the cleaning, it took a long time before she gave me any payment for the work I did. I never knew if she received any money for keeping me, some allowance or something; anyway, if she did, I never saw any of it.

But it was the end of my learning, never went to school again, got no education at all and couldn't do anything about it.

I eventually learned enough English to make myself understood; it took me about six months. I remember one funny story that happened to me in those six months. One morning Auntie Ella said to me, "I want you to go to the shop and get me some flour." So, I went off to the shops and came back with a bunch of flowers. "I didn't say flowers," she shouted at me, "I meant flour, baking flour." Served her right. I never forgot that, I was only twelve.

There was another time when I first got there that she really upset me, maybe I was angry more than upset. I had this toothache and had to go to the dentist. I was scared and said to Auntie Ella, "Will you go with me, I am frightened." I mean Mutti always went with me to the dentist, I never went alone. Well, she said to me, "I can't leave Robbie." She could have left him with someone or taken him with us but no, I had to go on my own without much English and all, I never forgot that. When I got to the dentist he asked if I had money, by that time I understood a little bit, and when I replied no, he gave me some tablets and that was it, never examined me or anything. They were lucky I never needed a doctor all the years I was with them!

The one comfort I had in the early years was Uncle Isadore, he was more like my father and I would wait every day until he would come to visit us. Of course, he came to see Robbie who was his grandchild but he also would spend time talking to me. I don't think my cousin liked that, maybe she was jealous, who knows. I mean one August we went to Blackpool on holiday, the whole family. We had a room there and stayed for a whole week. One day Uncle says to me, "Martha, I'll take you around the shops." We spoke German to one another; I don't think Auntie Ella liked that because she did not always understand everything we were saying. Anyway, he bought me a pair of sunglasses at Woolworths, I remember they cost about three pence. I came back with them, and was very excited, but when she saw them, she shouted at her father, "What have you let her buy sunglasses for?" Well, there was a right row, he shouted back, "I'm your dad, I do as I want, and I bought my niece a pair of sunglasses." The argument went on the whole day but anyway it was forgotten later. Imagine, over a pair of sunglasses, and I was so excited, I was only twelve, children's sunglasses.

Uncle got Alzheimer's and no longer knew who I was, it was very sad. He died in 1942, three years after I came to live with Auntie Ella. I missed him terribly, he was the only one like family, and when he was gone there was no one left to protect us.

Another memory I have of the early times was that the people around us were not friendly. Nobody would ask you to join in with anything and we were never asked to come into a house with the children who lived there. Maybe it was because Ella was such a cold person, she never had any friends over. I am different, I make friends very easily but the problem was she wouldn't allow me to go out of the house much so even if I met up with the children around us, I could not see them very often.

It was also very difficult after we arrived because it was war time. I remember we had an Anderson air raid shelter in the back garden and would have to go into it many nights. I don't really know what protection it gave us because if a bomb fell on our house that shelter would not have helped very much.

After Uncle Isadore died Uncle Ivan decided he was going to open a market store selling rugs, carpets and curtain materials and Auntie Ella told me that I had to go with him and help him in the store. I hated that time especially when it was very cold in the middle of winter and I was forced to get up very early in the morning and go off with Uncle Ivan to work; I was only fifteen and never got paid anything. One day however I had a win of sorts, I still laugh about it. Auntie Ella would make us sandwiches to take with us, I got lung in mine and Uncle Ivan got beef or some other kind of meat. Well, you know what they use lung for, they feed it to cats and other animals. This one day she mixed it up and gave me the meat and Uncle Ivan the lung. When he opened his sandwiches, he went mad and started shouting, "She gave me lung, I can't eat this, wait until I get home, I will tell her a thing or two." I of course said nothing, just sat quietly eating my sandwiches and enjoying them for a change. When we got home there was such a row, he was screaming at her and she was shouting back, I just went to my room, making sure they could not see the big smile on my face. They didn't speak to each other for a week but eventually made up. I never forgot that, ever.

In all the time I was there I never really stood up for myself. Strange though, when she eventually got over her stutter Margot did answer back, she turned out to be a lot braver than me. I think I was a coward all those years. There was this one time when a family that were friends of the Brauns in Altona managed to escape and come to England. They had two children, twins, and Mutti and Tatti told them where we were living. When they eventually got in touch with Auntie Ella, she would not allow then to visit us, that was very cruel and I should have said something but I didn't.

Another thing I have to tell you about my time with Auntie Ella, is that the Jewish people around us never bothered much with me. We were living in an area where there was a lot of Jewish people but I must be truthful they were very cold. They could have said, why don't you come in the house and play with my child, or here is some toffee, or a chocolate, but never. I saw them giving to other children but me, never. When kids with me had a piece of chocolate they didn't share, why, I really don't know. So, I didn't have any Jewish friends there at all.

Auntie Ella's family were not religious, I mean they went to synagogue on holidays and kept kosher but that was all. I remember when we lived with Opa Siegmund how religious he was, put on tefillin every day and Saturdays we weren't allowed to do lots of things we did during the week. Not at Auntie Ella's,

I mean Uncle Ivan never put on tefillin, not that I saw anyway. Another thing that hurt me, when we went to synagogue, they all had seats but never got one for me. So, I would go upstairs where the ladies were, and sit in an empty seat then someone would come up to me and say, "This is my seat." I had to get up and find somewhere else and it happened all the time. Where Margot was living with Leah they went to synagogue every Saturday morning, she was more religious than her sister.

I remember the time when I wanted to go to a Jewish club in Manchester, Maccabi, it was a sports club and I think I told you I was very good at gymnastics when I lived with my parents. I told Auntie Ella I wanted to join Maccabi and her reply was, "Oh no, you're not bothering, I never had a club when I was a youngster, you needn't bother."

So, it was very hard for me to meet any Jewish people and have Jewish friends.

My Contact with Tatti and Mutti

———◆◆———

After I first arrived, when I did not have to do housework or look after Ronnie, I spent a lot of time on my own in my room. When I was sure Auntie Ella was not around, I pulled my suitcase out from under the bed, took out the silver spoons, forks, and knife with Opa Siegmund's name on them and spread them out on the bed. Then I arranged the photographs Mutti had packed for me around the cutlery, and after carefully looking at everything I sat on the floor and read one of the books in German I had brought with me. It was the only way I could feel some connection to my family. Auntie Ella would not allow me to put the photographs on the shelf in my room so I had to keep them in the suitcase and took them out when I was sure she was not around.

I wore the watch, silver bangle and pendant that Mutti had given to me all the time, at least she never stopped me doing that!

Uncle Isadore helped me to send my parents letters through the Red Cross, you were allowed to write twenty-five words. I was feeling cold at night and I asked them to send me my coat which had been left behind because there was no space in the suitcase. I also told them I was unhappy.

I was so excited at the end of August 1939 when we got a postcard from Tatti, it was stamped 13th August, eighteen days before the war started. We never got another postcard after that, only the Red Cross letters. In the postcard Tatti told me that I should not worry because Uncle Isadore would always be there for me and that they would send the coat.

I have very few of the letters I received from Tatti and Mutti through the Red Cross because when I first got them Auntie Ella took them away from me. She said, "You are not keeping these letters," and destroyed them, destroyed them in front of me. I did, however, manage to hide some and still have them. When you sent a letter you first wrote down the twenty-five words on a form and gave that to the Red Cross. They then would type the words on a formal letter which you had to sign. I have one copy of a letter I sent to Mutti and Tatti in October 1941. The letter said, *"Dearest Mutti and Tatti, we are well. Mutti, I hope you can send me a recipe to make potato salad, sincerely, your loved ones Martha, Margot."*

I have another a letter from Tatti dated July 1941 in which he complained that Margot and me had not written for some time, in it he said they were both fine and had jobs. All the time we were writing to them and they were replying we hoped in a short time we would all be together again, but then, in January 1942, we got this letter from Mutti and Tatti, it said *"Beloved children, we are healthy, we are moving home to Selma. Give you a new address immediately and warm wishes to all your relatives and you."* I knew exactly what Mutti was telling me, just like Tante Selma had been forced to leave our home in Hamburg and go to Poland, the same thing was happening to them.

When I got that letter, at that moment I knew I would never see Mutti and Tatti again. Tante Selma and her family had disappeared, we never found out what happened to them. Now, the same thing was happening to my parents. I must have cried then; I don't remember, but I knew that I had to tell Margot, she deserved to know. I never showed her the letter but when I was allowed to visit her, just said, "I don't think we will ever see Mutti and Tatti again, they have been sent away to Poland." We both cried, it was terrible. It was the last letter we both got from our parents, we never received a new address, they had just disappeared, like Tante Selma. Maybe Margot still had hope in her heart that we would see our parents but I just knew that it would never happen; after that letter I lost all hope.

Then, in November 1945 my cousin, Auntie Ella, got a letter from something called the Refugee Children's Movement. I still have the letter, it said that Mutti was deported to Minsk on the 8th November 1941 and had not returned to Hamburg. When I came into my room that evening I saw the letter on my bed; she must have opened it, read it, and then taken it up to my room because she did not want to talk to me about it. I was like numb I think when I read it, didn't cry, left my room, and said I am going to Margot. It was the most terrible thing to go and tell my sister what was in that letter, we both cried our eyes out. I don't know if Margot got any support from Leah after that day but I certainly never got any from Ella.

In 1955 I wrote to the Jewish Community in Hamburg asking if they had any knowledge about what happened to our parents. They wrote back very quickly saying that they could confirm their deportation to Minsk on the 8th November 1941, but were unable to provide any information about what happened to them after that.

We also found out that Opa Siegmund had been deported to Theresienstadt in July 1942 and then two months later was sent to Treblinka where he was murdered in the gas chamber. My grandfather put on tefillin every morning, very religious he was, but it didn't help, did it, with all that he did, never helped! You know what I mean.

Margot and me were left with a few photographs, silver spoons, forks and a knife engraved with the initials SN, some jewellery, a watch, a postcard, some letters from the Red Cross, and our memories. We kept the memories of our parents alive, we never stopped talking about Mum and Dad.

I Finally Go Ice-Skating

———•◆•———

At times when I was on my own in my room I would think about home, not always the good things, also the bad. One of the memories that always upset me terribly was the day Mutti took me to the ice rink and we were told "no Jews allowed". I said to myself, when this war is over, I am going to get a pair of boots and go skating. I made the mistake of telling Auntie Ella about this dream and all she could say was, "Well you are not going to work and so you will never be able to buy skates."

Anyway, I put aside everything I could from the little bit of money I got for the things I needed, and when the Ice Palace opened in Manchester after the war, I found some second-hand skates in the newspaper. The Ice Palace was only up the road from where we lived so I could get there easily on the bus. The ice-skating changed my life. In the beginning I went once a week on a Saturday evening and it gave me something to look forward to. Not only that, I made friends there, not Jewish friends, English girls. I think I told you that at home I was a very good gymnast and so the skating came very easily to me. I was happy at the ice rink, I loved skating, it became my hobby.

There was this one time when the people at the ice rink decided that they were going to have an ice show and signs were put up inviting regular skaters to come and try out for a part.

Ten of us were chosen and I was one of them. I only got a part in the chorus but I was so excited. When I went home and told Auntie Ella I got a part in the show, all she was interested in was how many evenings I would be away from the house. When she heard the show was going to be on for a whole week, she immediately said I couldn't go, because she needed me in the house. We got into a real argument, I was then in my early twenties and I think for the first time I stood up for myself and told her I was going to be in the show and that was that. It was only for two hours between 7pm and 9pm and if I was not at the house for those two hours it really wouldn't matter. We never spoke properly for a long time after that. My ice-skating hobby helped me to eventually leave Ella and Ivan, but that is another story.

Being part of the show, called Xmas Pie, was marvellous. We had to dress up in these lovely hired costumes and every night was a great success with the audience clapping and cheering. Of course, Uncle Ivan and Auntie Ella wouldn't come and see me, would they, I mean this was one of the best moments in my whole life since I left Hamburg and they couldn't be part of it, could they. Not only that, they wouldn't even call for me afterwards in their car, it was only a twenty-minute drive. So, I had to come home on the bus on my own at 10pm in winter but I really didn't care, you know, I had finally done something for myself.

I eventually started going to the ice rink two nights a week, she wouldn't allow me any more. So even after me standing my ground against Ella that one time I was still too much of a coward to tell her that I was old enough to do what I want.

The Pig Farm

———◆◆———

I think I told you that Uncle Ivan started on the market, he sold rugs, and I had to work with him. In 1955 he suddenly announced, "I've got enough money and my wife has a friend who owns a pig farm so we are going to buy that farm." He never said what kind of friend but more about that later! Well, they bought the farm, a pig farm of all things, it was outside of Manchester in a place called Simister near Prestwich. Besides the pigs it had on it one cow, some hens, and a cottage where the farmer, Auntie Ella's friend, lived. His name was Richard, not married and a very untidy man. They made me go there every Tuesday to clean the house, the whole business took me a whole day. First, I had to take two buses and then there was a ten to fifteen-minute walk to the farm. I tell you, the only good thing about that day was I got a decent meal and at least Uncle Ivan came to pick me up and take me home in the car.

In the beginning she never paid me, then, maybe I complained I don't remember, I got half a crown. Before I ran away, they were giving me seven shillings and sixpence a week, you couldn't do much with that I promise you, even in those days.

I will tell you what kind of friend this farmer was to Auntie Ella, she started going out with him, secretly of course—

nobody knew except me. She would say to me in the morning, "You are coming out with me to the pictures, but you are not going, you are going to the park while I go and meet Richard." They would be out for about two hours and I then had to meet her again and we came back home. I never said anything, wouldn't have done me any good, would it.

    I was very angry about my treatment when I was living with Ella and Ivan but couldn't do much about it until I decided it was enough. I didn't have a good life, that's why I ran away. I tried to be nice to her at times, it never helped. Once or twice I said to her, "I would like to buy you some flowers." "Don't need no flowers, I can buy my own," that's what she used to say, a cousin, a first cousin. Took me nearly twenty years but eventually, I did it, I ran away.

I Run Away

---・---

I don't remember the exact date when I began planning to leave my cousin but it was around two years before I actually did it. It was one of my friends at the ice rink who finally helped me, we were together one day and she said to me, "You know, Martha, you don't look very happy." I looked at her and said, probably very sadly, "No, I am not," I mean I was already in my early thirties when this happened.

She squeezed my hand and said, "I am going to find you a nice home."

It was quite some time later when this friend told me about a couple she knew who lived in Chelmsford, which is in the country outside of Manchester.

"They have no children, are quite elderly, have a nice new house and own a garage. You would live with them, have your own room, and get paid for looking after them and the house."

This immediately sounded a little bit too good to be true; Auntie Ella never paid me anything for working in her house and looking after Robbie. I never got paid for going to the market with Uncle Ivan and finally got seven and six for cleaning Richard's untidy house. I was afraid though, and my friend must have seen that. She suggested I meet this couple and decide if I wanted to move in with them.

Well, it was arranged for me to have a meal with them. I liked them immediately; they were a lovely couple, their name was Black and we got on very well. I did have some doubts though, one being they were not Jewish; maybe it was an image of Opa Siegmund in my mind causing this, I really don't know. In the end I made my mind up because I thought, maybe my life will be different. I had no education, had not been to school; what would I do if I left my cousin, I could only be a home help or domestic worker. The Blacks were also quite persuasive, they must have liked me from the start because they really wanted me to move in.

When me and the Blacks finally agreed that I would move in with them I had to make a plan to run away. It was not easy, Ella and Ivan were always around so I had to find a time when I would be alone and then make sure the plan was kept totally secret. It was all a bit underhanded but what could I do.

I found out that Ella and Ivan were going to a show in Manchester, at the palace, on a Saturday afternoon so I immediately phoned my friend from the ice rink and told her that this was the only day I could leave. They very kindly arranged to fetch me in their car and take me to the Blacks' house in Chelmsford.

Well, that day after my cousin left the house and went to the show, I quickly packed up my things, I didn't have very much, and telephoned my friend to say I was on my own. They came with their car, I quickly got into it, and we drove away.

I had no mind of my own when I ran away, for twenty years I was bossed about and felt like a coward because I never stood up to them. So, I was not sorry to leave that house; it was

February 1960, I was thirty-three years old and had been there for nearly twenty years.

Well, there was a right to do after I left. I thought it was a total secret, that only my friend, the Blacks, and me, knew where I was going. I was wrong, somehow Ella and Ivan found out, maybe it slipped out to one of my skating friends, I don't know. Anyway, when she came home and saw all my things had gone and there was no note from me, my cousin must have known I had run away. She never knew much about my life at the ice rink but she did know I spent a lot of time there. So, I am guessing she went to the ice rink to check if I was there; it was Saturday night, the night I usually went skating. Probably she started asking around whether anyone knew where I was. Someone must have heard that I had gone to the Blacks and told her, I never found out who it was.

Anyway, the next day Ivan and Ella turned up at the Blacks' house and she came in and started telling me, "Martha, you can go to work, we will even get you a job at Marks and Spencer, I promise you no more housework, you can do what you want, but come back, I am missing you a lot, I love you and we think so much about you."

Mrs Black listened to all this and said to me, "Martha, don't go outside, once you get in the car you will be driven back to Manchester, don't do it if you want to stay." I looked at her and said, "I do want to stay," so I did, and never went back to my cousin's house.

I lived with the Blacks until I married—an Englishman, not Jewish. We have our own house and have had a good life together. In the end I would have loved to have been in a family where there were children, I would've liked to have had children myself, actually, because I love little ones. Anyway, these things happen, it's too late now, you can't go back. Thank you very much for listening and being such good listeners, I've never talked to anybody at all about this; I've got it off my chest, I've got rid of it now.

Epilogue

———◆———

Around twenty-four thousand German Jews were deported to Minsk between November 1941 and October 1942. On arrival many of the initial deportees were taken to a small village, Maly Trostinets, and gassed in gas vans. Other deportees were moved into the Minsk ghetto and housed in a special section. There they became slave labourers in factories that were situated both inside and outside the ghetto.

From the date the Minsk ghetto was established the Nazis conducted mass shooting Aktions and thousands of Jews were murdered. In August of 1943 the ghetto was liquidated and around four thousand Jews were transferred to Maly Trostinets where they were murdered in mass shootings. Any remaining residents of the ghetto were deported to the Sobibor death camp where they were gassed on arrival. We know that Daniel and Theresa were in the first group of German Jews deported to Minsk and given that there is no trace of them after that it would indicate that they could have been among the first victims murdered in Maly Trostinets. This is however conjecture, and like millions of other Jews murdered during the years 1939 to 1945 their exact fate is not known.

After Martha ran away from cousin Ella she settled into the life of a domestic servant and companion to the Blacks. This was a paid position and she was very happy there. Through the Blacks she met her husband who worked in their garage business. After her marriage Martha moved into her husband's house which they both eventually shared with his mother after she was widowed. Martha in fact insisted that her mother-in-law should move in with her. *"I said, you are not living on your own in the country in a cottage, you are coming to live with us, I've got a bedroom to spare. She lived with us for twenty years and we got on wonderfully well, no arguments ever, no words, none; and she knew I was Jewish. She was very religious, a religious church woman."*

What was the chain of circumstances that brought us to Martha?

Besides her ice-skating prowess Martha was also a keen swimmer. One day in the pool she saw a lady with an object around her neck that was somewhat familiar. Martha being the friendly soul she is approached this lady and said, "What's that around your neck, is it a magen david?"[86] The lady, whose name is Marjorie and happened to be Jewish, replied "No, it's a Chai,[87] have you heard of that?" Something in Martha's soul then prompted her to say to Marjorie, "I am Jewish," this, after years and years of having absolutely no contact with anything Jewish.

Marjorie's response was, "You are Jewish, I can't believe it," and the two became firm friends so much so that Martha told Marjorie many things about her life including that she had been on the Kindertransport.

The next link in the chain of circumstance is Marjorie's daughter Lisa Revivi, who lives in Israel. After hearing some of

---

[86] Star of David.
[87] Chai is the Hebrew word for life and a Chai is a pendant, usually on a necklace, made up from the two letters in the Hebrew Alphabet that spell Chai.

the very touching stories about Martha's life Lisa recognised that this was an opportunity to acquire testimony from a survivor of the Kindertransport and confided in Albee Kava, who is a guide at Yad Vashem and also a friend. He was immediately intrigued because his understanding of the Kindertransport at that time was based on stories with positive rather than negative endings. With Lisa and Marjorie's assistance, arrangements were made to interview Martha via Zoom and those interviews are the basis of this book. This charming and lovable lady's opening comment to us when we first met on Zoom was, "You can ask me anything," and we did.

ILLUSTRATIONS

*Apartment building where the Braun family lived,
21 Grune Strasse in Altona*

A page from "Prayers During Wartime for Our Jewish Soldiers," printed by The Nissensohn German-Hebrew Lithographic and Book Printing Company

Daniel and Theresa Braun, date of photographs unknown

Kindergarten in Altona attended by Martha and Margot. The River Elbe is in the background

Altona synagogue attended by the Braun family

Braun family portrait circa 1930

The Braun family enjoying a day on the Elbe River beach circa 1932

Martha enjoying the water with Daniel circa 1930

The Bismarck Bad where Martha learned to swim

Nissensohn family photograph taken at the Bar Mitzvah of Joachim Freiburg circa 1937

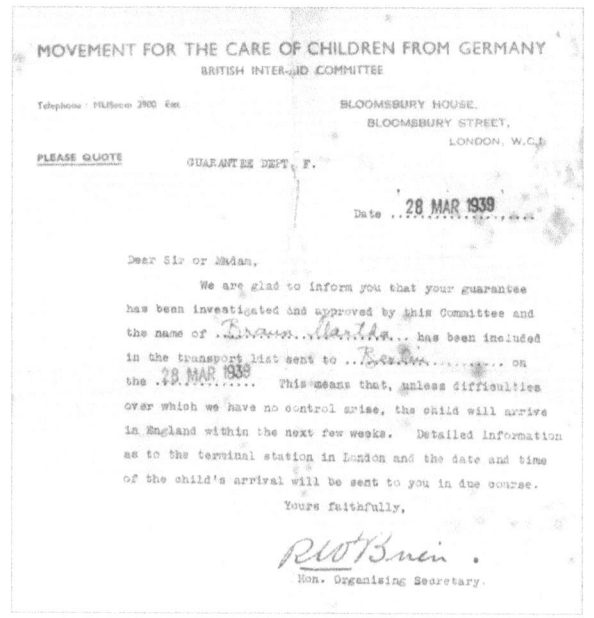

Initial letter approving Martha's inclusion in the Kindertransport list

ILLUSTRATIONS

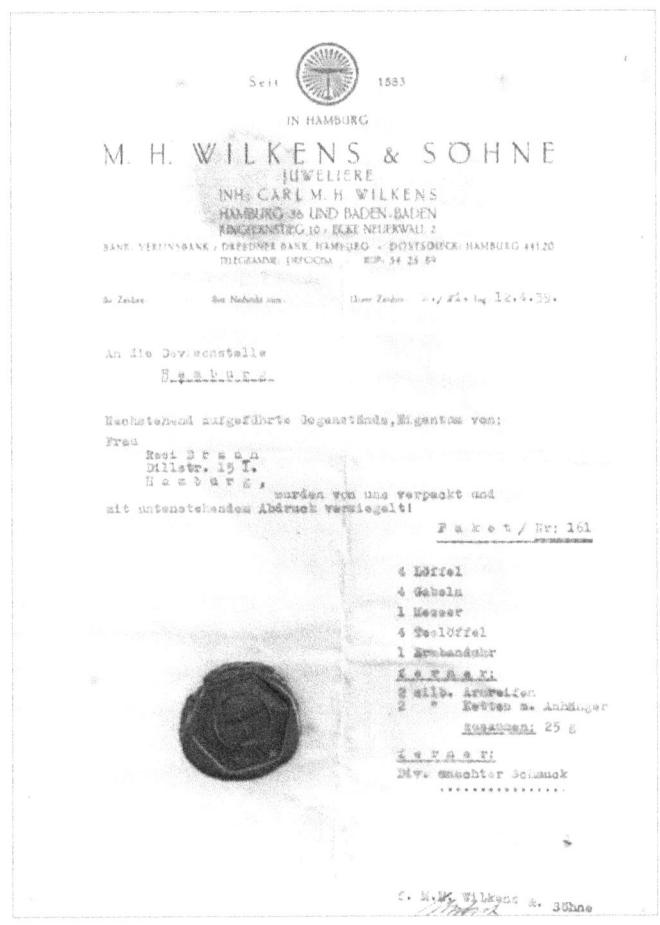

This document is a declaration by a jeweller certifying the contents of a package numbered 161. It states that the property listed is owned by Resi Braun who lives at Dillstrasse 15 in Hamburg. It also certifies that the package which contained four spoons, four forks, one knife, four teaspoons, one wristwatch, two silver bangles, two silver chains and pendants was sealed by the jeweller, M. H. Wilkens and Son. The listed items together with some sundry items of fake jewellery weigh twenty-five grams.

The jeweller's declaration listing the inventory of goods to be removed from Germany was taken by Theresa to the office of the Chief Financial Officer Hamburg. It was stamped at the back with "a one-time approval", given for one month only, for the listed goods to leave Germany. The girls left Hamburg two days after the approval date.

ILLUSTRATIONS

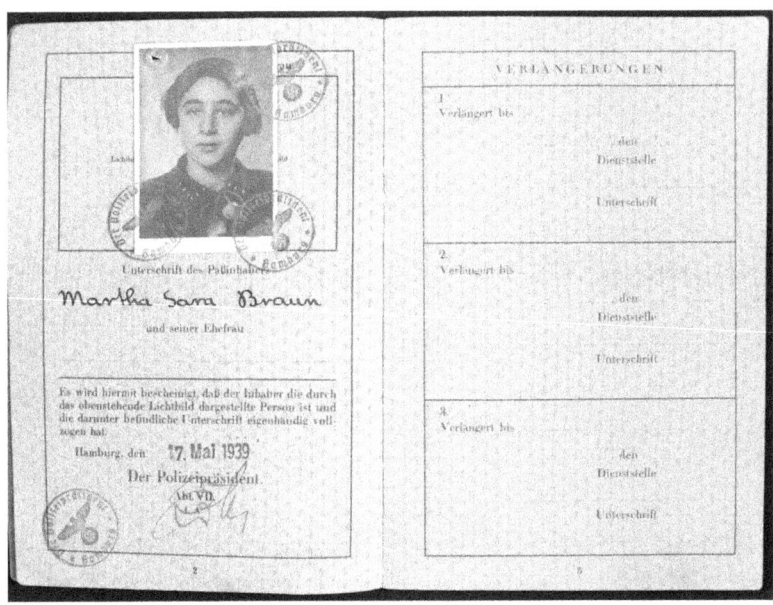

On the 17th May 1939 Martha had to sign this document in front of a representative of the Hamburg police chief which proved her identity

Deutsche Reich Reisepass - Martha's passport issued on the 15th March

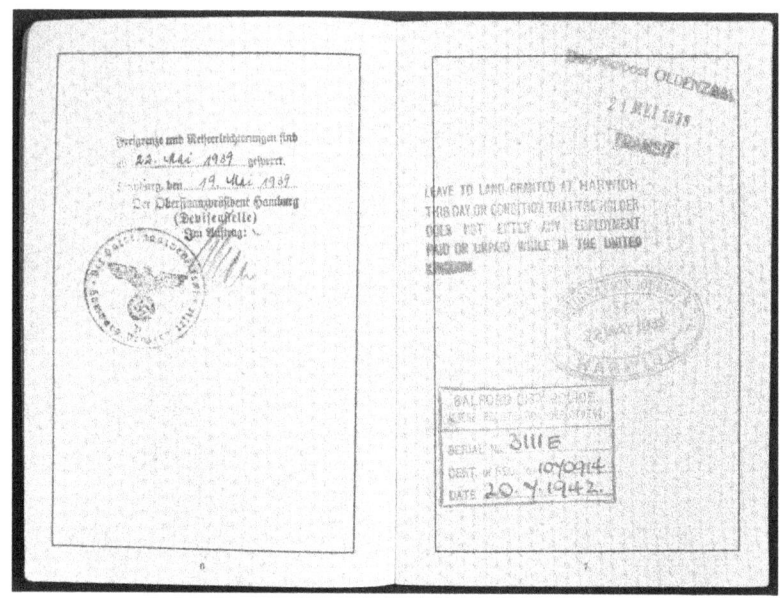

Entries in Martha's passport recording her journey to England. She was given approval to transit through Holland on the 21st May 1939 and given leave to enter England at Harwich on the 22nd May. The approval to enter forbid any paid employment. Permission to remain was given again 20th July 1942.

> **JEWISH REFUGEES COMMITTEE**
> MANCHESTER BRANCH
>
> Please address all communications to
> The SECRETARY
> Telephone: BLAckfriars 5437 & 4933
>
> Our Ref. S/ HR/PM
> Your Ref ....
>
> 1, BRAZENNOSE STREET,
> MANCHESTER, 2.
> 16th November, 1945.
>
> Miss M. Braun,
> 2, Bispham Grove,
> Hr. Broughton,
> S A L F O R D, 7.
>
> Dear Miss Braun,
>
>   Re: Daniel and Therese BRAUN.
>
>   With regard to your enquiry for the above named, we deeply regret to have to inform you that Mr. and Mrs. Braun were deported on 8.11.41, from Hamburg to Minsk and have not returned to Hamburg.
>
>   We can assure you, however, that we will continue the search for them, and if we have any further information we will pass it on to you immediately.
>
>   Yours sincerely,
>   JEWISH REFUGEES COMMITTEE
>   Search Department.

Letter to Martha's sister Margot informing her about the deportation date of their parents

JÜDISCHE GEMEINDE IN HAMBURG
Körperschaft des öffentlichen Rechts

HAMBURG 13, den 19.12.55.

Unser Zeichen Li/Se

Frau
Martha Braun
2 Bispham Grove,
Hr Broughton,
Salford 7.

Wir bestätigen den Empfang Ihres Briefes vom 9.Dez. und bedauern Ihnen mitteilen zu müssen, daß wir keinerlei Unterlagen besitzen, aus denen hervorgeht, wo Ihre Eltern zuletzt gewesen sind. Wir können lediglich bestätigen, daß Ihre Eltern am 8.11.1941 nach Minsk deportiert wurden.

Wir möchten Ihnen noch anheimstellen, sich evtl. mit dem Internationalen Suchdienst, Arolsen, Krs. Waldeck, in Verbindung zu setzen.

Hochachtungsvoll
JÜDISCHE GEMEINDE IN HAMBURG
i/A:

Letter advising Martha that the Jewish community of Hamburg have no information regarding the last address of her parents

APPENDICES

FIRST INTERVIEW WITH MARTHA BRAUN

Edited transcript, interview conducted via Zoom 18/8/21

Interviewers: Albee Kava and Leon Duval (Martha is in Manchester at the home of her friend Marjorie Nadler. Albee and Leon are in Israel. During the interview Martha was accompanied by Marjorie.)

Albee and Leon introduce themselves and explain to Martha that they are both guides at the history museum of Yad Vashem, the World Holocaust Remembrance Centre in Jerusalem. They explain to Martha how important it is for her story to be documented. Martha responds by saying, "Not anyone I know ever asked me about it (her story)," to which Albee and Leon reply, "We are going to make up for that today, because you will be shocked at how many people will be interested."

AK: We'd like to start from the beginning. Can you tell us about your family, the city where you were born and something about your earliest memories.

MB: I was born on the 19th July 1926 in Hamburg. My parents' names were Daniel and Theresa Braun.

AK: Did you have siblings?

MB: I had a sister, Margot, she was eighteen months younger, born 18th December 1927.

AK: Was she on the Kindertransport with you?

MB: Well, I'll tell you what happened. Me father was the youngest of eight, he had family *(brothers)* in England, quite a lot of family but much older. The family in England were already all grown up with children much older than us, not even teenagers already in their 20s and 30s. My father kept saying we are going to get to England. Anyway, *(one of)* his brothers did everything he could for him, my father was an upholsterer, he made furniture. This brother got him a place to work and then he *(my uncle)* goes on the bus from Manchester into the town and he died on the bus; that was the end of that. His brother got everything ready for him *(but then, we couldn't go)*.

AK: What year was it that your uncle died and what was his name?

MB: It was either 1936 or 1937, his name was Morris Braun. There was another one who died, Solly Braun. Anyway eventually, we came over in May 1939, my sister and I, the two of us on the Kindertransport. Have you heard of Reverend Carlebach, the Uber Rabbiner Carlebach from Hamburg? Well, his wife, she was amongst the nurses that took us over, two hundred children at once, and she took us as far as London and then she went back to her family. Then we had to get from London to the train to Manchester and that took us in those days five hours. We arrived about eleven at night. We had big labels on the front of us, our name and the address *(we were going to)* because we couldn't speak English. My uncle met us at the station, it was about ten past eleven at night, he spoke good

German, he never forgot it. So, we were alright *(because we could talk to him)*.

AK: Martha, forgive me, I'd like to just go back a little bit to when you were leaving Germany. We would like to know what you remember as a young girl of twelve saying goodbye to your parents. When did you expect to see your parents again? Did you ever see your parents again? What was it like when you boarded the train with your sister? What was it like with the group of children you were with? Could you go back to that period of time?

MB: I can go further back, to 1937, it was July near to my birthday. My father bought a big scooter for me and other toys, and he stuck them under the settee; and the Nazis came, they were all over the road, shouting about Jewish people, it was terrible, and I was frightened, and was going under the settee *(to hide)*, and my father said ooh you mustn't go under there. I says why? You can't 'cause there's toys there! That was one of the occasions, and they *(the Nazis)* were marching in the street and were shooting, and fetching people out of their houses. I don't know where they were taking them to, I can't even tell you that, I don't know, I was only about ten years old in those days. About coming to England, well me mother got a letter that we were going to leave on the 21st May 1939 to come to England, it was my mother's birthday but we couldn't alter the date, no way. So, we did go, we went to the station, and we *(were told)* not to kiss one another, not to hug one another, and we must get on the train and not go near the window and don't wave. We had our names on us with a ticket *(and)* where we were going, and everything like that. There was a hundred of us, I was twelve, and most were just under twelve and one or two were about sixteen. We travelled up to Holland, slept overnight on a boat; that was alright and I think we had something for breakfast. Then we were taken to London. We all had to wait in a great big hall while people were calling for us, then just four were left, that were my sister and I and another two children, we were all going to Manchester, on our own, without any language we knew, and nobody with us. We got there though.

AK: When you left Hamburg when were you expecting to see your parents again?

MB: I don't know. Oh, I said soon, I hope soon otherwise I am not going. I was very stubborn. I said soon, it's choking me up now, *(Martha is having difficulty expressing herself because of emotion overwhelming her.)* I said I am not going without you. So, they said, well you've to go, you and Margot have to go.

AK: Did your parents explain to you that this had to do with the fact you were Jewish?

MB: Oh, I knew I was, I knew all that from school, because I went to a Jewish school, actually I came from Altona which is outside Hamburg, and we went to school for about three years there and when I was nine, we moved to Hamburg to my grandfather's. He was very religious and we went to a girls' school in Hamburg. But we only went for two years and then the Nazis came and chucked us out and we had to go to the boys' school which was right near where I lived. We went there for about six months and after that I came to England. In the meantime, they were throwing stones at us we couldn't play in the street, couldn't go into a shop, it was terrible.

AK: Did you wear anything on the street that identified you as a Jew?

MB: No, not in those days. When I came to England my mother wrote to say she had to wear a J on her cardigan. No, we didn't, funny enough, but we had to have an injection before we came, can't remember what for, an injection in our arm, something that was going about, we were alright though.

AK: Considering your background and the fact that you stayed at your grandfather who was religious and your parents…*(at this point Martha interjects)*

MB: Very, very religious, he went to the synagogue every week, never missed at all on Friday night. On the morning, we left, my mother said what do you want for breakfast? And I said I'd love an egg, so we had a boiled egg and me grandfather, we lived with him, comes into the kitchen and says to me mother, Theresa, how can you send your children without you? *(Martha is having difficulty expressing herself because of emotion overwhelming her)* She says, well I am trying to save their lives. *(LD interjects at this point saying "that is a very powerful memory", and Martha continues.)* He banged the door then, and we never saw him again. He was seventy-six, very, very, religious; every morning he put tefillin on. And he was a clever man, he worked, had a printing works in Hamburg with his wife. I never met me grandma, she died, that's why I've got her name. They had six children, four girls and two boys, four of them went to concentration camps. I tell you, my cousin Marion, she was two years younger than me, she went to the same school, and the Nazis came one morning and they said, is Marion Bierman here? They said yes, and they called for her, and put her on a wagon, she was six years old, and she had to go on a wagon to our house where we lived in Dillstrasse Hamburg and her parents were waiting to go to Poland, that was terrible.

LD: That was the expulsion of the Polish Jews?

MB: Yeah, that was either 1937 or 1938.

LD: It was in 1938.

MB: Not long afterwards my mother sent them a case of some stuff. I don't know where she *(cousin Marion)* went, they *(she and her family)* never came back.

AK: Were your parents of Polish origin?

MB: They were German, but my aunties' husbands they were both Polish and that's why they were sent, my father and mother were born in Hamburg both of them....

LD: *(interjects)* And your grandfather, Martha, was also from Hamburg, born in Hamburg?

MB: Yes, and he had a good printing works, he did everything in Hebrew, he was a very religious man. *(Martha then tells us about things she took on the Kindertransport that reminded her of her grandfather.)* Mother sent with us four teaspoons, two tablespoons, and a knife, everything in silver. He *(grandfather)* always had silver when he got married and he had his names put on, initials SN, his name was Nissensohn, Siegmund *(and his wife's name)* Martha.

LD: Your memory, Martha, is incredible; I just want to tell you that.

MB: You can ask me any question; I can remember only I get choked up, that's the problem.

AK: Take your time, we get choked up as well listening to some of this. So, you take your time and the three of us will get choked up together!

MB: We had the most wonderful toys as children. Up to the age of about seven I had everything you could think of, sledge, prams, skates, swings, everything; he was that kind of a man. He loved having photographs taken of us, we had school photographs, we had all sorts of things like that, we were short of nothing up to the age of eight, then it started!

AK: When you left were you sent with photographs of your family that you keep to this day? Do you have those documents?

MB: *Martha responds with an affirmative saying she has photographs with her and then proceeds to hold some of these up to the camera. One of these is a photograph of the two memorial stones placed outside her parents' home in Hamburg, one in memory of her father and one for her mother. The stones are engraved with this message:* "Here lived Daniel Braun born in 1883, deported to Minsk 1941, murdered. Theresa Braun born in 1887, deported to Minsk 1941, murdered".

AK: So those were put by the government in front of the building where you lived?

MB: Yes, I've been back *(to Hamburg)* four times; I've seen them and I'm in one photograph. You've got to polish them up, *(the memorial stones)* I did. Now this is the whole family of me mother's side at a Bar Mitzvah, I'm not in it, we were in bed. *(MB then shows another photograph of a very large family group.)*

AK: What year was that photograph taken?

MB: Around 1937. That was the family, everybody Jewish of course; and me grandfather in the middle, right in the middle between the girls.

AK: Did any of them *(the people in the family photo)* survive the war beside yourself?

MB: *Martha's initial response to this is,* "No, only Margot and myself." *She then corrected this saying:* I am telling you a lie. This girl *(points to someone in the photo)*, let me tell you about her. Her name was Carmen and she was seventeen. She worked for a solicitor learning to type and all that sort of thing, a German solicitor not Jewish. And he says "Carmen, I am very fond of you, I know your father *(Herbert Friedberg)* is in concentration camp, I'll see what I can do for you, I'll try and get him out. If you are able, would you and your mother *(Paula Friedberg née Nissensohn)* go to Brazil?" "Oh yes, we will," she says, "anywhere, to get out." So, he got them out, they went to Sao Paulo in Brazil. They got the father out of concentration camp eventually, and the family went to Brazil. Eventually Carmen got married and her son, who is now about forty-odd, he got in touch with me from Sao Paulo.

LD: And those are the sole survivors from that photograph?

MB: Yes, that's it, the girl, Carmen, the mother Paula, *(sister of Theresa Braun)* and the father Herbert, those are the sole survivors. *(Martha then moves on to another story from her youth.)* Did you know about Reverend Carlebach, I can tell you his story, I've got a big paper about it. Did you know about him from Hamburg, the Uber Rabbiner, Dr Carlebach. He had nine children I went to school with one of the girls. She stopped at our house, I stopped at hers. *(She lived)* in a very big house in Altona and he, Rabbi Carlebach, was very well known. Eventually he went to Hamburg, you had to go to Hamburg, and the whole family moved to Harris Strasse in Hamburg. We *(Rabbi Carlebach's daughter and Martha)* still kept on *(as)* friends. His wife *(Rabbi Carlebach's)* took us to England and then she went back again. *(returned to Hamburg). Martha then began telling us about the fate of this Carlebach daughter who was her friend but her explanation was not clear. Apparently, she was sent to Israel, lived in Tel Aviv and became some sort of teacher in an institution for which Martha did not know the name. Our subsequent research suggests that possibly Martha was referring to Miriam Carlebach who became head of the Carlebach Institute, Bar Ilan University.*

Martha then continued to tell us what she knew about the history of the Carlebach family.

At home there was three children left with Dr Carlebach and his wife. They took them into the woods and they shot them one by one, got a paper about it.

AK: I want to ask you before we move on to your life in England as a young teenager. What did your parents do to try to get out, or were they just trapped, they couldn't get out?

MB: Well, my mother wouldn't leave her family, she wouldn't leave her father on his own. Me father kept saying I've got my family in England *(a brother the one who she told us died on the bus in Manchester).* They *(her parents)* tried to get out about 1938, that was a bit late, they couldn't no way. So, my mother says well, we'll send the children. My grandfather was annoyed, they got in a real argument he banged the door; *(he said)* "You can't send the children to a strange country, you can't do a thing like that. I know they are relations but they don't know them." Anyway, we went.

AK: What was the fate of your parents, do you know?

MB: They went to Minsk I've got it in black and white, I have it in writing.

LD: What happened in Minsk, how long were they there?

MB: That I don't know, I can't tell you, they died in Minsk that's all I can tell you, concentration camp.

AK: In your childhood when was the last time you heard from your parents?

MB: It's on a little letter.

AK: *Returning to Martha's travel experience from Hamburg to England.* Tell us what happened. So you get to England?

MB: I went to England; I was with one cousin. Me uncle, he could speak German very well so we got on alright. *(Isadore Braun who had also moved to England. Martha boarded with his daughter Ella who was married to Ivan Ruby.)*

AK: Were you frightened on the journey?

MB: No, I wasn't frightened, I don't know why I wasn't frightened. There was a hundred of us, I didn't like it, I was crying a lot. I got over it eventually and when I got to London me uncle was waiting in the station at eleven at night. They were slow, the trains, five-hour journey to Manchester. I went to one daughter *(Ella Ruby)* who was married with a boy of four *(Robbie)*, and me sister went to the other daughter *(Leah Steen)*. Now they *(the two sisters)* were well off, they had cars, not second-hand ones. One stood *(at the)* markets, *(Ivan Ruby)* the other one had a factory making clothing and later air force clothing or army clothing *(Morris Steen)*. I wanted to learn English and get to school, so I went to school for six weeks but I couldn't speak much English. Then *(Auntie Ella)* says, "Oh you are not to go to school again, you are going to do housework and help me in the house." And that was the end of my learning. But I said I would like a job. "No I don't need you for a job you can stop at home and do housework." I never had a job, ever, till I got married. I never had a job at all ever! And Margot was the same.

AK: These were your relatives who said to you, you don't go to school?

MB: Well, it was war time. You must remember the war started September 3rd and school finished the end of July in summer. So, I never went back to school. I was four weeks in school before July and I couldn't speak English, I couldn't do anything at all because I couldn't read.

Martha abruptly switches the situation here and tells us about one of her earlier experiences with cousin Ella. She (Ella) says, "I want you to go to the shop and get me some flour." I heard of flour so I come back with a bunch of flowers. "I didn't say flowers, I meant flour," *(she said)* she meant baking flour! Served her right, I never forget that; I was only twelve then. It was my cousin but I had to call her Auntie. And then, she put all the food in the middle of the table and said, "Yours is at the side," because mine was margarine, theirs was butter. Mine was always different to theirs.

AK: Why was that?

MB: *Martha's response was not clear, she appeared to say was that she did not know why, but her food was always put on the side, away from the food in front of Ella's family. Her food included bread and margarine, whereas theirs was bread and butter.*

AK: Where you and your sister went, they were relatives? I am not certain if I understood correctly. The people who sheltered you, brought you into their homes, were they relatives of yours?

MB: They were proper first cousins. Where me sister went, they had a maid living in and Margot and this maid they slept in one single bed together and yet, she *(the cousin)* had a front bedroom with furniture not used, never gave her *(Margot)* a room of her own.

AK: Did your sister continue in school?

MB: Well, she had about twelve months but she couldn't talk, she stammered, she started stammering after the first week, couldn't talk at all just stammering. It took her about three years to get rid of it but she didn't do anything at school, she couldn't talk. I never went to school *(after being there)* a month.

LD: It was because of the war, that was the reason why you couldn't go to school?

MB: The reason, she wanted me for the housework, cleaning. I said *(to her)* I've never cleaned before. She didn't like housework; she was a very smart woman with high heels walking around posh and all made up. And she said, "I'll show you how to do housework." I said I want to learn something; I want to earn a bit of money and pay you back for keeping me. Now *(Martha asks us)* would she have got paid to have me do you think, I don't know about that, would she have got some allowance?

AK/LD: We really don't know.

MB: *(Referring to her father's family in England Martha says)* They all died anyway, the whole family on me father's side *(in England)* there must have been about thirty of them, they all died naturally and in fact there is only me living, my sister's died now, I'm from the whole family nobody else. *Given an aunt and her family escaped to Sao Paulo, Martha must have been talking about the family in England.*

AK: Did you have friends when you were an adolescent *(growing up in Manchester)*?

MB: I soon make friends very quickly but I was not allowed out much so the friendships didn't keep long. *Martha then reminiscences about an episode during her childhood.* My mother used to go ice-skating in Hamburg, and so I says to her, "Oh mum, I would love to go." So, she says, "I'll take you." *(When we arrived, the sign says)* "no Jews allowed", so we couldn't go ice-skating. *Martha then shifts to an experience when living with her cousin in Manchester.* I knew where the place was *(the ice rink)* so I said, right after the war I am going to start ice-skating, it's something I always wanted to learn. At the ice rink I made quite a few friends. *Martha then began explaining the circumstances leading to her leaving the cousin's home.* And one of them *(a friend)* said, "You know Martha, you don't look very happy." And I said "No, I am not really," so she says, "I'll find you a very nice home." It took me about two years to make me mind up and this *(new home)* was in Chelmsford, in the country outside Manchester, a good way outside and a lovely couple. They had no children. I left them *(my cousin and her husband)* a note. *Martha then explained how she met up with the couple she was going to live and how she escaped.* I knew they were going to a show in Manchester, this couple and her husband, on the Saturday afternoon. So, I said *(to them)* right I've got one date I can give you if you want to take me, this Saturday. So, I went *(met them and left with them)*. I got to know the people before, they took me for a meal and I got to know them. They owned a garage, they were very comfortably off. I made me mind up yes, maybe I will go, maybe my life will be different; so, I did.

AK: Did your cousin know you were leaving?

MB: Nobody knew, it was a secret, I didn't tell anybody.

AK: Did they come looking for you?

MB: Yes, they did the next morning, somebody's given it away over at skating, where I might have told one of the girls, can't remember, must have done. They *(Ella and Ivan)* came the next morning to the garage. They *(the family she was moving in with name of Black)* had a house in the country, you know it stands on its own ground, a very nice house; they had no children. And my cousin came and said, "Martha you can go to work, you can do what you want, but come back, I'm missing you, I'm missing you a lot and I love you and we think so much about you." She came in the house *(the cousin)*, we let her in. So, Mrs Black said, "No, don't go outside Martha, once you get in the car you will be driven back to Manchester. Don't do it if you want to stay." "Oh, I do want to stay" *(replies Martha)*, so I stayed, and never went back.

AK: Did you stay in touch with your cousins?

MB: No, not at all, and with nobody, only me sister. And she knew where I was going.

AK: And when you think back to them what are your memories like of them? Considering you left the way you did.

MB: They were horrible memories, I was not a bit happy there, I tell you. When there was a meal, they put things in the centre; mine was margarine, theirs was butter, mine was always different to theirs. I said *(to them)* my mother never used to do that when my cousins came, we all had the same! So, they did things like that and that annoyed me to think I am having second *(rate)* food. Well, then they go to markets selling rugs, carpets and curtain materials; so, she says *(the cousin)*, "Right, you can go with my husband to market.". So, I went with him, and it was cold, it was war time, mid-winter, it was terribly cold and she *(the cousin)* used to send sandwiches. Well one day she sent them *(the sandwiches)*, she sent me lung sandwiches, you know what lung is, cats have it, animals, well they were sent for me. And it was beef or some kind of meat for her husband. Well, they were mixed up, I got the beef sandwiches and he got the lung sandwiches! Well, there was a right to do, there was such a row, he says how dare you send me lung sandwiches. "I didn't," *(she says)* "I sent you meat sandwiches." I had them, they were mixed up, I had proper sandwiches, I don't forget that ever. They didn't speak to one another for a week and then they made it up again.

LD: Did you have contact with your parents in the beginning, did they call you at all?

MB: Yes, for two years I had contact, twenty-five words only, and they were typewritten, you couldn't write them but you could sign, put your name. Me parents did the same twenty-five words and the last one, I have kept it, says, "We are moving to Auntie so and so." I knew exactly where that was, Poland, *(it)* means they were going to Poland. My Mutti said to me *(when we left)* read between the lines, you are big enough *at this point Martha chokes up struggling to speak*, read between the lines. I knew that meant they were *(going)* to Minsk, I knew exactly where they were going because her sister went to Minsk, and died of course eventually, with her children.

AK: When you received the last notification from your mother about reading between the lines and then going to Minsk, you were still living with your first cousins. You must have shared the news with them, did they give you support, did they understand *(your angst)*?

MB: No, I never had support, they didn't give any support.

AK: So, you are getting the notification about your parents and their fate, what happened to them. So, emotionally you are very much by yourself or possibly, with your sister, with no support at all from the people that are supposed to be taking care of you?

MB: Me uncle, he was great, but he died and I couldn't do much about that. But when he was alive and he was well he was great. He was more like me father but I didn't know him for long cause he was ill and he died. But me cousins, they were hard, put it that way, they had no feelings. When I got there the first day, she *(cousin Ella)* was looking after her child, he was about five then. I went upstairs and I come down from the bathroom and I was crying she could see I was teary. What are you crying for *(she asked)*. Because I am missing me mum and dad. Oh, you are a big girl, you are twelve years old, what do you mean you are missing your mum and dad. I got told off about that cause I was crying, so that made it worse for me. But when she lost her mother years after, she broke her heart, but I didn't say nothing to her though, no point in me bringing it up, waste of time.

AK: Did you spend a lot of time with your sister at this point? Were you able to support each other?

MB: No, she lived round the corner, I could get there in about three minutes but we did not see each other every day because they would not let me out, and not let her out, every day. We were children then really. We went to school together, well to say for a month we walked to school together, but I couldn't speak English then. And we went to a school, there were four class rooms in one room. I had never seen that before, each corner had so many of the class. I couldn't speak a word, well the odd word, I couldn't converse and Margot, she started stammering and that lasted three years then she got over it. She was what you call a mummish girl.

LD: Have you managed to still remember the German or has it gone?

MB: Yes, I can read and I can talk. I've got one or two German books from school, children's books, I brought them with me, for girls maybe around ten or eleven, two books with me. I've read them over and over again.

LD: How long did it take to learn English?

MB: I should think in six months, not very fluently, but I could speak it because I was living with a family. Mind you, we spoke Yiddish and that's how we got on *(in the beginning)* they could speak a bit of Yiddish you see, but not German.

AK: When you moved on to the second family was that a Jewish family?

MB: Oh, they were English they weren't Jewish.

AK: Were you at all, considering your background, the way your parents raised you, the education that they gave you, the sentiments of your grandfather and your parents, did you have any conflict at all, personal, about the fact that you were now living in a non-Jewish home?

MB: Would I think about it? Well, I did think about it, but I couldn't do anything about it. I still do today *(think about it)* but I can't do much about it. I am married to an Englishman actually but I told him my story *(Martha chokes up)* he said I don't want to know; I want you, not what you are. Yes, he is full of understanding, he was. He was a bit frightened being in touch with you *(to Albee)*, he says, "You know you can't trust people these days." We were very nervous, actually. And Marjorie, I am in her house now, she says, "Oh don't worry about things, they are perfectly alright." Anyway, he is alright today about it and I couldn't wait to get here quick enough. I wanted to get rid of it and tell you all about it.

AK: What was it like when you moved into the second home, you were still an unmarried young woman. You also never not got the education you hoped to get as an adolescent?

MB: No, I got no education at all. I went ice-skating because I loved it and they chose me in a show, not on me own, about ten of us together and I really enjoyed it. I made a lot of friends *(at the ice rink)*. I just couldn't do anything about it *(my education)*. I was happy enough there *(at the ice rink)*.

AK: As Jewish holidays, came *(referring to the time when Martha had moved from cousin Ella to the Blacks)* not necessarily shabbat, like Yom Kippur, Rosh Hashanah, Pesach.

MB: No none of that no, not when you move in with English people you don't have that. I had that in Manchester, yes *(when living with Ella)*.

AK: Were you associated with any kind of local Jewish organization *(when living with Ella)*?

MB: No, they *(Ella)* weren't interested in those days. When I was younger in Manchester, I said I would join Maccabi, a Jewish club. *(Ella's response was)* "Oh no, you're not bothering, I never had a club when I was a youngster, you needn't bother." So, I never got anywhere so I started ice-skating, that's how I met friends, but not Jewish.

LD: This is a very difficult question but I would just like to ask you this. If you had a more supportive environment in Manchester with your family, do you think that would have changed the way your history developed as a person, how you *(personally)* would have developed?

MB: Yes, I think so, I think it would. They *(Ella and family)* weren't religious, I mean they were kosher yes, they went to synagogue on holidays only. They all had a seat but they didn't get me a seat you know; everything was different what I did. *Martha proceeded to explain what happened when she went to the synagogue in Manchester, a place she described as being very beautiful. Her explanation was difficult to follow word for word, it has been edited for clarity.* In the synagogue ladies sat upstairs and men downstairs. I would sit in a seat in the ladies' section and someone would come to me and say, "Excuse me, that's my seat," so I had to get up and find another seat. I shifted from seat to seat. *Martha then switched to another painful memory from the past.* And they were lucky I never had a doctor all the years I was with them, I just didn't have to have a doctor, I wasn't ill!

AK: What has been your work experience, outside of your home?

MB: *Martha's response was that she has no profession, none at all, and then said, skating or swimming, that was my hobby. She then said,* I met Margie, *(Marjorie Nadler)* whose house I am in now, at swimming.

AK: How long did you live with the second family *(the Blacks)*?

MB: Till I got married, twelve years I think it was.

AK: And over the years did you seek out any kind of Jewish organization to get involved in?

MB: No, none at all. I missed that!

AK: Did you miss it, in the sense that you would have liked to join?

MB Yes, I would yes, definitely. *Martha's reply required editing for clarity.* When I was younger, around twelve, I remember that people weren't kind enough to ask you to join in. They wouldn't even ask you to come over and have a cup of tea with the children in their house. When I went to school *(for the short time after arriving)* I was in a Church of England school with six other Jewish children. There were no Jewish schools *(in Manchester)* in those days, it was 1939. I don't know why they weren't friendly enough; they were all well off and all, everyone had a car in those days.

AK: Did you stay in touch with anyone from the Kindertransport?

MB: There was only four *(in Manchester)* and the other two were younger and I didn't know them. They went to the country somewhere, to the grandparents. No, I've not been in touch with anybody at all.

AK: Were you in touch with your sister?

MB: Oh yes, until she died, oh yes, every day, in fact we had holiday together, we did everything together, we had no secrets from one another, very close.

AK: And with your sister, did your sister follow a similar path, or did she somehow stay involved with the Jewish community?

MB: No, she stayed there *(at the Steens)*, she never left, she wouldn't leave, no. *It is not certain what Martha meant because in later comments she told us that Margot was living with other people.*

LD: Did your sister marry?

MB: No, she didn't get married, in fact she wasn't one hundred percent, half the things I am telling you she didn't even know about. Nothing wrong with her, but she wasn't sharp enough. She wouldn't read, she hated reading, so she didn't read anything; and I picked up reading very quickly.

AK: Did you ever celebrate any Jewish holidays with your sister *(when you were)* in your 40s and 50s; *(in other words)* later on in life?

MB: No, *(only)* when I was young when I was living *(Ella)*. *Martha then spoke about the place where Margot boarded with the Steens.* Where she was living, the woman there *(cousin Leah)* was religious to a certain extent, went to shul on Saturday morning. *Martha then changed the subject and returned to her own experience with Ella.* But eventually she *(Ella)* started *(at the)* market, so she left the shul. This is what I call a hypocrite, that's what I called her, that was my cousin. *Martha then proceeded to say this about both cousins.* They were all well off, they owned cars, not second-hand ones you know, new cars, Austen. They weren't that poor, the people I lived with. Eventually they bought a farm, a pig farm of all places, this was two years before I left. So, I had to go, this is in the country two buses away, I had to go and clean the cottage out because a man lived there on his own. So that was my job, cleaning the cottage out in the farm, not for money, eventually she gave me 7s 6d a week; so, I couldn't do much with 7s 6d, couldn't do much with that. I didn't have a good life that's why I ran away.

AK: After you received the news about your parents going to Minsk, did you try to keep in touch with anyone else in the community in Hamburg?

MB: No, I didn't know anyone in those days, nobody at all. And then years after when I got to Chelmsford, I got a letter from somebody who my parents knew, they knew them very well. He was Jewish and she was German but they were married, very happy, and had four children. They asked me to come over *(to Hamburg)*. I was in Chelmsford then *(with the*

Blacks), I had left Manchester, and I said *(to the Blacks)* I'm going to have a week in Germany, do you mind? And they said no, we'll take you to the airport. I went on me own to Hamburg and they *(the couple referred to)* met me.

AK: What was it like to walk back, what was it like to go back to Hamburg?

MB: Terrible, terrible, because I went to the house where I come from.

AK: I am guessing your first time back in Hamburg would have been sometime around the early 1960s?

MB: Yes, it was about 1965, I didn't know anyone then, only the couple I went to. I didn't know them but they met me at the airport, I was on my own, not with my husband. They gave me a lovely fortnight; they made me feel good and they have died since.

LD: Did you ever try to trace what actually happened to your parents in Minsk?

MB: Yes, I did try but all I got to say was they died in concentration camp. I got nothing else. I've even sent photographs but I've never got them back. It didn't matter, I've got more of them.

AK: Martha, I want to ask you a personal question, did you ever have any thoughts throughout your adolescent life, your adult life, did you ever continue to question why your parents did what they did? Do you struggle with the fact that your parents sent you away; is that something you remained angry with them about; is it something you found you had to forgive them for? What was it like when you think about the fact that your parents sent you away?

MB: No, I can't because me mother, she said, "I've got to save the children." She had an argument with her father about it, my grandfather, he was very, very religious, very frum.[88] She says, "Look, Dad, I've got to send them away; I don't think we can come, there is no way we can get over, I can't get any permits, but I've got to save the children and seeing that this Dr Carlebach's wife offered to take them, I'm going to send them." Well, he went berserk and he went and banged the door. me grandfather, he was about seventy-six, oh it was a terrible morning, yeah. And *(at)* the station we couldn't kiss them goodbye and I wanted to ask her one or two questions which I couldn't.

AK: What questions did you want to ask her?

MB: Well, they were personal, a girl's question, put it that way, I was twelve you see, I couldn't ask them, *(Ella)* nothing, no. I've never told this to anybody, never mentioned it to anybody; I mean that's really private, isn't it?

LD: Do you ever think about the terrible burden this placed on your mother having to send her children away?

MB: Oh, I've thought about that many a time, terrible, yes. I *(will)* tell you what they did *(my parents)*. They didn't go home for a fortnight. We had a *(friend)*, German man married to a German woman, elderly, and they lived in a cellar outside Altona. And they *(my parents)* went there for a fortnight. It was cramped in the cellar *(but)* they lived and slept with them for a fortnight, lived with them, couldn't go back home! I had that in a letter, they just couldn't go back home, just couldn't face the empty house, the beds and all the rest of it. This I have in the letter; they were always in German of course. They *(the cousins)*

---

[88] Observant of Jewish laws and traditions.

destroyed them *(the letters)* I couldn't even take them with me when I ran off. I never saw them again. I kept the odd postcard but not the letters, they were in German of course. So, my grandfather was left on his own in the flat, he had to look after himself I suppose, that's all I can think of. *(He)* never cooked before but he must have had to do something. He was a very religious man.

Based on subsequent research we think Daniel Braun was not living in the family home when the girls left Hamburg, he had been sent away to a labour camp at Buxtehede. This makes Martha's account even more heartbreaking because fixed in her memory is an image of her father accompanying them to the train station. Examine her testimony carefully, she talks a lot about how her mother prepared the girls for their journey and for the day of departure, however there is no mention about the participation of the father.

LD: Did you feel any real anger towards the relations you were living with, about the way you were being treated?

MB: Yes, I was very angry but I couldn't do much about it, very angry. That's why I ran away eventually, took me twenty years to run away. They were that strict, never let me out much, so I was very frightened to do it *(run away)* but I made this friend at the ice rink and they persuaded me to do it. I says *(to the friend)* they are not Jewish, *(but)* it doesn't matter who they are so long as I can be happy there.

AK: And were you happy there?

MB: Yes, I was, but eventually, this is very funny. I looked after her *(when she was ill)* and she says to him, "Before I die, buy Martha a car, she is going to learn driving." So, he says, "Yes, I'll buy her a car." She died and he says, "Draw some money out and you can buy yourself a car." That was me own money I drew out so he didn't buy me the car after all that! But anyway, I did learn driving, I passed, and that's how I met my husband eventually.

AK: Do you keep in touch with that family?

MB: No, they've died, they've all died, they had no children. I had a good life, I must admit. The food was perfect and I was very happy there until she died.

AK: Did you have children?

MB: No children, I got married late in life, late 40s, so we never had any children. No, I've got nobody.

LD: And your sister?

MB: Well, she's died, she had no children, she wasn't married. I am the only one left of the whole family and it was a big family, its only me that's left.

AK: What are the lessons in life you would like people to know? You have gone through something very unusual. At the age of eight or nine all this blatant hate coming at you, you see the world coming apart against you and your community. You get shipped away, you wind up with a family where you are not treated very well, you're keenly aware of the fact that you're second-class within that household. You move on to a family where fortunately they seem to have cared for you and treated you well. What would your message be if you had to sum up your life's lessons as to moving on to the next step in life, your attitude.

MB: I'd have loved to have been in a family where there's children. I would've liked to have had children meself actually, because I love little ones. I am very fond of children, yes. It's too late, I am ninety-five, there is nothing much I can do about that.

AK: You look decades younger.

MB: I was ninety-five a fortnight ago.

LD/AK: Happy birthday!!! Where did you meet Marjorie?

MB: I started going swimming with a friend and Marjorie was in the water and she wore a chain around her neck (*Marjorie interjects – a chai*). So, I says to her in the pool, "Excuse me, what is that around your neck, is it a magen dovid," which is what I called it because I had one. She says, "No it's a chai," and I say, "What's that?" And then before she can reply I tell Marjorie, "I am Jewish." "You are Jewish, *(she said)* I can't believe it," and that's how we made friends. But I don't go swimming now, I'm too old, water's too cold, I've stopped going swimming.

LD: It's a very nice story about how you met.

MB: And Marjorie sends me the Jewish Telegraphs with a friend and I've got three at home at the moment and I enjoy reading them.

AK: Was Marjorie your first Jewish friend in your adult life in England!?

MB: Yes, she is. I tell you, the Jewish people never bothered much with me, I must be very truthful, they were cold. I mean they could have said sometimes, "Come in the house and play with me child," or "Have some toffees, have some chocolate." One couple, lived right near us where I lived, there was a Jewish quarter and in this quarter they (*the people living in the quarter*), would see a child and give a chocolate, *(but)* they never gave me a piece. I used to get needled, I was ready for a piece of chocolate but they didn't share it, no. So, I didn't have any Jewish friends there at all until I met Marjorie, I couldn't believe it when she had this thing around her neck.

AK: When you were leaving Germany there are many stories about parents giving guidance to their children as to how they hoped they would conduct their lives and one of the common themes was of course parents telling their children, "Remember that you are Jewish, (and) we want you to have certain values."

MB: Yes, they did that, definitely. But me grandfather was very religious. Every morning, he put on tefillin and all that, every morning, about six o'clock, I think. He didn't go to work because he had his own printing works; and he gave that up years ago. *Here Martha is recalling the time when her parents had moved in with the grandfather probably around 1925.* And he did that *(put on tefillin)* every morning. But it didn't help did it with all that he did, never helped! You know what I mean.

LD: The one thing amongst all the other parts of your story that probably angers me a lot is the fact that the community in Manchester was so cold towards you.

MB: Yeah, very cold they were honestly, I never went to anybody's house.

LD: Many Jewish communities are not like that, it's very, very sad that you experienced it.

MB: Yeah, they were, I couldn't believe it myself. I mean my cousin was just as cold because she never had any friends in the house and I didn't know anybody at all. In our school, it was a church school, class divided into four, one room divided into four classes, ridiculous, I couldn't speak English then. There were four Jewish children going to school besides Margot and I, there were six of us and when it came to morning prayers, we just went out the room because they had an English morning prayer.

LD: Do you think that maybe the community attitude towards you was because you were in the Christian school and not in the Jewish school in Manchester?

MB: There was no Jewish school in those days, no, I don't think there was one Jewish school in Manchester in those days. This is 1939, 1940 even. *Marjorie Nadler interjects at this point saying, there weren't any Jewish schools, my husband went to a non-Jewish school and the Jewish boys there stood against the wall and were sometimes knocked about. He learned to punch very quickly, he learned to fight very quickly!*

LD: Were a lot of children sent away from Manchester, into the country, during the war years. Or, were the children kept inside the community?

MB: No, I don't know that; I can't answer you on that one, I don't know.

Marjorie: They were, a number were sent away because of the bombs, they were sent to the country.

MB: We had an Anderson air raid shelter; we went into that at night.

AK: Your sister stayed with the other cousin, correct?

MB: Yes, but she ran away eventually as well, when I ran away, she copied me, to an English couple not Jewish. She was quite happy there, had a good life. She met the son there, he wasn't Jewish, but she was happy enough. She wasn't married but she was happy enough, she wasn't short of anything.

AK: She stayed involved in the Jewish community?

MB: No, no she met an English boy, we both went with English people, yes, but she had a happy home.

AK: Have you ever visited Israel?

MB: No.

AK: Do you have any desire?

MB: No, I never did have, I was frightened tell you the truth, I was frightened. With suffering so much in Hamburg about Jewish people I thought no, I'm not going to Israel ever. That's the only reason, no other reason.

AK: Any last stories you'd like to share that come to you?

MB: You ask me questions and I might remember better!

AK: I think you must be an extremely strong person, really, from the way you, from the ordeal you went through and the spirit that comes through of who you are. I think you must be a very strong woman.

MB: I would have been happy if I had nice people to live with but they were nasty that's why I ran away, really. She would never let me go anywhere, meet anybody, or go to work and earn a bit of money. I said I would like to buy you some flowers, you know, at the end of the week. "I don't need no flowers; I can buy me own," that's what she used to say. That's a cousin, a first cousin. Anyway, these things happen it's too late now you can't go back.

AK: Well, you have a beautiful smile and a very nice spirit, really, it's amazing. I want to thank you very much. I just want to add that sitting together with Lisa (Marjorie's daughter) several months ago she began to tell me the story of how the two of you met and saying that Martha had had this history of being in the Kindertransport and yet most of her adult life had never associated in any way with Jews or Jewish organisations. I think that it is a very unique story. I think what you went through is a very tough situation as an adolescent and you can see how it all plays out to where life led you, but it was a very unusual story. I thank you; we want to thank you for sharing.

LD: I've got to say that your story is very emotional, I am feeling very emotional about it but you are an inspiring lady and I thank you so much for sharing that with us. It really meant a lot to me, thank you.

MB: Thank you very much for listening. I've never talked to anybody at all, then I've written down my life story when I came to England. I can have it copied and you can see it then. I've got it off my chest, and I've got rid of it now. Thank you for listening and being good listeners.

Second Interview with Martha Braun

Edited transcript, interview conducted via Zoom 23/11/21

Interviewers: Albee Kava, Leon Duval, Tal Hartuv (who is also a guide at Yad Vashem)

Martha is at her home in Manchester, Albee, Leon, and Tal are in Israel. Also present during are Martha's friend Marjorie Nadler and her daughter Lisa Nadler Revivi. Events and impressions documented in the first interview were not recorded in this edited transcript of the second interview.

AK: Several people have read your story and everyone has been incredibly moved by it. You need to know that, it's very special and you sharing it is much appreciated. Now whatever you would like to start with, we would like to hear. What you have been thinking about, anything you didn't emphasise last time.

MB: You ask me questions and I'll answer them.

LD: I just want to make one comment. Martha you should know that Albee and I went to Yad Vashem after he had spent time with Lisa going through the documents you sent us. They are excited and moved by *(your story)*. We want you to know that.

MB: Thank you so much, I have had them *(the documents)* for years and nobody bothered about them.

AK: Well, we are hoping in around three weeks to have a ceremony on Zoom, officials from the museum on one end and you on another. They are going to formally accept your documents and present you with a certificate of recognition and thanks for your contribution to the museum.

MB: Thank you very much, I don't know how to thank you. *Martha then holds up two pictures, one is a perspective of a small town, the other, a large building which she explains is a house.* This is a story about my father *(she explains)*, the town is Buxtehude, a place where they were digging canal. He had to dig them, they lived in two months at a time and he was allowed to come home for one weekend. This was happening when I was still in Hamburg, in 1937.

AK: You remember your father being sent away even while you were living at home?

MB: Yes, I remember it all, he was sent away two months at a time[89] and came home for one weekend and we managed to see him for one weekend. He wasn't the only one, there must have been about twenty to thirty *(other men)* digging canals.

AK: To tie together what we spoke about last time when you described the separation at the train station. Was your father at the train station when you were going away?

MB: Yes. *Martha continued to describe what happened on the day she left Hamburg. The story was documented in the first interview therefore the only dialogue recorded is anything that adds to an understanding of the event.* It was Sunday 21st May 1939, my

---

[89] Martha contradicted herself about the time in another discussion. There, she said it was one month.

mother's birthday, she said how do you want to go to the station? I said I have never been in a car; so, she got a taxi. We went to the biggest station in Hamburg *(Hamburg Hauptbahnhof)* lots of others *(were)* there. We were not allowed to hug, not allowed to kiss our parents, they were not allowed to go near the train. It was eleven o'clock in the morning and straight on to the train. *(We were told)* "Don't go near a window." That was the end of that.

AK: When did your father first start to be taken away for labour?

MB: He was taken away in 1938 early on, January or February until May when we left. *In the previous interview Martha said it was 1937, possibly she got confused with the years because this happened at the end of 1937 just before the 1938 year.*

AK: How did your family support itself while your father was taken away?

MB: I can't answer that, I've no idea.

LD: The building you showed us, was that where they were digging the canals?

MB: Yeah they were living there, I don't know how far the canal was, they were living there in this place probably about twenty to thirty men. *(MB shows photographs of the place where they were accommodated).*

AK: You were very young, did your father describe how many days he worked?

MB: No, I can't tell you that at all, my mother wouldn't let us listen to that, she was very fussy about that, "You are too young to hear things like that."

AK: We want to ask you some questions to clarify some of the things you went through when you came to England.

Your father had several siblings already living in England, correct?

MB: Yes, he had four brothers, all were married with children.

AK: Did you know all your uncles?

MB: No. His favourite brother wrote to him, sending him tickets, but he died on the bus on the way to Manchester.

LD: What was his name?

MB: Morris Braun.

LD: Morris had died before you came to England?

MB: Yes, he died in 1936 or 1937.

LD: When you arrived in London an uncle met you?

MB: No, we arrived in London *(he was not there to meet us)*, there was about one hundred under fifteen years old and one baby of six months who came in a suitcase. I don't know the name of the baby.

LD: When you got on the train to go to Manchester there were four of you, yourself, your sister and two others?

MB: We got to London and then we got a train to Manchester, the four of us with big placards on our front with our name and address where we were going.

LD: When you got to Manchester *(they arrived at London Road Station in Manchester)* an uncle met you there?

MB: Yes, Uncle Isadore.

LD: Was Isadore the father of the cousin you went to stay with?

MB: Yes, I had two more uncles there but I didn't go to their houses.

LD: What was the name of the cousin you stayed with?

MB: Ella Ruby.

LD: Were the (*two daughters of Uncle Isadore*) born in England?

MB: Yes, they were born in England.

LD: What happened to the son *(Ella's)?*

MB: He died about ten years ago.

LD: Did you have anything to do with him?

MB: He came to see me when I got married, only once. I didn't fall out with him.

LD: Did he get married?

MB: Yes, and he had four children.

LD: And you have nothing to do with them?

MB: I don't see them at all.

LD: That's strange that he didn't want to invite you into his family.

MB: The two older children I knew, they went to shul with us when I was in Manchester. But the two younger ones I never knew. When I ran away the others were born later. That's a long time ago.

AK: On your mother's side, her sister Selma was deported to Poland. Was that because she married a Polish Jew?

MB: Correct, (*she was deported*) with three children.

AK: And did you through some kind of documentation, investigate *(what happened to them)*.

MB: No, I know nothing. The only thing is my mother said…you were allowed twenty-five words; this is war time through the Red Cross…And she put on, *(one of the letters)* "We are moving to Tante Zelma," which is her sister; and me mother said, "Read between the lines," she told me that before I come to England, and I knew where they were going.

LD: The twenty-five-word message from your mother, was it a letter or a telegram/telegraph?

MB: It was typewritten, looked like a telegram.

LD: It was probably a telegram, that's why it was only twenty-five words.

TH: This letter/telegram, was it enabled by the Red Cross?

MB: Yes, through the Red Cross, I've got one.

AK: Your sister Margot, you said she began to stammer, that was upon arriving in England?

MB: Straight away, shock, it must have been shock. She was what you could call a mother's girl, she was her mother's baby, she was ten. She lived with her mother, well we both did, but her more than me really. I was a father's one she was a mother's one.

AK: And you remember clearly in Germany her speech was fine?

MB: Absolutely perfect, on the boat, train, we got to Manchester, perfect. The next morning, she was stammering.

AK: And that lasted for several years?

MB: *The response from Martha was confusing because she appeared to be saying that she and Margot spoke Yiddish between them and that is unlikely, they would have been speaking German. I believe what she was trying to tell us is that the two girls spoke Yiddish with the cousins who were unable to speak German.* Of course, she *(the cousin)* couldn't speak German *(and so)* we spoke Yiddish between us, well in a certain way, it's a bit like German Yiddish is. I tell you one thing, she *(Margot)* got to the house, they are people who have a brand-new car, they weren't poor, and they had a maid living in a single room with a single bed. And they put me sister in the same bed with her.

AK: How long did your sister live with them?

MB: Same as me, about twenty-odd years.

AK: And the whole time she had to share a room?

MB: No, the maid had to go in the war, she was called up, then she *(Margot)* had the room to herself.

LD: Did you have your own room?

MB: Yes, I did, I had a very nice room but not very good food, that was the worst of it, I was always hungry.

TH: What did they call you?

MB: They called me Martha.

LD: Could you tell us again the story about the food?

MB: When we got there first night, she *(Ella)* didn't give us anything at all. Where me sister lived, we had a meal there; it was fish, cooked fish. I couldn't eat it was 11.30 at night. *Martha now turns to her experiences at Cousin Ella's.* Me cousin, she used to say, "Look Martha, your food is at the side of you, don't take off the centre table, that is for us." So, mine was bread and margarine, theirs was bread and butter. Mine was always a bit different to theirs. She sent me some lung sandwiches; she sent them twice *(to the market stall where Martha worked with Ivan)*. I had to stand markets with him *(Ella's husband Ivan)*, that was in Hyde market in Manchester, I was about fourteen then.

LD: And when you went and were forced to clean that house when they bought the farm, what happened? Did they give you food when you went there, how long were you working in that place?

MB: I'll tell you about the farm. After the war he'd made some money *(Ivan)*, he sold rugs on the market. I was with him to help sell these rugs; I had nothing to do with the money though. Anyway, he said, "I've enough money, and me wife has a friend whose got a farm; we are going to buy a farm." They bought a farm and it was a pig farm of all farms, one cow, and pigs and hens with a cottage. And this man, a single chap, was living in the cottage. Now me cousin started going out with this single man unbeknownst to anybody else. She said to me, "You're coming out with me to the pictures, *(but)* you're not, you're going in a park, while I go and meet Richard." She was out *(for)* about two hours and I had to meet her back again and come home. So, *(coming back to the farm)* we had to clean the place, the cottage, he lived on his own. He was very untidy, I had to clean the place. I got no money for it and then she gave me half a crown a week, years after. And then up to seven and six but then I left.

LD: How long did it take you, was it a whole day thing that you had to travel to the place, clean and then come back?

MB: I had to get two buses and a walk of about quarter hour in the country, it was outside Manchester, real countryside; it might have built up now. I've not been back for sixty years. It's a long time.

LD: When you were living with the Blacks, did they pay you?

MB: Yes, a wage.

LD: What did you do for them?

MB: Well, I just helped out in the house, ordinary house work, and I went everywhere with them as a daughter, put it that way. I was very much like a daughter but I did help in the house and they included me in everything. I had a very good home. *(Before)* she died she says, "She is learning to drive Sid, buy her a car." So, he says "right" and after she died and things were sorted out, we went to Manchester and he bought me a brand-new car, a Ford, and he says to me, "You can draw some money out." And I says, "You are supposed to buy me the car," which he didn't. I drew money out which I got compensation from Germany.

LD: So, the compensation from Germany came to you, did it?

MB: Yes, it was two thousand *(pounds)* for Margot and two thousand for me. I used one thousand for the car.

LD: And that was all you ever got in restitution?

MB: About four years ago I got another three thousand pounds from America. *(I never got)* no pension.

LD: Your father worked in Germany, didn't he?

MB: Yes, he worked for Otto Nagel in Altona, he made furniture that was his job. There were twelve men working making furniture, and he was sort of the main one in the twelve; he rang the bell at dinner time, I don't know what you would call that.

LD: So let me get this right. In all the time what you got from Germany was a total of four thousand pounds for you and your sister?

MB: *Martha at this point says she can't remember very clearly; it could have been five thousand but not more definitely.* No pension, I tried for a pension, too late. I was in hospital, in the late 50s or 60s I think it was, I had cancer. So, we found out you could get money from Germany. We went to a Jewish chap in Prestwich in England, he said, "I'm afraid you left it too late." I said I was ill and didn't know anything about it, but I never got it anyway. I get no pension at all, English but not German. The

English *(pension)* I only get three-quarters because I didn't have a job, I didn't pay stamps. She says *(cousin Ella)* to me, "Martha, I'm keeping you, I am not paying any stamps, you don't have to pay any stamps for you." That was me cousin. So, I never paid stamps, so now I get three-quarters of an English pension, that what I get.

LD: Can I ask you about the family in Sao Paulo, that was your mother's family?

MB: Me mother's sister's husband was taken to concentration camp in 1938 while I was there in Hamburg. Their daughter, she was about sixteen or seventeen, worked for a German solicitor and he was very fond of her; her name was Carmen. He says, "Carmen, I can help you, I'll try and get your father out of concentration camp, I am well in with people and I'll get him to Sao Paulo." (She replied) we would do anything to get out of the country, and they did. So, two days before we came to England me mother's sister and daughter went to Sao Paulo in Brazil.

LD: And you've had some contact with them, you actually met up with them?

MB: I met up with them about 1967, I went to Hamburg on me own, I wasn't married then, and I met them. They've died since.

LD: And what about children, are any children alive at all?

MB: They had one daughter, now she's died since as well. She had two sons that I've been in touch with. One rings me up, he's got two children, girls, Jewish, they keep Jewish, they *(went)* to Jewish schools. They are older now, one goes to university, and one goes to school. But they are in touch with me, not very often but they are in touch.

LD: Was your grandfather also deported to Minsk or did he die before your parents were deported?

MB: No, he was sent to Theresienstadt.

LD: And did he die there?

MB: Yes, he must have done.

LD: And his surname was Nissensohn?

MB: Yes, he had a Jewish printery in Hamburg. He had a printing works; he did a lot of things for the Talmud Torah Schule in Hamburg.

LD: It does make sense that he went to Terezin because they did send a lot of the older people *(German Jews)* there.

MB: He was seventy-four or seventy-five when I left him.

LD: What was the name of the Carlebach daughter that you were friendly with, *(the one)* who went to Israel?

MB: Her name was Ruth. *(It was later established her name was Carmen, Ruth never went to Israel.)*

AK: Just out of curiosity, you mentioned that you had two favourite books you kept from Germany, that you came to England with, and you would read them over and over again. Which book, and what story was it?

MB: About schools really, about four girls in a club going swimming, skating, and things like that.

AK: It's a child's book about friendship?

MB: Yes about eight- or nine-year-olds.

AK: And you still have them?

MB: *Lotte and the Club of Four* (*MB translates the title*), that is one of them, the other *(is called) I Remember When I Was Four*, something like that. I've not read them for a long time but I still have the books. I have a posy book, that means you write your name, schoolfriends put their names in, an autograph book, yeah. I've got that. Me grandfather even wrote in that, me parents and me school friends, it was a Jewish school I went to.

AK: I want to ask you some personal questions and while I know I might be crossing a line here, forgive me. If you are not comfortable answering I certainly understand *(MB interrupts, I am very comfortable)* I am not comfortable asking but we so want to know the details of your story, I am compelled to ask.

AK: Here is the first question. Your neighbours today, your circle of friends besides Marjorie, the people in the neighbourhood you say hello to, the people you pass every day, maybe people when you go shopping, we all have common faces in the neighbourhoods we live in. Any one of them aware, or identify you, or do you identify in front of them as a Jew?

MB: No, not where I live now in England, in Wilmslow.

AK: Is that intentional?

MB: The odd one does know, but they don't bother.

AK: I mean, before I came to Israel, I had neighbours in a community in the US and I generally knew the backgrounds of people even if I wasn't close with them. So, the question is, do you intentionally, is it your intent, that you don't want people to know you are Jewish?

MB: Oh no, not like that at all, they know I came from Germany as a Jew. I don't hide that, no use hiding that.

AK: As a family with (your husband), do you attend the Anglican Church?

MB: Not really, we don't go to church and I don't go to shul either. I have been to church but very rarely. I did belong to a club in Wilmslow, an English club in a church, but I left it about two years ago.

AK: When Jewish holidays came around, you talked about celebrating them with Margot, were these British (public holidays) or Jewish or both?

MB: No, Jewish.

AK: So, until Marjorie's passing you would celebrate Jewish holidays with her?

MB: No, not then, definitely not. When I moved to Chelmsford, when I moved out of Manchester, I never had any Jewish holidays at all.

AK: So, you really haven't celebrated Jewish holidays for....?

MB: No, none at all for sixty years, I was brought up very religious (*however*). No, I've not spent a seder, me grandfather used to do that, oh it was wonderful that was. I can still say Mah Nishtanah, I know it all, me sister couldn't say it, I had to say it, I could read Hebrew.

AK: *Edited for clarity.* I have another very personal question, I apologise before I am asking it, I know I am crossing a line but it's things we want to know about you, intimate things, *(that are)* meaningful to you. My parents were both Holocaust survivors, my father had a number on his arm, he came out of Auschwitz; he was liberated at Dachau. My mother was a partisan, underground fighter. Before my parents passed, I had an idea of what they wanted the world to know about them and so I, knowing what was important to them when they were buried, created a tombstone for them. On the borders of my parents' tombstones are the names of their siblings. On my mother's tombstone it says she was a partisan survivor, and on my father's, that he was a Holocaust survivor. So, with that background I'm going to ask you this. We all ponder thoughts about our mortality and so, *(I want to ask)* if you have considered whether you want to be *(buried)* in a Jewish cemetery, or if it *(is something that)* doesn't matter. Do you want to be marked as a Jew so that in the future people will say, "Martha was Jewish, this was important to her"? *(I am saying)* how important is this considering the tragedy of your life, and how you led your life. Again, I apologise, I know I am entering personal ground, but if you could just expound that a little bit, it would really give us a great insight as to how you see yourself today.

MB: *(A bit taken aback)* I don't know how to answer you. *(Marjorie interjects)* When you die, where do you want to be buried, *(or)* do you want to be cremated?[90]

MB: Cremated. Me sister was cremated. *(Marjorie explains)* Margot's ashes were taken out to sea by the Royal National Lifeboat Institution. *(Martha continues)* Margot was living with people associated with that organization, *(her cremation and scattering of ashes)* was five years ago.

AK: Is that how you envision a final resting place?

MB: I'm not really *(sure)* I was surprised when that happened to her. *(Marjorie then asks do you want it to happen to you and Martha responds)* Oh, I am not bothered at all. *(Marjorie asks again, do you want to be buried in a Jewish cemetery, it would have to be paid for and done and Martha responds)* I can't answer you honestly, I'm ninety-five. It would be left to my husband.

AK: Well, no, it is really left to you. Would it be important enough in your framing of yourself? Would it be important to say, I was a Holocaust survivor? Because you are!

---

[90] Cremation after death is against traditional Jewish law.

MB: Yes, I would, yes. Like you say, I am a Holocaust survivor, of course, yeah.

LD: It's a very deep question, I think we are going to leave you with that question. Your story is so important and it needs other people to know about it. We are thinking of two possibilities and we need you to think about it and give us approval. First, we had a thought that because your story was initially a children's story that we would try and write a children's book around your experiences and your life. Tal, who is a very talented artist, will also illustrate that book. It will be Martha's story aimed at children ten to eleven years old, telling what it is like for a young girl of twelve to be put in a train and sent away from her family. The other thing that we would like to do is to write "Martha's story", and we would like to put that in a place where people can read it, exactly where, we are not sure yet. None of this would be done without your approval and nor would we do anything until you had seen what was written.

MB: You've got my approval, definitely.

LD: Thank you, we will begin doing something on that; and anything, before it goes to any public place, will come to you so you can look at it.

MB: Thank you very much, thank you for thinking about things like that.

AK: And when you went off to England and your parents went through this terrible period where they couldn't even go home.

MB: They stopped a fortnight in Altona. She (*referring to the people the parents stayed with*) was Jewish and he was German; but they were a wonderful couple we've known them forever, since I was small. And they *(Martha's parents)* lived in a cellar, the cellar is still there.

AK: Do you have letters your parents might have written to you from there describing their loneliness.

MB: No letters from there, no. I've a lot of postcards but not from there.

AK: When did you first understand or learn about where your parents had gone, spent a month in this cellar.

MB: Me mother wrote me that. She didn't say cellar, she just said with Auntie so and so. I knew, my mother had said "read between the lines".

AK: Do you have any of the letters or postcards describing that?

MB: No, they destroyed them all. Me cousin *(Ella)* said you're not keeping these letters, she took them off me, destroyed them. First cousin! I had to call her Auntie, much older than me. When I got there the first week, she is bathing the child, I come down the stairs and she says to me, "What's the matter with your eyes, you look as though you've been crying. Big baby, crying *(because)* your mother's not here." That hurt me a lot. That's the first week, a big girl of twelve crying for her mother. I can't talk, it chokes me up.

LD: *(Holding up a picture)* Martha is this Miriam Carlebach, the one who went to Israel?

MB: Yes, Miriam, that's her name, I was friendly with Ruth, her sister.

LD: She *(Miriam)* did very well here, she was in charge of an Institute named after her father.

MB: Yes, I've got that in black and white, I've got a letter from her. She kept writing to me then she lost her eyesight and couldn't write and read anymore. So, then we lost touch about five to six years ago.

LD: She is so well known, here in Israel. The letters she wrote to you are very important historic documents.

MB: Don't know if I've got all of them, have to have a look through.

MB: I'll tell you the story of the three younger ones *(Carlebach children)*. They went to the woods and they shot them; Reverend Carlebach and his wife, the three younger ones, one was my age maybe eleven or something like that, and two younger ones. They shot them one after another in front of the parents, and then they shot the parents.

AK: *Edited for clarity. AK had asked Martha about the photograph she had shown us in the first interview, the one taken at the family bar mitzvah.*

MB: *(The whole family was there)* bar me sister and I; we had to go to bed, we were too young. (*The photo was taken)* in our house, the clock is there. It was taken in 1937, the time was 12.15pm.

LD: When you got married was it a large wedding?

MB: No *(not)* a large wedding at all, it was in a registry office in Macclesfield. And *(then)* about six miles away in a café, we had about fifteen people for lunch.

LD: And I understand you got on extremely well with your husband's parents, that in fact your mother-in-law came to live with you.

MB: Yes, for twenty years she lived with me. Her husband died and I said you are not living on your own in the country in a cottage, I says, you are coming to live *(with us)*. I've got a bedroom to spare, we've got only two bedrooms, you have the second bedroom. And she lived with us for twenty years and we got on wonderfully well, no arguments ever, no words, none; and she knew I was Jewish. She was very religious, a religious church woman.

LD: It's very amazing that you managed to do that because it's not easy that sort of relationship; it's a great compliment to you.

MB: I wasn't happy at me cousin's, she was nasty with me always, till the very end.

LD: Was it difficult for you to make that break?

MB: It was at first because it wasn't a Jewish house you see. *(Marjorie interjects what he is asking you is whether it was difficult for you to run away?)* It was done underhanded because I knew they were going to see a show in Manchester, in the Palace, me cousin and his wife. So, I rung up my friends and I said this is the only day I can go without them seeing me and that's how I went. It was a Saturday afternoon and they *(friends of Martha that she met at the ice rink)* called for me in the car.

LD: How old were you?

MB: I think I was thirty then or twenty-nine when I ran away. *(I had)* no mind of me own when I ran away, bossed about, I was a coward, I just didn't leave the house. But that day they *(Ella and Ivan)* were away and I phoned them *(the Blacks)* in Chelmsford where I was going and told them I was coming and I was there ever since.

Marjorie: Who arranged for you to go to Chelmsford, was it the girls that you were skating with?

MB: No, I had *(a friendship with)* a lovely couple, he was an instructor at the Ice Palace, and he and his wife got very fond of me. They said, we will help you to go somewhere to have a good home, and they did. They took me to Chelmsford this particular day, 1960, in February.

Marjorie: So, they were the ones that persuaded you to go?

MB: Yeah but they've both died now.

LD: Martha, when I transcribed the last interview, at times I was so emotional that I had to stop. I felt your pain.

MB: I don't believe it. I've never found anybody with a lot of love *(that)* they give you a good hug and all that.

AK: Oh, we'll give you a good hug as soon as we see you!

MB: Marjorie has been a wonderful friend; I know I don't see her that often but I'm in touch with her.

Marjorie: We did swim together but that's *(ended now)*.

MB: I stopped swimming about four years ago because it was too cold, the water, but I was a good swimmer. I liked gym, that was my hobby and skating, that's how I met everybody, skating. That's how I come to move to Chelmsford and then got married. I just enjoyed it. Me mother was teaching ice rink. We went to Hamburg, she said I'll take you skating, this was in 1936. So, she took me to the rink right near the school where I was. They said you're Jewish, no Jews come here to skate. So, I didn't go. That was the end of that; but she went as a youngster herself because she was born in Hamburg.

LD: Tell us about the time you were chosen to be in the show.

MB: I soon picked it up *(the skating)*. But I wasn't the main one, I was in the chorus, there was ten of us in the chorus. I've got a photo of that. I enjoyed that but they *(Cousin Ella and husband Ivan)* wouldn't go and see me at night, it was only on for a week, between seven and nine, but they wouldn't go see me, they couldn't be bothered. I was dressed *(up)* you know, they gave you fancy dresses to put on for the show.

LD: How old were you?

MB: Early twenties, I think, can't remember.

LD: And they wanted nothing to do with this, a really wonderful moment for you?

MB: It was my hobby *(ice-skating)* and I was proud of being picked in the show out of so many girls, and I was so happy about it. But she *(Ella and Ivan)* said, "We are not going to see it." No, they didn't go. I went skating twice a week, wasn't allowed anymore.

LD: You weren't allowed to go out more than that?

MB: No, twice a week, not to go out at night *(they told me)*. That's why I never met anybody and where I was skating there weren't many Jews, there was one or two Jewish but not many. I had a lot of girlfriends but not boyfriends at all, not me.

LD: But you didn't feel that because they were telling you, "You can't go out," that you just didn't care, and would go out?

MB: I didn't answer back, I cried, but I never answered back. My sister would answer back but I did not answer back that was my problem. How I left, I don't know how I did it, February 20 1960 I left; underhanded, they had a note.

LD: Not going back was a very good decision, because it changed your life.

MB: It changed my life. I know *(there were)* no Jewish people *(but)* I had plenty of food to eat, I didn't have separate food, *(at cousin Ella)* mine was always different to theirs.

Marjorie: Where you went skating, the girl who took the lead part *(in the show)* became the head of the Jewish school in

Manchester. She was a relative of yours! (*apparently through marriage*)

MB: Oh yes, my father's nephew had a son and this girl married the son. (*Her married*) name would be Braun.

AK: This was one of your friends when you were skating?

MB: Yes, I didn't know anything about it then but I found out she married me cousin and her name (*became*) Braun.

AK: Did you remain in touch with her?

MB: No, she lives in London now.

TH: Can I ask you a question about skating, it's really fascinating that you like ice-skating. How old were you when you first went skating and how did you get to ice-skate? Did somebody say hey, let's go to the ice rink?

MB: No, me mother, she spoke so much about ice-skating when I was a child. (*And so*) I said (to myself) when the war is over, I am going to start getting a pair of boots, save up for a pair of boots. "Well, you are not going to work, you'll never." (*a comment from cousin Ella*). I says I'm going to save up for a pair, so I got second hand ones out of the paper.

TH: But you went ice-skating before the war as well?

MB: No, no, not allowed to, no.

TH: How old were you when that (happened)?

MB: Was about ten, me mother loved skating, she was a gymnastic teacher and very fond of gymnastics. I was good at that in school, I was top of the class in gymnastics nothing else, and I was good at Hebrew. They opened the Ice Palace in Manchester after the war, up the road from where I lived, only had to take a bus. So, I went once a week to the Ice Palace, I made friends quickly, English friends not Jewish, English girls.

TH: Do you remember any activities that you as a ten-year-old child was not allowed to do, like, if you went to the movies?

MB: We weren't allowed anything, nothing at all, not from ten years onwards. *(MB then repeated the story about the Nazis rampaging through the streets of Altona before her birthday and the toys under the settee where she dashed to hide. The following insight was new though).* They were knocking on doors and they were fetching people out. *(Martha then talks about her father.)* He was the most wonderful father; we had every toy you could think of, prams, scooters, bikes, you name it we had it, not short of toys up to the age of about eleven, and we had to give it all up.

TH: Did you take any toys with you when you went?

MB: No, we weren't allowed anything, not even a doll no, not even a teddy.

TH: And did you remember when you left, did you ever think when you got to England, oh I wish I had that toy?

MB: All I thought about was me mom and dad, didn't think about me toys at all. I brought two books with me, school books, and I still got them.

TH: But obviously you would say your mother tongue is English. What language do you count in?

MB: English better than German, oh yes now. I don't know anybody to speak in German at all round here where I live, there's nobody in German. Yiddish is like German that's how *(I spoke to)* my cousin where I lived, she spoke in Yiddish while I understood a bit cause it's a bit like German but she couldn't speak any German. I went to school for five weeks but I couldn't speak any English then. *(MB then repeats story about the class structure that Marjorie confirms was universal in wartime Britain.)*

TH: *(Referring to the school experience)* That must have been very scary.

MB: Oh, it was very scary and I was always hungry, she didn't give me enough to eat. I want this for me little boy (she would say), he's only a baby, only three. I did pinch a slice, there was sliced bread in the bread bin, before I went to bed, I always pinched a slice of bread, nothing on it, and always took it to bed for a long time, at least two years. Things got better then, but I was always hungry the first two years. I never had a doctor; I was there two years never had a doctor so I didn't know any doctors. Had a dentist but not a doctor, I wasn't registered *(for a doctor)*.

TH: Can I ask you a question about the document you got at the end of the war, about Minsk. When you actually got that as a young lady, when you saw that for the first time, how did you feel in your head? Were you frightened that you couldn't remember what they *(your parents)* looked like, what they sounded *(like)*?

MB: No, no I wasn't frightened, I knew what they looked like, it never left me mind never, nor me sister. We never stopped talking about our mum and dad and I've got a photograph in front of me. *Martha's response here is not clear, but it appears that cousin Ella would not allow public display of the photos Martha brought with her from Germany. So, she hid them in a case in her bedroom.*

AK: Tal, what you asked was so incredibly insightful. Martha, what was it like, if you could put yourself back in 1945, you receive news that your parents were sent to Minsk, we haven't asked that. What is that like for a fourteen- or fifteen-year-old, to get such a letter, that you are never going to see them *(your parents)* again? Its unimaginable!

MB: Oh, it was terrible, and I had to go and tell me sister. She had nothing sent; it was sent to me. I had to go around and tell her; we cried our eyes out. But we knew she was going there, "read between the lines, we are going to Auntie Sel." *This is a direct quote in code from her mother's telegram. It was designed to inform the girls that the parents were being deported to Poland just like Auntie Selma had been deported to Poland when the Polish Jews were expelled from Germany in October 1938.*

TH: So, when you had to tell your sister, none of us can ever imagine what you've been through, do you remember what you said to your sister when you got the news? Did you say...I mean, how did you word it?

MB: "I don't think we will see Mum and Dad again; I don't think so, they've been sent away to Poland," I said. She cried, I wish I'd never said it, but she cried. I didn't show her the letter. I don't remember exactly what I said but *(something like)* she was sent to Tante Selma, because we knew exactly where they were sent. Me whole family were sent to Poland bar me grandfather, he was sent to Terezin, he was seventy-four or seventy-five.

TH: OK you were in England for a big chunk of your life as a girl, right, it's like I know you and your sister spoke about your parents every day. Were you ever fearful of forgetting what they looked like or sounded like?

MB: No, no never. I think about them every day, no I wasn't fearful about that at all, no definitely not. They were really the most wonderful parents.

TH: And when you got that letter the end of the war, you know somebody said the last thing to die is hope, did you, up until that letter was there, *(have)* hope in you. As children we always think our parents are invincible, I think that's natural for every kid, like mum and dad will never die type thing. Was there that hope in you until you got that letter. Or had you like resolved yourself to you *(are)* going to get some bad news. What was your state of mind leading to that letter?

MB: I knew I would never see them again; I was sure of that. When I read Minsk, I knew exactly where they were going because you see me mother had three sisters, one went to Brazil, the other two went to Minsk. So, I knew exactly, she said "read between the lines", so I knew what was going on.

Marjorie: You didn't think they would survive?

MB: Well, me mother's sisters' husbands were Poles as it happened. So, I thought, well they were sent, but me father was German! But they *(my parents)* were still sent just the same.

Marjorie: Did it ever occur to you that they might survive the camp?

MB: No, it never, no it didn't occur to me at all.

TH: So, you as a child, because you are obviously very perceptive, you read between the lines. So, from the moment you know they are in Minsk you know it's not going to end well. But then take that moment when you realise what is happening. What were your thoughts about your parents, what were your memories, what did you like to think, special moments that you remembered, your mom's cooking, was it your dad (*MB interjects "everything" and TH responds and says pick one*).

MB: Everything from the age of about five.

TH: What would be the memories that you as a child, for want of a better word, you indulged in. Like you know your parents are in Minsk, you know they are probably dead, so you as a child are probably thinking wow, I remember how Mummy used to do this or Dad did this. Can you think of a memory that...

MB: From me father, yes. *(Martha recalls her father saying "I want you to go swimming and I'm going to take you to the baths, you are going to have private lessons. I've saved two little girls.")* He saved two little girls at a seaside place we went to, don't think it's there anymore, it's on the Elbe *(River)*. Anyway, he saved two little girls and he said, "When I have children, they are going to learn swimming." So, he took me to the Bismarck baths in Altona, had private lessons for three months. I'd forgotten about that; I picked it up in two months so I could swim. And he took Margot swimming, she wouldn't go, frightened of the water and wouldn't go, so she never could swim.

TH: When did you stop swimming as an adult, you said you stopped only a few years ago.

MB: About three to four years ago because it was too cold.

TH: Let me ask you another question about swimming. As an adult when you are swimming did you ever think about your dad like?

MB: Yes, I do, always do think, he was such a wonderful father, don't think anyone had a father like that, he was marvellous; I never got smacked. I never forget them somehow, never, I just can't forget things; I've got a good memory. When I go to bed I think about things, I go to bed early most nights *(and)* me mind goes back to Germany.

TH: What do you think about exactly, is it a repetition thing, one particular?

MB: All sorts of things about me mum and dad. They were the happiest couple, we never got shouted at or anything like that; I've never seen parents like that; I've never known that.

Marjorie: Did you think about things, about playing or playing outside, playing on your bike?

MB: Well, we could only play up to the age of eight, the Germans stopped us then.

TH: They stopped you from playing outside?

MB: Oh yes but I played with friends, German and Jewish friends. Ruth Carlebach, that was one of the daughters, she lived with us for about two nights many a time, we were very friendly, she played out with me.

TH: You've had your hot toddy, you've had your Scotch and orange juice as they say in Scotland, you're gonna go to sleep. So, you always think about Germany. Are these thoughts about Germany before your head hits the pillow, is it about the good things?

MB: Not the bad things no, I don't think about the bad things, I wouldn't sleep then. The good things definitely. Me sister is the same, we were the same, very close.

TH: If I could push it a little. If you are lying there before you are sleeping and suddenly you have like an unhappy thought about what happened...

MB: Yes, I get that sometimes, I do.

TH: And what do you do in those moments, do you say, Martha I have to think about something else or do you get up out of bed; like what do you do to walk through on....

MB: I don't do anything, I really don't do anything, no. I've never spoken to anybody like this before, no one has ever asked me questions like that about me parents.

TH: It's their loss, we've won the lottery!

Marjorie: They've won the lottery because they are talking to you.

TH: Yeah, we are the richest people in the world at this moment.

MB: Thank you for having me on anyway (*she is quite overcome from the attention*) it does me good to get rid of it; it does me good to talk about it.

TH: Martha you are passing it on, you know, it's your legacy, it's your life. And think of how many people want to hear your story, it's going to be so amazing.

MB: No, they are not interested, the girls I went skating with, they weren't interested!!

TH: Now listen to me, young lady, you thought nobody was interested then you met Leon and Albee and I didn't go on the Zoom last time. I'm so interested, I didn't want to miss this for a million dollars.

MB: Well, you're the first people ever. Marjorie, she was interested, especially with this round her neck; she started it off.

TH: So, Martha, when you say nobody is interested, you mean nobody except for Albee, Leon, Marjorie, myself and Lisa, that's already five, pretty good going.

MB: I'm a coward. The dentist I went to, had toothache when I was twelve not thirteen yet. My teeth were seen to before we come (*this statement seems to have been contradicted later*) and he says (*the dentist*) have you got any money on you, and I says no. I could hardly speak English, I have no money. And he was a Jewish dentist, I understood what he said, and do you know he gave me anodynes and that was it for the toothache. I thought maybe it needed taking out or seeing to but he didn't do that cause I had no money.

Marjorie: Why weren't your teeth seen to before you came to England?

MB: Well, they were Nazis, you see, we couldn't go to the dentist *(after they came to power)*. We went every three months up to the age of eight, every three months me mother took us, she was, and me father was, very strict with dentists. And after ten *(conflicts with the eight previously mentioned)* I didn't go at all. She *(cousin Ella)* let me go on me own to the dentist, she should have gone with me, she didn't. So, he gave me a packet of anodynes. I said, "Auntie Ella will you go with me; I'm frightened, come with me?" *(She said)* "I can't leave me son," he was about four, but she could have left him with someone or take him with her, but she didn't. I never forgot that. This was in 1939.

TH: It's amazing how you remember each year.

MB: No but I do remember that with the dentist. We were evacuated *(1940)* actually *(to)* Bowlea in the country. *(It appears that they stayed on the same farm which the cousins' family bought later.)*

TH: Do you have photos of the places you were in England or not?

MB: No, none of them, but the house *(Ivan and Ella's home)* was a nice modern house, three bedrooms, garden front and back. No photos, they didn't believe in photographs. It was a modern house, they had a new car not a second-hand car, so they weren't poor, were they. Her mother lived right opposite, number one and she *(cousin Ella)* never did any cooking. Her mother was Russian, she left all the food across to us, the meals, the hot meals not the teas. Auntie Ella wouldn't cook.

LD: Her mother was your aunt?

MB: Yes, my father's brother's wife.

LD: And you had no relationship with her?

MB: Oh, I did, she was alright, can't say she was wonderful, but she was alright.

LD: How long after you moved in with this cousin did your uncle die?

MB: Me uncle died about three years after I lived there. He spoke good German and he was like me father; he was wonderful to me. We went to Blackpool, it was a holiday, the whole family in August and we all went, whole family went, and we had a room there. We were there for a week, it was good weather and he says "Martha, I'll take you around the shops," we spoke German to one another, and he bought me a pair of sunglasses, Woolworths, about three pence they were. I come back with them, very excited, and she says, *(cousin Ella)* "What have you let her buy sunglasses for," she shouted at her dad. "I'm your dad, I do as I want, and I bought me niece a pair of sunglasses." There was a whole argument going on the whole day. Anyway, it was forgotten later; over a pair of sunglasses. I was so excited, I was only twelve, children's sunglasses.

TH: Have you read other children's stories about the Kindertransport?

MB: No, I've never seen one at all, no.

The interview ended with Martha saying, "Thanks everyone for having me on, I was so excited overnight."

Notes

Taken by Lisa Revivi during interview with Martha, 3/1/22

Memories of the family home in Altona

Martha recalls this as an old-fashioned building with three stories. In the living room, there was a cast iron stove with a metal chimney attached. She and her sister Margot shared a bedroom which was furnished with one wardrobe. Martha also remembers that the beds they slept in were like big cots because there were bars around the four sides.

Schools and schooling Altona

Martha recalls attending a kindergarten situated adjacent to the Great Synagogue of Altona.

Her lower school in Altona was around a ten-minute walk from her home. Martha remembers walking to lower school with her Mutti but returning home on her own. The school day ended at 12.30pm.

Memories of life in Altona

Martha says that her parents were very cuddly and warm, they always kissed the children goodbye when they sent them to school.

Martha remembers that she had between eight and nine non-Jewish friends. They would play together in the street because most families did not have private gardens.

Martha says that after Hitler came to power in 1933 these non-Jewish friends refused to play with Jewish children and some of them would even throw stones. It is not known if this occurred immediately, or after a period of time. When Hitler came to power Martha was six and a half.

When this began Martha said that she was afraid to go to school and so their Mutti always walked them.

Martha also recalls that when she was around eight years old (1934) the non-Jewish children in the neighbourhood would shout, "You are Jews, we don't play with Jews."

Martha recalls an incident which we cannot date nor verify. She insists that it happened after Hitler was made Chancellor. Nazis were running amok through the streets of Altona shooting and yelling "Juden Raus". The girls started crying and ran inside the house. Their parents immediately shut the front door and hugged their terrified children. After the riots the girls didn't go to school for around four days because they were scared. When they did eventually leave the house, she says there was broken glass everywhere.

Memories of the family home in Hamburg

Martha's family relocate to Hamburg around 1935 to 1936. Martha is ten years old, Margot between eight and nine.

The address of the apartment they move into is Dillstrasse 15 in Hamburg's Grindel quarter. The apartment is on the second floor of the building and Martha does not really recall how many rooms it had. Martha's grandfather Siegmund Nissensohn, by this time a widower, had moved into this apartment and the Braun family moved in with him.

Martha recalls that the girls shared a room, and that the beds they slept in were normal, without bars!

Schools and schooling Hamburg

School was six days a week. Jewish children studied on Sunday instead of Saturday. That's how people knew they were Jewish. Martha stopped taking her satchel because people would know she was going to school on a Sunday and therefore was Jewish. She felt ashamed to show she was a Jew.

Memories of life in Hamburg

Martha recalls signs on shop windows saying no Jews allowed. Because of this Martha said that she doesn't know how her Mutti was able to buy food.

Daniel and Theresa were very particular about the dental health of the children, however Martha recalls that because of the situation Jews were confronting in Hamburg she was unable to go to the dentist after the family moved there.

Martha was twelve years old on the 9th November 1938, the start of Kristallnacht. She says that there was no school for three months afterwards and when they did go back it was to the boy's Talmud Torah school. Martha also insisted that after Kristallnacht the sisters had to wear a Yellow J about four inches long sewn on to their coat sleeve. They were not allowed out without it. She also recalled that when the girls went to England their Mutti made sure that they did not take the coats with "J" on them. *(This memory appears to be in conflict with the historical facts.)*

Jewish traditions in Martha's family

Martha couldn't follow prayers in synagogue and used the time she was in attendance to catch up with friends. Although she was unable to follow the service Martha says that she could say the Shema Yisrael.

Martha remarked that her Mutti was fully conversant with the content of the Jewish prayer books and able to follow the synagogue services.

Martha did recall that when she was in the synagogue, she remembers being grateful that her Mutti was alive not dead.

When they went to synagogue the girls wore white linen hats, and they had matching dresses with aprons. Martha remembers that all their clothing was bought because their Mutti did not know how to sew.

A very pleasant memory of the Jewish holidays was Simchat Torah, when the girls went to Grandfather Siegmund's synagogue and were allowed to be in the men's section where they would receive sweets.

Martha recalls that her Mutti had beautiful challah covers and silver candelabras inherited from her grandparents. She remembers Shabbat meals with wine chicken soup, mostly chicken and sometimes beef.

The deportation of the Polish Jews

Martha and her cousin Marion were in the same school in October 1938. Martha's Tantie Selma was Theresa's oldest sibling, she was married to Josef Bierman whose origins were Polish. The family was among the Jews in Germany deported to Poland in October. From the window of her classroom Martha saw Marion put onto the back of an open lorry. Marion was the only child taken and Martha recalls her crying, screaming, and holding onto the edge of the truck trying prevent them from putting her on the back. All the class saw this happen.

Daniel is sent away to do forced labour
When Martha was eight her father was taken away to a place called Buxtehede where he and others were pressganged into doing forced labour. He was allowed to return home once a month for two nights. The family was allowed to visit him once a month and Martha recalls how hard it was to say goodbye after each visit. In Buxtehede the only accommodation available was with a childless couple where the wife was Jewish, the husband not. There were no beds, the Braun family had to sleep on the floor.

Memories of the journey to England
Martha remembers the Gestapo coming on to the train before crossing the border. The children were terrified and Lotty Carlebach calmed them down saying there is no need to cry, you will see your parents again. The Gestapo opened all the cases of the children except for those of Martha and Margot. Before their departure Theresa had gone to the Gestapo and requested they inspect and seal the suitcases that her girls were taking. As a result, the Gestapo didn't open their cases.

There were twenty to thirty children in each carriage which Martha recalls as being packed.

The destination of the boat trip was Harwich. Martha recalls them being given breakfast on the boat.

ABOUT THE AUTHOR

Leon Dwolatzky Duval was born in Johannesburg and at age twenty-seven emigrated to Melbourne, Australia with his wife Denise and their two young daughters. The Victorian culture they confronted in the days before Australia became ethnically diverse prompted them to change their surname to Duval in order to avoid constant requests for instructions on how the name Dwolatzky was pronounced or spelt.

An accountant and management consultant by profession, Leon discovered that many of the clients he looked after in his early Melbourne days were Holocaust survivors. These relationships exposed him for the first time to a Jewish community with roots in pre–Holocaust Poland. The stories told and the underlying trauma their narrators still carried with them stimulated in him a yearning to search for greater understanding of his Jewish inheritance and antisemitism's underlying causes.

After retiring from professional life and moving to Jerusalem, Leon undertook an extensive course to train as a guide for the Yad Vashem history museum and is now a committed amateur historian spending many hours researching the history of the Jews in Europe and that of his own family which has its roots in Lithuania.

Leon has a Master's degree in business accounting and a PhD in management studies, both awarded by Monash University in Melbourne. He is a fellow of the Australian-based Institute of Certified Management Accountants and was its foundation president. In the year 2000 he was awarded a centenary medal by the Australian government recognising his efforts to introduce the study of ethics into the curriculum, leading to membership certification by the accounting profession in Australia.

www.ingramcontent.com/pod-product-compliance
Lightning Source LLC
LaVergne TN
LVHW021928280225
804817LV00013B/188